YALE
and the
MINISTRY

*A history of education for
the Christian Ministry
at Yale from the
founding in 1701*

Roland H. Bainton

*Line drawings
by the author*

HARPER & BROTHERS
PUBLISHERS, NEW YORK

YALE AND THE MINISTRY
Copyright © 1957 by Roland H. Bainton
Printed in the United States of America

FIRST EDITION
C-G

Library of Congress catalog card number: 57-7344

To my colleagues of the Yale Divinity School
and in particular three
nearest to me in age:

ROBERT LOWRIE CALHOUN
HELMUT RICHARD NIEBUHR
PAUL VIETH

Their friendship has helped to
make the days of my years
labor indeed but not sorrow

CONTENTS

ILLUSTRATIONS

Preface

The founding fathers of Yale were committed to "the grand errand" of propagating "the blessed reformed Protestant religion in this wilderness" whereunto they deemed the religious education of suitable youths a chief expedient. The pursuance of this grand errand at Yale, from the foundation in 1701 to our own time, is the theme of this book. Anything approaching an adequate portrayal becomes a history of the religious life and thought of southern New England, because Yale was the creation, instrument, and leader of an entire community embracing the Connecticut valley as far north as Northampton, and taking in the southern fringe of Massachusetts and Rhode Island. This community was so well integrated that throughout the nineteenth century many of the Connecticut pastors, alumni of the school, were quite as influential in forming the minds of the students as were the actual faculty; and until 1822 these ministers were engaged in the teaching process, though not in the college halls. Students after the four-year undergraduate course made their specific training for the ministry in the homes of pastors who supervised their studies and inducted them into the practical work of the ministry. These alumni pastors thus constituted a veritable graduate faculty.

Even after the establishment of the Divinity School in 1822, some of the neighboring ministers who were never on the teaching staff such as Lyman Beecher and Horace Bushnell, made nevertheless a profound impact upon the students. For this reason the present student includes sketches of leaders beyond the immediate confines of the school.

The religious life of southern New England for the last two centuries and a half exhibits a significant and unique development in the degree to which the major Christian themes were held in balance. Theology, piety, and social concern did not part company. They tended to do so elsewhere in the eighteenth century. The two great movements of that age disparaged the theology of the Reformation. The Enlightenment admitted only that measure of theological affirmation which is simple and universally accessible to the meanest intelligence. This was the religion of "common sense." The Pietist movement in Germany and its counterpart Methodism in England looked askance at theological formulation as desiccating for religion. As for the social concern, the Enlightenment indeed stimulated humanitarism, but ran the risk of eliminating the religious motivation. And though Pietism sensitized the conscience, nevertheless personal salvation was often stressed at the expense of social reform.

In the New World the three were nowhere so fully held in conjunction as in the Connecticut valley. The Unitarians around Boston, under the impact of the Enlightenment, rebelled against Calvinist theology. The Presbyterians at Princeton retained it, but with little hospitality to the Enlightenment; and the Methodists and other exhorters deprecated an educated ministry.

But in southern New England the theology of the Reformation stemming from Calvin was perpetuated in a vital, changing, and unbroken continuity. At the same time the Enlightenment was appropriated at the point of the philosophy of Newton and Locke, and the science of Kepler and Herschel. Pietism found expression in the first and second Great Awakenings, but did not lead to any dilution of the ideal of the trained ministry.

The social concern had been the very marrow of the Puritan holy commonwealth. In the eighteenth century the struggle to maintain the external framework of the religious oligarchy sometimes obscured the purpose for which it existed, but the sense of a commonwealth in covenant with God was never obliterated and found expression in the reformatory movements of the nineteenth century.

These three threads, then, theology, piety, and social reform, run through this story. They are not at all times equally apparent in the pattern and certainly not in the narration, but they are continually recurrent.

The greatest change in Yale's pattern has come in the extension of the terrain from southern New England to the nation. The holy commonwealth has come to be not New Haven or Connecticut but the United States and in a measure the entire globe. As the scope expands the treatment in this book is forced to contract. One can portray Yale as the center of a community so long as the community is compassable, but when, as in the twentieth century, the lines have gone out to the ends of the earth, attention has to be restricted to their point of origin. Hence, though the Yale Divinity School operates today in a widely ramified society the narrative is of necessity focused on the school itself.

The point at which to end this survey presents a problem. During the last twenty-five years the Yale Divinity School has increased in numbers, quality, and influence, but a detailed treatment of this period is precluded by considerations of space and by reason of the author's involvement. Therefore, the last quarter of a century will receive only a succinct and impersonal account. This means ending with Dean Brown's administration. But even this point is not clear. There were during his administration three age groups. The older men are accorded here somewhat detailed treatment. The men in the middle bracket receive but cursory mention. They are Dahl, Archer, Weigle, Robert Seneca Smith, and Latourette. The younger men are not mentioned at all unless it be to illustrate a point in some other connection. This group includes Calhoun, Richard Niebuhr, Jerome Davis, Shedd, Malone, and Bainton.

YALE
and the
MINISTRY

CHAPTER I

This Grand Errand

Yale was conservative before she was born. The reason for its founding was to conserve and to revive the ways of the fathers. In the opening years of the eighteenth century New Englanders were christening their children Ichabod, because of that verse in I Samuel 4:21 which reads: "And she named the child Ichabod, saying, The glory is departed from Israel." The pillars of the first generation were dust, and none had arisen to replace them. Christians were so far degenerate as to frequent taverns, consort with the lewd, desecrate the Sabbath, and profane the name of the Lord. The younger ministers regarded as mere trifles those tenets for which their fathers had relinquished pleasant livings across the sea and braved a "wast and *howling Wilderness*." Since the death of that "apostolical man, Old Mr. Eliot," the missionary enterprise among the Indians had been "dwindling and dying." And, bemoaned Increase Mather, Harvard, the very glory of New England, was sending forth degenerate graduates who were at once recognized as the visible tokens of paradise lost.[1]

According to some modern historians, Yale was founded to offset the defection of Harvard. This need not be assumed, for Connecticut had long felt the need of a school nearer at hand, and she had besides reason enough for regarding herself as a degenerate vine without casting aspersions upon Massachusetts. Had not the very founder of the New Haven Colony, John Davenport, withdrawn to Boston in dudgeon over the defections of Connecticut?

Today one may wonder whether the dirges were altogether warranted.

2YALE AND THE MINISTRY

Prophets are notoriously prone to chide their own generation by the example of some other idealized time or clime.

Yet certain changes were indisputable. The menace of the frontier had receded almost to the Hudson. The coastal cities enjoyed a measure of that prosperity which is never conducive to rugged piety. Cotton Mather quoted approvingly the dictum, in Latin of course: "*Religio perperit Divitias, & Filia devoravit Matrem: Religion* brought forth *prosperity,* and the *daughter* destroyed the *mother.*"[2] Solomon Stoddard, the grandfather of Jonathan Edwards, similarly bewailed the mighty clogging of the work of reformation. Merchandise had prospered, but as for reformation, "Laws have been inacted, Sermons have been preached, Covenants have been made, but all endeavors have had a miscarrying Womb; there has not been one Sin generally reformed these twenty Years."[3] The plain fact was that some of the saints were sermon glutted. They had not suffered the restrictions imposed in the Old World upon their fathers, and the sons of exiles can never be expected to share the fervor of their forebears.

In addition, one notable and depressing change affected the colonies: the restoration in the 1660's of the Stuarts and the Anglican Church in England. In the two previous decades the emigrants had identified themselves with the English struggle trusting that the example of the "*golden Candlesticks*"[4] shining in the wilderness might favorably determine the outcome of the Puritan Revolution in the old land. However, the return of Charles II and the re-establishment of the Church of England blighted such hopes and led to the era of colonial isolationism in New England. The Congregationalists had now to pursue their own course without hope of exerting influence or of receiving aid. They might rather expect to be subject to obstruction and interference if not flat negation.

Yet apart from these alterations in their situation, the New Englanders of the third generation were the heirs of problems inherent in the very structure of the first settlements, problems which their forefathers had adroitly managed to defer to their successors. The founding of Yale College occurred in the day of reckoning. The old theocratic structure was crumbling and the founding of a school was one of the devices for resuscitating the holy commonwealth.

The original plantation had been conceived in the audacious hope of rearing in this land unsown a covenanted society. The optimism often ascribed to these early Americans sprang not primarily from the richness of the soil, but from the stupendous confidence of men who braved repellent shores that here they might erect some semblance of God's kingdom. The marrow of their hope was derived from John Calvin, who believed that the sovereign Lord had a plan for the ages to be achieved through His chosen people. The renovated Church should be the kingdom of God. Calvin did not quite venture an identification of the Church actual with the divine society, envisaging rather a purification and a realization. God would bring it to pass in His own good time, and there was reason to assume time enough because Calvin projected the second coming of the Lord Jesus into a vague futurity during which the God who led Israel from bondage to the land of promise would again establish His chosen in this New Canaan.

Here was the pattern of the distinctively Protestant theocracy, based not on soil and blood like the Hebrew nor on sacramentalism and sacerdotalism like the Catholic, but on predestination, the assumption that from before the foundation of the world God had chosen some for eternal salvation and to them would He commit the erection of a divine society upon earth.

Then came the question how the elect could be recognized. Here New England parted company with John Calvin. Both agreed that no infallible rule of identification could be discovered. There were, however, certain presumptive tests. For Calvin these tests were three: orthodox faith, a godly deportment, and participation in the sacraments. If these conditions could be met, a man should assume his election and stop worrying. What good did anyone ever achieve who was everlastingly agonizing over his destiny?[5]

The New Englanders altered the third test. Attendance on the sacraments was not for them a sign of election, but a privilege accorded only to those assumed to be already of the elect. Candidates for church membership were required to give evidence of an inner experience of regeneration, evidence that "they have been wounded in their hearts for their originall sinne, and actuall transgressions, and can pitch upon some promise of free grace in the Scripture, for the ground of their faith, and that they finde their hearts drawne to beleeve in Christ Jesus, for their justification and salvation."[6] Whenever was a theocracy based upon a ground so intangible and therefore so unstable, tantalizing, and tormenting?

The case would have been much less difficult had this inner experience been the test only for church membership. Instead it was the requirement also for the full enjoyment of citizenship. Church members alone exercised the franchise. So it was at Boston, and so it was at New Haven, where only one-tenth of the population were members of the church-state and the rest simply inhabitants. A tract entitled A *Discourse About Civil Government in a New Plantation Whose Design is Religion* (1663), composed by John Cotton and published by John Davenport,[7] averred that "in a new plantation, where the most considerable part purposes to enter into church fellowship," only Christians should be magistrates and only Christians should vote for magistrates. The holy commonwealth was thus an oligarchy of the saints.

One would suppose that those who launched so daring a design would never have started without a homogeneous constituency. But they had not been willing to leave behind their servants, and were hardly in a position to finance such voyages without the aid of merchant companies composed of "profane men, who, being but seeming Christians, have made Christ and Christianity stink in the nostrils of the poore Infidels."[8] The very *Mayflower* carried saints and strangers, and the famous Compact was a charter not of liberty but of restraint. Bradford recorded that when the ship was found to have landed outside the confines of Virginia, there were murmurings and mutinous speeches from the mouths of some who declared that when they got ashore "they would use their own liberty." The Compact brought these strangers into submission to God's holy will and incidentally to God's chosen saints.[9]

During the first generation the maintenance of control over the strangers was not too grave a problem because through lack of property they never had enjoyed the franchise in England. The mischief came when the sons of the saints became classed among the strangers. When the son of a minister could not vote for militiamen, there was murmuring in Israel. How should the holy commonwealth hold its children? To make

Abrahams out of Isaacs is not always easy, particularly if the sons have been sacrificed on the altars of their fathers' devotion. One solution of the problem was to let down the bars to the level of the people. The other was to raise the people to the level of the bars.

Both ways were adopted. The standards concerning the two sacraments were progressively relaxed. First as to baptism: in the early days it was administered only to the children of the presumably elect, baptism being regarded as primarily a pledge that parents would rear their children in the fear of the Lord. Thus if the parents were not qualified the children were denied the rite. The Half Way Covenant formulated in 1662 leaped over a generation and granted baptism to the grandchildren of the elect. The chances of adequate religious instruction were thereby diminished and the danger was introduced that birth in the flesh should outweigh birth in the Spirit and the elect degenerate into the elite. The question of the franchise early ceased to be involved because in 1691 the test of church membership was abrogated in Massachusetts, and the Connecticut Colony had never been so rigid.

Regarding the second sacrament a vastly more radical innovation was introduced by Solomon Stoddard of Northampton. Stoddard argued that there is no infallible test of regeneration and election, therefore all those sincerely desirous should be admitted to the Lord's Table: that the sacraments be deemed a saving ordinance, a means of regeneration, not a reward or a token of a chosen state. Here was a return to the practice of Calvin, which, taken in conjunction with the stand on baptism, incurred the danger that the church might be composed of the decorous rather than the devout, since some individuals might seek full church memberships for social prestige or political influence.

For this imminent danger Stoddard had his antidotes. While on the one hand he would lower the requirements, on the other he would elevate the people by revivals. Though he would receive all to communion, he did not pretend that respectability is regeneration nor that preparation is saving conversion, for during preparation sins are not mortified but "are like Vermin in Winter, stupifyed but not dead."[10] Though he did not venture to identify the elect, he did exhalt a heartfelt commitment which he was ready to induce by threats of hell or feeding at the table of the Lord.[11] If only the Spirit would pluck the lyre, all quibbles about halfways and wholeways would lose their point. Solomon Stoddard gave substance to his words. His ministry was repeatedly punctuated by ingatherings of the sheaves, notably in the years 1697, 1683, 1712, and 1718.[12]

Another expedient was to tighten the watch of the churches over one another. If a particular congregation were diluted, then the associated churches might exercise the office of reproof and counsel. This principle, as Stoddard recognized, conflicted with the theory of the complete autonomy of the local congregations. "The supream Ecclesiastical Authority doth not lye," said he, "in particular Congregations . . . [God promised to take whole nations into covenant] . . . if there be no National Church, then every particular Congregation is absolute and independent, and not responsible to any higher Power: This is too Lordly a principle, it is too ambitious a thing for every small Congregation to arrogate such an uncontrollable Power, and to be accountable to none on Earth . . . it is more probable that in a whole Country, Persons may be found that may rectify the Miscarriages of particular Congregations, than that particular Congregations will not miscarry, this absoluteness of particular Congregations is a dignity that the primitive churches did not enjoy."[13]

Still another antidote in the judgment of all New England was the education of the people through a trained ministry nurtured in "schooles of learning." So wrote Charles Chauncy in 1655,[14] and Cotton Mather was clear that the decline which he bemoaned could best be arrested through schools and colleges. In ancient Israel, said he, Samuel was the founder of colleges, and Josiah showed great respect to the college at Jerusalem. "When New England was poor, and we were but few in number comparatively, there was a spirit to encourage learning and the college [Harvard] was full of students, . . . but it is deeply to be lamented that now when we are become many, and more able than at our beginnings, that society, [Harvard] and other inferior schools are in such a low and languishing state."[15]

New England as a whole was ready for some or all of the above measures, Boston no less than Northampton or New Haven. The Boston area made the first move to consolidate the congregations that restraint might be exercised over particular churches. The movement miscarried principally because state aid could not be enlisted since the governor had Episcopal leanings. In Connecticut it was different. Here Governor Saltonstall was a minister transplanted from the pulpit to the capital. The Assembly likewise could be counted on to support the churches.

Regarding the franchise, the Connecticut Colony centering at Hartford had always been more liberal than either Boston or the independent colony of New Haven. When then in 1664 New Haven morosely succumbed to incorporation with Connecticut, Davenport seceded to Boston. Inasmuch as the ancient lineaments had been effaced, how much greater the need of the churches to strengthen their hold upon the community by exercising a sharper supervision over their own members! This was acutely felt at New Haven, and from this area were recruited the prime architects of the Saybrook Platform which from 1708 to 1784 established in Connecticut a mildly Presbyterian polity. The churches were brought into consociations "for the mutuall affording to each other such assistance as may be requisite upon all occasions ecclesiasticall" and that cases of scandal should be adjudged by what amounted to church courts. The 1680 Boston Confession of Faith was endorsed, which set forth unflinchingly the doctrine of the immutable decrees.[17]

Yet all of this reform would be of little avail without men trained to cope with lethargy in the Church and secularism in the State, to rally the new Israelites to a renewal of the Covenant. The very ministers who fashioned the Saybrook Platform in 1708 had seven years earlier founded a collegiate school at Saybrook, subsequently transferred to New Haven. The desire to offset Harvard cannot be altogether excluded as a motive, for the aid of the Boston conservatives, lately unhorsed at Harvard, was enlisted and unstintedly given. Cotton Mather it was who secured the initial grant from Elihu Yale and proposed Yale as the name for the college.[18] On the other hand, neither opposition to Harvard nor regard for the present exigencies wholly explained the maturing of a plan long since cherished. John Davenport had purposed that there should be a school "for the better trayning upp of youth in this towne, that, through God's blessing they may be fitted for publique service hereafter, in church or commonweale."[19] When the plan, at first deferred because of deficiency of funds, was finally realized in 1701 almost the very words of Davenport were incorporated in the act of foundation of the collegiate school! "For the educating and instructing of youth in good literature, arts, and sciences; That so by the blessing of Almighty God they may be the better fitted for publick Imployment both in Church and in Civil State."[20] More explicit aims were specified in the memorandum of the trustees. "Whereas it was the glorious publick design of our now blessed fathers in their Removal from Europe into these parts of America, both to plant, and under ye Divine blessing to propagate in this Wilderness, the blessed Reformed, Protestant Religion, in ye purity of its Order, and Worship, not onely to their posterity, but also to ye barbarous Natives: In which great Enterprise they wanted not the Royal Commands, & favour of his Majestie Charles ye Second to authorize, & invigorate them. We their unworthy posterity lamenting our past neglects of this *Grand errand,* & Sensible of our equal Obligations better to prosecute ye Same end, are desirous in our Generation to be Serviceable therunto. Whereunto the Liberal, & Religious Education of Suitable youth is under ye blessing of God, a chief, & most probable expedient."[21]

The school, be it observed, was not to train men solely for the ministry but also for the magistracy, the ministers and the magistrates to study together, not so much that the ministers might be broadened through association with men of the world as that the magistrates might be instructed in divinity. The school was to be the servant of the theocratic society, with all leaders equally bound to uphold the Covenant. The sources of its financial support were indicative of its relation to the entire community. Some funds came from the churches, some from the legislature, and some from private benefaction.

At the outset the institution was designed to ground men in the New England way. The ten ministers who established the school in 1701 lugged forty ponderous tomes to a house in Branford. A modern historian has somewhat derisively referred to these books as "dusty theological folios." They were not dusty, and their owners would rather have parted with ten cords of cut wood. Those volumes had been handed down from father to son and encased the marrow of the holy commonwealth in covenant with the Lord. They came from the Reformed tradition of Continental Protestantism. Surprisingly, there were only two works of

English Puritans and possibly one from Luther, the bulk of the forty volumes coming from the Swiss and Rhineland theologians: Bucer of Strasbourg, Gualter and Bullinger of Zurich, Musculus of Berne, Beza of Lausanna, and Calvin of Geneva.[22] These were the Continentals who had molded English Puritanism and in whose works one finds delineated the contours of the covenant society.

The actual curriculum centered on the traditional excercises with the traditional tools. The Scriptures should be read daily, the Assembly's Catechism recited by heart in Latin, and careful attention devoted to the works of that Puritan most influential in New England, William Ames.[23] This attempt to recover the Golden Age by studying the classics of early Independency did not, however, properly meet the present situation. The original Latin of Ames's *The Marrow of Sacred Divinity* had been published in Amsterdam in 1648. It insisted on the complete autonomy of the local congregations[24] and therefore ill-comported with the Saybrook Platform. Evidently conservatism would have to be innovating. The departed glories could not be reinstated with the departed devices. Yale College, sensing the inadequacy of the resources, commissioned Jeremiah Dummer to solicit from England gifts of further books. His success proved to be profoundly disconcerting because the donors were mostly Anglicans and the works designed to restore the Puritan commonwealth occasioned rather a defection.

Jeremiah Dummer approached Elihu Yale, the original benefactor, who rejoiced at the progress of the college bearing his name, "Saving that he expresst at first some kind of concern, whether it was well in him, being a Church man, to promote an Academy of Dissenters. But when we had discourst that point freely, he appear'd convinc't that the business of good men is to spread religion & learning among mankind without being too fondly attach't to particular Tenets, about which the World never was, nor ever will be agreed. Besides if the Discipline of the Church of England be most agreeable to Scripture & primitive practice, there's no better way to make men sensible of it than by giving them good learning."[25] In other words, Elihu Yale entertained apparently the slight hope that his donation might subvert the holy commonwealth.

Yet the collection, when it finally arrived, aroused no immediate suspicions. There were works of philosophy and natural science irrelevant to the controversies, among others John Locke's *An Essay Concerning Human Understanding*,[26] Robert Boyle's tracts *About the Cosmicall Qualities of Things*,[27] and Newton's *Principia* and *Optice*,[28] contributed by himself. The collection was not narrowly Anglican, and Puritan divines were well represented,[29] but with these reassuring titles appeared works on both sides of the controversy regarding conformity to the

Samuel Johnson

Church of England. The Puritan side was well presented in three volumes by Edmund Calamy, *A Defence of Moderate Nonconformity in Answer to . . . Mr. Ollyffe and Mr. Hoadly*, printed at London 1703 to 1705.[30] And on the other side, there were two volumes by Benjamin Hoadley, the Bishop of Winchester, *The Reasonableness of Conformity to the Church of England* and *A Serious Admonition to Mr. Calamy* printed at London in 1703 and 1705,[31] as well as the works of the Bishop's cohort John Ollyffe, consisting of the first, second, and third *Defence of Ministerial Conformity to the Church of England: in Answer to . . . Mr. Calamy* printed at London in 1702 to 1706.[32]

These works fell into the hands of the rector of Yale College, Timothy Cutler, and some of his tutors, notably Samuel Johnson, later the founder of King's College, subsequently Columbia University. The books were not solely responsible for the defection of these men because they were already troubled as to the adequacy of their congregational ordination and their nonconformity to the Church of England. The arguments used in colonial Puritanism had commenced to recoil. The contention then had been that the Puritans were not separatists from the Church of England but only secessionists, cast out not by their mother, the church, but only by "little-souled ceremony mongers, . . . into the horrid thickets of America."[33] Since the Restoration, however, the Anglican Church had manifestly allied herself with these ceremony mongers. Either then the New Englanders must return to obedience or proclaim themselves in a state of separation. Moreover, Johnson was troubled by the frequent ineptitudes of extempore prayer and had the temerity to supply himself with the Anglican liturgy. We read of student murmurings against the tutors, conceivably on these very counts.

Then arrived the cases of books assembled by Dummer for the library. Johnson records that he avidly devoured the Calamy-Hoadley exchanges and then pushed on to extensive studies of the early church in which he was convinced episcopacy had prevailed since the days of the apostles.[34] Rumors became rife of Arminian leanings among the tutors. Wherefore, after commencement in 1722, the trustees summoned the rector and the tutors to the library and instituted an inquiry in the expectation that the suspects would clear themselves and dispel the "dark apprehensions." Instead they proclaimed themselves converts to the Church of England.[35] There could not have been greater consternation in the colony if the French had taken Boston.

Several of the tutors were amenable to persuasion, but Cutler and Johnson were firm. "How is the gold become dim!" bemoaned the grandson of John Davenport, "and the silver has become dross, and the wine mixt with water!"[36] The offenders were required to resign, and to forestall any such future defections, the trustees decreed that every rector and every tutor henceforth must subscribe to the Saybrook Confession of Faith.[37] This rule continued in force until 1823.[38] Elisha Williams, onetime head of the Weathersfield secession, became rector.

But the menace of Anglicanism was not so easily dispelled. The love of Samuel Johnson for Yale was not diminished because he now considered the College to lie within the province of the Society for the Propagation of the Gospel in Foreign Parts. He approached Bishop Berkeley with a solicitation for another gift of books. There were rumors that the Bishop was well disposed because he thought Yale more likely than Harvard to turn Episcopalian.[39] At any rate, he said that Yale bred "the best clergymen . . . in America" and that from Yale had graduated those Presbyterians lately turned Anglican.[40] He presented the college with a very handsome collection, which the trustees were exceedingly loath to accept. "Behold the gratitude of dissenters!" exclaimed Samuel Johnson.[41] But whether out of deference or a sense of futility, they did accept. This was in 1732.

When Yale, founded to vindicate the ancient order, behaved thus, one can understand that the churches and the state would wish to institute controls. Thomas Clap, who became rector in 1740, was resolved that the college should conduct its own purge and establish its own safeguards. Church, State, and School should serve and support one another, but in mutual independence. Unwittingly perchance he was the heir of a medieval tradition that society be built around three co-ordinate and mutually independent institutions, the State, the Sanctuary, and the School, corresponding to the three offices of Christ as teacher, priest, and king. This tradition was perpetuated by John Calvin in the form of Church, State, and Academy under the leadership of the parson, the prince, and the professor. Calvin's great fight had been for the independence of the Church from the control of the State. New England Congregationalism had to fight for the independence of the college over and against Church and Commonwealth.[42]

At first Clap bore the title of rector. In 1745 he came to be called president, and president he meant to be. He would repair the breaches and heighten and tighten the stockade. A gift of books from a donor of "erroneous" religious opinions was rejected because of the stipulation that the collection be made available to all the students. When some of the seniors took up a subscription for a reprinting of Locke's *Essay on Toleration*, Clap demanded a public confession of sin on penalty of nongraduation. One boy refused and found his name omitted on commencement day. He secured his degree only by appeal to the King in council.

Clap proceeded to revise the constitution of the college in accord with his theory that "the principal Design of the Institution of this College, was to educate persons for the Work of the Ministry." Therefore, "if any Scholar Shall deny the Holy Scriptures or any Part of Them to be the Word of God . . . continuing Obstinate therein after the first and Second Admonition, He Shall be Expelled."[43] Episcopalians might attend and take degrees—a liberty which Oxford and Cambridge did not accord to Dissenters—but Episcopalians at Yale must conform to all the requirements of a Congregational foundation. Parents of the Anglican communion strenuously objected to enforced attendance at services at Center Church when only next door, Trinity Church was conducting worship in accord with the *Book of Common Prayer*. In part to obviate this plea Clap severed the connection of the College with Center Church, and a separate service was instituted in the college chapel to be conducted by the newly appointed Professor of Divinity whose sermons would be so largely of a theological nature that attendance might be justified as an academic exercise. In 1765 Clap was driven to relent to the extent of allowing the Episcopalians to attend their own services but warned that "should they take Pains to infect the Minds of their Fellow-Students with such pernicious Errors, as are contrary to the Fundamentals of Christianity, and the special Design of founding this College, so that Parents should justly be afraid of venturing their Children here, it is probable that some Notice would be taken of it."[44]

Clap's action in withdrawing from Center Church made the College distinct from, and in a measure independent of, the churches.

Independence of state control was less simple because both the charter and financial grants came from the State. When Clap sought to convert Yale into a training ground primarily for ministers of Congregational persuasion, he was challenged on the ground that the original purpose had been to train men for every walk of life. His various religious restrictions were also naturally the subject of complaint. The dispute became acrimonious and personal, and appeal was made by the president's opponents to the Assembly at Hartford to conduct a visitation of the college.

Clap stoutly rallied to the defense of his regime and in 1754 published *The Religious Constitution of Colleges*.[45]

As for the plea that Episcopalians should be excused to attend their own services on the ground that the Episcopal Church was the established church, he answered that it was established only for England, Wales, and Berwick-on-Tweed, not for the colonies. Some complained that he was violating religious liberty, the plea being the more plausible after the English Toleration Act of 1689, but he replied that colleges must reflect the conscience of the founder. Then came the rejoinder that Governor Yale and Bishop Berkeley, two of the greatest benefactors, were members of the Church of England, to which Clap scornfully inquired whether by their donation they had purchased the college. In other words, the original foundation determined the character, and subsequent donors, aware of its nature, must subscribe unconditionally. The contention that the College received state support and ought therefore to minister proportionately to the predilections of the entire population was unequivocally rejected. The College was founded on an idea, and those who chose to attend must conform. Finally and most important of all, the Assembly of the State of Connecticut enjoyed no right of visitation. The College could take care of itself. Here was the claim of an institution to serve the community but not to be dominated by the community. Clap cannot be dismissed simply as an irascible pettifogger, as some portray him. He transmitted a great tradition and thereby set the pattern for many schools of religious foundation throughout the nation, schools responsible to the public but independent of control from the Church and from the State and from opulent donors. However petty the squabbles which evoked these formulations, the principles themselves were of vast import.

Yet as an antidote for the disintegration of the old theocracy Clap had little more to propose than a reform in congregational singing. In the current Congregational practice the women were silent while the men sang without reference to time or pitch. Clap advocated singing by rule as the only way to negotiate the "numerous Turns and Quavers."[46] By so doing he alienated those reared in the old way who felt that he was appeasing the Anglicans and introducing further regimentation, as if the Saybrook Platform with its presbyterianized polity were not more than enough! Should now Psalm singing be made to conform to Scotland, if not indeed to Canterbury and Rome?

A more pertinent question would have been whether there were not something more vital than singing in tune, turn, and time. The answer was to be given by Jonathan Edwards.

CHAPTER II

The Great Awakening

Jonathan Edwards inherited the problems of his grandfather Solomon Stoddard, who had lowered the standards as to baptism and the Lord's Supper and sought to retrieve the holy commonwealth by consolidating the churches, educating the clergy, and reviving the community. The first two points were covered by the Saybrook Platform and the third by the successive harvests in his parish, but the last had occurred in 1718 and during the ensuing nine years there had been no further ripening of the grain. The veteran evangelist might well attribute the failure to his diminishing powers, and rejoice that the church at Northampton invited his grandson, Jonathan Edwards, to become his colleague.

The young man had had his schooling at Yale in the turbulent days when the seat of the school was as yet indeterminate. He had shared in a secession to Weathersfield. Returning to New Haven in 1721, he reported, "Monstrous impieties. . . . In the Colledge, Particularly stealing of Hens, Geese, turkies, piggs, Meat, Wood, &c,—Unseasonable Nightwalking, Breaking People's windows, playing at Cards, Cursing, Swearing, and Damning, and Using all manner of Ill Language, which never were at such a pitch in the Colledge as they Now are."[1] The first week in New Haven was marked by despondencies. "I have now," he said, "abundant Reason to be convinced, of the Troublesomeness and Vexation of the World, and that it will never be another Kind of World.[2]

Yale taught Jonathan Edwards to know the depravity of man, but yet at Yale came his own awakening, the new sense of the glory of divine things. On the completion of his graduate study he was for two years in a pastorate, then for another two years a tutor at Yale. In 1727 he became a colleague of his grandfather. As the two men sat behind the pulpit, the generations were met. The one was eighty-four, the other twenty-three. Both were patricians, Solomon Stoddard, "the Pope of the Great River," a venerable figure; Jonathan Edwards, slight of frame, with a finely chiseled face, and a voice somewhat languid with a note

Jonathan Edwards

of pathos. Within three years the great Elijah was gathered to his fathers, and the young Elisha, then twenty-six, assumed the mantle.

The problems confronting the young minister were: How might Northampton be quickened? How might Yale College be touched? How might New England be revived? To a generation emancipated from Calvinism such questions appear unanswerable on the basis of Calvinist presuppositions. If God at Creation had predetermined the number of the elect, no human effort would alter the quota. And if conversion is a condition of election, and the election is absolutely fixed, then God must will to convert those whom He has chosen; and man can in no way contribute. Yet manifestly Calvinists never acted on this assumption; the very survival of the holy commonwealths depended on winning the stranger within the gates and the children within the portals. Moreover, efforts to that end did appear to have been efficacious. God would seem to have ordained not only that there should be conversions but that there should also be preparation for conversion.

But what sort of preparation could man make? Recognizing that he has no claim on God[3] he can only subject himself to those disciplines and influences through which God has been known commonly to work:

read the Scriptures, observe the Sabbath, engage in self-examination. All this the seeker can do. The shepherd of souls, however, can do much more. Grace is never bestowed without knowledge,[4] not mere theoretical knowledge but "the sense of the heart." The information that honey is sweet differs from the tasting of it.[5] The role of the minister, then, is to preach theology: to let man know where he stands, to make him acutely sensible of God's majesty, of the wonder of His mercy and the terror of His wrath, of man's dire sin and perilous plight, of Christ's proffered redemption.

There was nothing new in the content of this message. The new note appeared in the exceptional manner in which Edwards presented his theology. In southern New England of his day he was the supreme exemplar of a unique combination of elements from the Renaissance, the Reformation, the Enlightenment, and Pietism. Edwards communicated a Calvinistic theology enriched with Pietistic fervor. His aim was so to impart knowledge as to cause his hearers not simply to assent to a fact but to be swayed by a conviction. His forcefulness sprang from his ability to communicate his own experience. In his seventeenth year during his graduate study at Yale, he had experienced "a new sense of things." According to his own narrative, the "inward sweet delight in God" came to him on the reading of the words I Timothy 1:17, "Now unto the King eternal, immortal, invisible, the only wise God, be honor and glory for ever and ever. Amen." "As I read the words, there came into my soul, and was as it were diffused through it, a sense of the glory of the Divine Being; a new sense, quite different from anything I ever experienced before. . . . I thought with myself, how excellent a Being that was, and how happy I should be, if I might enjoy that God, and be rapt up to him in heaven, and be as it were swallowed up in him forever!

"The sense I had of divine things, would often of a sudden kindle up, as it were, a sweet burning in my heart; and ardor of soul. . . . I walked abroad alone, in a solitary place in my father's pasture, for contemplation. And as I was walking there, and looking up on the sky and clouds, there came into my mind so sweet a sense of the glorious *majesty* and *grace* of God, that I know not how to express.

"The appearance of everything was altered; there seemed to be, as it were, a calm, sweet cast, or appearance of divine glory, in almost everything. God's excellency, his wisdom, his purity and love, seemed to appear in everything; in the sun, moon, . . . and all nature. . . . I often used to sit and view the moon for continuance; and in the day, spent much time in viewing the clouds and sky, to behold the sweet glory of God in these things; in the meantime, singing forth, with a low voice, my contemplations of the Creator and Redeemer. And scarce anything, among all the works of nature, was so sweet to me as thunder and lightning; formerly, nothing had been so terrible to me. . . . But now, on the contrary, it rejoiced me. I felt God, so to speak, at the first appearance of a thunderstorm; and used to take the opportunity, at such times, to fix myself in order to view the clouds, and the lightnings play, and hear the majestic and awful voice of God's thunder, which often times was exceedingly entertaining, leading me to sweet contemplations of my great and glorious God. While thus engaged, it always seemed natural to me to sing."[7]

He who had been thus so singularly lifted up was greatly exercised to know what "contrivance" God had ordained for promoting harvests among others. He marveled at the coldness of men's hearts. The need, he concluded, was not that men should "have their heads stored, so much as to have their hearts touched." How should it be done?[8]

Edwards found the clue in John Locke's *Essay Concerning Human Understanding*, where the mind is said not to be endowed with any innate ideas but to receive everything by sensation from without. For that reason, Edwards argued, the preacher must be "sensational," literally creating a "sensation." However, Edwards' interpretation differed from Locke's. For the latter, sensations result from the impact of things material upon the senses; for Edwards, the only reality is idea, sensations being therefore ideas resulting from the impact of God upon the mind. The sensation which results from preaching is then nothing other than God at work. Can the preacher prepare those conditions which are favorable to the working of God? The answer is that the preacher can impart only the truth. The natural man may thereby be given a view of God's natural perfections, the heinousness of sin, and the frightfulness of the punishments denounced against sin. The spiritual man may gain a sense of the excellency, beauty, and sweetness of divine things.[9]

God, His glory and excellency; man, his capacities, depravity, and peril; Christ, his compassion and the work of redemption—these are the truths to be declared. The manner of the declaration should be matter-of-fact because these are matters of fact. Yet the voice, though subdued, must be surcharged with emotion like that of the judge who pronounces sentence of death or reprieve to life.

The first word is about God. Here Edwards fused two traditions and thereby made God more accessible. The first came directly from John Calvin, the second from Cudworth, the Cambridge Platonist. The Calvinist strain, derived mainly from the Old Testament, pictures God in personal terms as the great Sovereign of the universe, the King of Kings, the Potentate of time and eternity, who shows forth His glory in the creation and government of the world, and elaborates His purpose in the course of history. His justice is displayed in consigning the rebellious to the fate which they deserve and His mercy by granting to some the compassion which they in no way have merited. All of this is in Edwards, and this is the reason why he is rightly regarded as a Calvinist. It is a formidable picture.

At the same time, there is a more approachable view interfused with Neoplatonic strains of God conceived less as a person than as a being with an inner necessity of self-diffusion, a fountain gushing streams or a radiance emitting shafts of light. This is the reason for the elaboration within the being of God of the Trinitarian structure.[10] This self-diffusion of God issues in the creation of the world which is pervaded by the effulgence of His glory. God's end in creation was the "infinitely perfect union of the creature with himself."[11] This is the point at which God becomes more approachable. If He be the sovereign, man can only bow and obey. But if He be self-diffusive being, there is then the possibility of the return to God of that which came from God, so that man can be united with God and share in the excellency of His nature.

The picture of God affects the picture of man. In accord with this Neoplatonic strain, long since appropriated by Christian mysticism, Edwards held that the end of religion is the participation on the part of man in the divine nature. The very reason for the incarnation was that as God became man, so man might become God. The pledge of such union was the combination of human and divine in Christ so that in communion with him the believer might partake of divinity.

This type of thinking, completely alien to John Calvin, was character-istic of his great opponent, Michael Servetus, who thought not to degrade God but to elevate man by union with God. To Calvin any such fusion must demean deity.[12] Odd that New England's greatest Calvinist at this point sided with one whom Calvin regarded as a monstrous blasphemer!

Yet Edwards actually combined this view, so repulsive to Calvin, with Calvin's own picture of man. The result was that for Edwards the depravity of man was heightened by the capacities of man. If he be capable of union with the divine and rejects his opportunity how much the more is he vile! Such defection is not to be considered merely the negation of good in Neoplatonic terms. Rather like a Hebrew prophet, Edwards portrayed sin as rebellion, malice, venomous hate, warranting the comparison of man to a poisonous insect.[13] Sin is a fire as intense as the fires of hell, and the wicked will have no principle of corruption in hell save that which they take with them.[14] This fire may be smothered or restrained, but given an opportunity it will flare forth. Man hates God. He hates His very mercy because it is holy and puts man to shame. If man does not hate God, it is only because he has constructed for himself a God whom he does not need to hate. If man continues God's enemy until death, he will always remain an enemy. "When you come to be a firebrand of hell . . . you will be all on fire, full of the fire of God's wrath: and you will be all on a blaze with spite and malice towards God. You will be as full of the fire of malice, as of the fire of vengeance. . . . Then you will appear as you are, a viper," no longer disguised.[15]

All men so behave, granted the opportunity, because owing to the fall of Adam, they are venomous by nature. The reason is not so much a hereditary taint as a solidarity of the human race with itself and with its progenitor. This theory of social cohesion is only one example of Edwards' theory of identity in the midst of change. From Newton he had learned that physics has an unsolved problem in that the atoms of a particular object adhere instead of flying apart. Edwards' answer was that they are held in cohesion by an unceasing act of God. Likewise the persistent identity of a changing individual is a work of God, who by continuous creation preserves continuity in the context of change whether from the acorn to the oak or from the infant to the aged. Just as the atoms of any particular object are held from flying apart by divine power, just as the successive moments in an individual existence are held in cohesion by an ongoing creation, similarly individual men adhere within the entity of humanity through God's embracing activity. For God is really the only substance in whom and through whom all things subsist.[16] Thus in Him humanity is one.

But humanity is sinful. If, then, any men are capabale of union with God it can only be because they have been extricated from this nexus of corruption and their very nature has been transformed. The conversion which turns a viper into a saint must be drastic. The language of the new birth is therefore more than a metaphor. It is a description of the sheer miracle of religion. It consists in a pure and disinterested delight in the excellency of God as He is in Himself. True saints are "inexpressibly pleased and delighted with the sweet ideas of the glorious and amiable nature of the things of God. And this is the spring of all their delights, and the cream of all their pleasures . . . [a] ravishing entertainment . . . in view of the beautiful and delightful nature of divine things."[17]

But once again, how shall they, who are without relish, taste and see that the Lord is good? Not directly. Herein lies the necessity for the self-disclosure of God in Jesus Christ. The preacher is not to dwell unduly on the majesty of God but is to disclose the excellency of Christ. "A sight of the greatness of God, in His attributes, may overwhelm men, and be more than they can endure; but the enmity and opposition of the heart may remain in its full strength, and the will remain inflexible, whereas one glimpse of the moral and spiritual glory of God, and the supreme amiablness of Jesus Christ, shining into the heart, overcomes and abolishes this opposition, and inclines the soul to Christ, as it were, by an omnipotent power; so that now, not only the understanding, but the will, and the whole soul, receives and embraces the Savior. . . . [And] the sight of the glory of God, in the face of Jesus Christ, works true supreme love to God."[18]

Here again mere information does not suffice. There must be an apprehension by the sense of the heart. At the same time, "holy affections are not heat without light, but evermore arise from an information of the understanding."[19] When Christ caused hearts to burn, it was through the opening of the Scriptures,[20] and it is only by the discovery of the beauty of the moral perfection of Christ that the believer is led into the knowledge of the excellency of his person.

Therefore, it is well to begin by a contemplation of him who is both the lion and the lamb, infinite in elevation and infinite in condescension, infinite in justice and infinite in grace, infinite in glory and infinite in humility, infinite in majesty and transcendent in meekness. "His infinite condescension marvellously appeared in the manner of his birth." There was no room for him in the inn because none would give up a room.[21] The squalor of his birth was a foretaste of the agony of his cross where he was tormented in his love and pity by the fire of our sins which he so took to himself as to feel himself forsaken by God. "This was infinitely terrible to Christ."[22] And in all this he continued to exercise dying love to his enemies.[23]

Thus did Christ consume our sins upon the cross. Our redemption consists in being joined with him as he is joined with us. Justification by faith has reference to no mere belief, nor even acceptance. We must be one with Christ as the members with the head, as the branches with the stock, which is the ground of their partaking of the sap, as the wife with the husband, which is the ground of her joint interest in his estate. Because of the union of the believer with Christ, God deems it meet that the merits and benefits of the Redeemer should be conferred on the redeemed.[24] As there is solidarity with Adam in corruption, so is there also with Christ in newness of life.

Why then are not all saved? Why should the law of solidarity be more potent for the lost than for the found? Depravity follows the principle of social cohesion but regeneration is individualistic and atomistic. No doubt one reason for Edwards' view was that he retained the traditional Calvinist scheme. But to say this is only to push the problem back to Calvin and his predecessors. The final reason is a rugged realism with regard to the tougher facts of life. So far as we can see, all are not saved. "How insensible and unmoved are most men!" cries Edwards . . . "How they can sit and hear of the infinite height, and depth, and length, and breadth of the love of God in Christ Jesus, of his giving his infinitely dear Son, to be offered up a sacrifice for the sins of men, and of the unparalleled love of the innocent, and holy, and tender Lamb of God, manifested in his dying agonies, his bloody sweat, his loud and bitter cries, and bleeding heart, and all this for enemies, to redeem them from deserved, eternal burnings, and to bring [them] to . . . everlasting joy and glory; and yet be cold, and heavy, insensible, and regardless!"[25] But the plain fact is that they are.

Nor are we to suppose that God is subject to any sentimental leniency in dealing with the rebellious; rather, as a lion He breaks our bones. It is all very well to talk of death as a benefit to wean us from the world, but what shall we say of the deaths of infants which exceed in number those of any other age (that was true in Edwards' day), and why should children before dying be tortured by disease? These things happen, and God does not stop them. Harriet Beecher Stowe well said that "Nature . . . is a more inexorable Calvinist than the Cambridge Platform,"[26] and the Puritans were too ruthlessly honest to dilute the vinegar of life. One wonders only why they felt constrained to project the tragedies and the inequalities of the temporal into the eternal.

On this point Edwards was clear: grace is available to some, and they are free to accept it. His "Treatise on the Freedom of the Will" undertook to vindicate freedom, though at the same time to conserve God's all-sufficiency without which man would be plunged into cosmic insecurity. God is in control but man is free. The reconciliation is effected by a subtle distinction between the will as choice and the will as inclination. Man is free to choose though he will choose in accord with his inclination and the inclination is determined by his very nature. The inclination to choose the good can result only from a change of nature and this is effected by the Holy Spirit infusing whom it will. All then comes back to God's arbitrary and immutable determination to damn some according to their desert and to save others according to His mercy, and Edwards said it plainly enough on occasion. But at the same time he exhibited again the paradox of Calvinism that it should be both predestinarian and revivalist. Ardent pleas were addressed to the congregation on the assumption that they could accept the proffered grace.

That was the whole point of the celebrated sermon on *Sinners in the Hands of an Angry God.* It was a revival sermon, designed to create a sensation in Edwards' sense by placing before men the fact of their condition, for "the bow of God's wrath is bent, and the arrow made ready on the string, and justice bends the arrow at your heart. . . ."[27] The God that holds you over the pit of hell, much as one holds a spider, or some loathsome insect over the fire, abhors you. . . . He is of purer eyes than to bear to have you in his sight; you are ten thousand times so abominable in his eyes, as the most hateful and venomous serpent is in ours. You have offended him infinitely more than ever a stubborn rebel did his prince: And yet, it is nothing but his hand that holds you from falling into the fire every moment." This is the point. God is holding back. He is giving you another chance, "O sinner! Consider the fearful danger you are in: It is a great furnace of wrath, a wide and bottomless pit, full of the fire of wrath, that you are held over in the hand of God. . . ."[28] How dreadful is the state of those that are daily and hourly in danger of this great wrath and infinite misery! But this is the dismal case of every soul in this congregation that has not been born again, . . . O that you would consider it, whether you be young or old! . . . And it would be no wonder if some persons, that now sit here in some seats of this meeting-house in health, and quiet and secure, should be in hell before tomorrow morning."[29]

Before the close of that sermon "there was a great moaning & crying out through ye whole House . . . ye shrieks & crys were piercing & Amazing. . . . Several Souls were hopefully wrought upon yt night. & oh ye cheerfulness and pleasantness of their countenances yt receivd comfort."[30] The Great Awakening was under way in New England. "Surprising conversions" spread from Northampton up and down the great river to Northfield, Deerfield, Hatfield, West Springfield, Hadley, Windsor, Coventry, Lebanon, New Haven, and even unto Yale.[31] Among the students to experience the new light was David Brainerd.

CHAPTER III

New Lights and Old

The Great Awakening had effects foreseen and unforeseen, coveted and lamented. The churches were quickened and out of the kindled zeal came a great missionary effort first in the home field and then in the foreign; the social conscience was aroused to a new sensitivity, and an ecumenical tendency was fostered in that confessional lines were blurred when the quickened Congregationalists became aware of their affinity with sectaries and Pietists. Yet at the same time the Congregational churches were split into the New Lights and the Old. The fabric of the old theocracy was demolished rather than restored, for unless the franchise were again to be narrowly restricted—and that no one contemplated—the State would have to comprise even the infidels, whereas the Church on the side of the New Lights would be reduced to convinced communicants and the Old Lights would no longer be the whole Church. Jonathan Edwards both restored and shattered.

One of the immediate effects was a heightened enthusiasm for missions to the Indians. The outstanding figure at this point was David Brainerd, converted while at Yale College through the Great Awakening. When Jonathan Edwards attended a Yale commencement Brainerd sought him as a spiritual counselor and the several visits in the Edwards' parsonage issued in the engagement of David to Jeshura, daughter of Jonathan. Brainerd's piety has a distinctly Edwardean stamp. He too sought the solitary places and greatly dejected in spirit endeavored vainly to pray until walking in a thick grove unspeakable glory enveloped his soul.

He "stood still, wondered and admired. . . My soul was so captivated and delighted with the excellency, loveliness, greatness, and other perfections of God, that I was even swallowed up in him."[1]

He became at once an evangelist and commenced upon his fellow students, venturing even as a sophomore to confront upperclassmen with an inquiry as to their spiritual condition. Samuel Hopkins whom he thus approached at first resented it, but afterward was quickened and to Brainerd owed his own awakening.

The desire to give to others that which also he had received prompted Brainerd not only to approach his fellow students but also to dedicate himself to the winning of the Indians. There was nothing new in this concern. The Puritans had early felt an obligation to bring the Gospel to the poor infidels. Cotton Mather surmised that "the devil decoyed those miserable savages hither, in hopes that the gospel of the Lord Jesus Christ would never come here to destroy or disturb his *absolute empire* over them."[2] In this he was foiled by John Eliot. When no immediate successor arose to this "Apostolical man," Solomon Stoddard posed the QUESTION, *Whether God is not Angry with the Country for doing So little towards the Conversion of the Indians?*

"Our hearts should yearn toward these Poor Heathen . . . who from generation to generation . . . go down to hell."[3] Brainerd with yearning offered himself to the Missionary Society. No modern board would ever have commissioned him, for already in college he was spitting blood and was plainly tubercular. The open-air life, to be sure, might have been his mending had he been certain of food and shelter. His first mission was to the Indians near Albany. Later he was transferred to the area near the forks of the Delaware. His entire missionary career was less than four years in duration. His labors among the Indians were not ineffectual but their chief impact was upon subsequent missions as Brainerd's story became known through the publication of his journal by Jonathan Edwards.

His journeyings were often without the shelter of a cabin: in the open, in wigwams, in huts of his own devising; his diet bread, often mouldy. His travels were interspersed with periods of intense weakness the description of which suggests not only tuberculosis but also malaria.

Debility alone was enough to induce depression apart from the loneliness which caused him to realize the wisdom of the Master in sending out disciples two by two. But there was also a theological ground for despondency. Why is it, Brainerd would inquire, that with the utmost striving man cannot fulfill the law of God? Christ enjoined us to be perfect as the Father in heaven is perfect. "These, I feel, are the sweetest commands in God's book, . . . and I shall break them! Must I break them? Am I under the necessity of it as long as I live in the world? Oh my soul, wo, wo is me that I am a sinner, . . . [who continually] grieve and offend this blessed God, who is infinite in goodness, and grace! Oh! methinks, if he would punish me for my sins, it would not wound my heart so deep to offend him; but tho' I sin continually, yet he continually repeats his kindness to be my own. . . . But, alas, . . . I find I cannot be thus entirely devoted to God—I cannot live, and not sin."[4]

Brainerd was never equal to Luther's lusty paradox that man can be at the same time a sinner and saved.

Yet for all his debility and despondency Brainerd never faltered. When it seemed more expedient that his Albany Indians be transferred to Stockbridge, he turned to the Delaware. Language presented a continuing difficulty. Because of the multiplicity of Indian tongues, what he had acquired at Albany was not transferable and in the new field he discovered as many as seven or eight languages. The only possible recourse was to an interpreter and here it was easier to find one who could talk about wampum and whiskey than about regeneration. The conversion of the interpreter was one of the first palpable encouragements. In addition, there were all the problems of keeping contact with migratory people, and of diverting them from powwows to prayer meetings.

Finally there appeared the disconcerting discovery that the greatest obstacle to the whole missionary enterprise was the white man himself, who wishing to exploit and exterminate the Indian, maligned the missionary as a deceiver seeking to assemble the natives in numbers that they might the more readily be enslaved and transported to England. The Indians pointed out that the whites would lie, defraud, steal, and drink worse than did the Indians.[5] They recalled that they had already been driven from the seacoast and now suspected Brainerd as contriving some new device for their further displacement.

He scarcely realized the gravity of the problem and how inadvertently he was perhaps contributing to it. For his plan was not only to convert but also to civilize the Indians as an aid to stabilizing their conversion. If they would live in communities, till the soil, and become instructed they would be easier to hold in the Christian way. But this was precisely what the praying Indians had done in New England and in consequence in the wars between the whites and the reds, these Anglicized natives on the outskirts of the English towns were regarded by the other Indians as apostates and by the English as still the children of the Amorites. Distrusted and decimated by both sides, some of them sought a new place of security by migrating to the West and settling in Michigan.[6] Brainerd was very much exercised that his converts should not be despoiled of their goods for drink and of their lands for debt. He scarcely saw that to Anglicize the Indians was all the more to jeopardize their existence.

But had he seen, he would not have discontinued his efforts on behalf of their souls. His aim was to spread the Great Awakening among the children of the forest. He aimed at a conviction of sin and would then display the exceeding mercy of God in the atoning death of Christ. No sermons were so effectual as those which dwelt upon the passion of the dying Saviour. There were no harangues of terror,[7] yet the spirit came in a "swelling deluge."[8] There were no excesses, no screaming, no swooning, only an "affectionate melting"[9] evidenced by tears. And the fruits of righteousness ensued. In a period of eleven months there were thirty-eight converts, and Brainerd was able to bring to the Lord's Table those thus spiritually begotten of his loins.

But his own strength was ebbing. Forced to return home he rode to Boston and there was joined by his fiancée, Jeshura Edwards. Together the two rode from Boston to Northampton where among the Edwards family Brainerd spent nineteen months, nursed by Jeshura. At family devotions his petition was "That we might not outlive our usefulness."[10] Jeshura outlived him but shortly and died in her eighteenth year of the disease contracted during the nursing.

A jotting in his diary in the wilderness sums up his endeavor. "My faith lifted me above the world, and removed all those mountains that I could not look over of late; I thought I wanted not the favour of man to lean upon; for I knew Christ's favour was infinitely better; and that it was no matter *when*, or *where*, or *how* Christ should send me, or what trials he should still exercise me with, if I might be prepared for his work and will."[11]

The Great Awakening not only stimulated missions, but likewise served to obliterate barriers between Christian confessions by drawing into fellowship the quickened spirits of divers confessions and lands. A close affiliation developed between the Great Awakening in New England, the Methodist revival in Old England, and the Pietist movement in Germany. Whitefield stayed in the home of the Edwardses at Northampton and incidentally, seeing Mrs. Edwards, wished that the Lord would discover for him another such daughter of Abraham.[12] John Wesley read with enthusiasm Edwards' *Narrative of Surprising Conversions*[13] and curiously the copy of this work in the Yale Library of 1742 was sent back from England by Isaac Watts. In New England great admiration was felt for German Pietism and Edwards lauded the work of August Hermann Francke with whom the Americans were in close correspondence.[14]

The Great Awakening both welded and clave. If those of like temperature in zeal were fused those of unlike were repelled. The very pillars of the Church were divided into the once and the twice born. Even deeper became the rift when the twice born abandoned all decorum. Itinerant evangelists, Whitefield from England, Tennent from the Jerseys, and the James Davenport, great-grandson of the founder of the new plantation, went from parish to parish indulging in a type of preaching which would be called sensational in a non-Edwardian sense. Charles Chauncy, of Boston, reported with dismay the preaching of Davenport, who at the top of his lungs would bellow out to a congregation, "You poor unconverted Creatures, in the Seats, in the Pews, in the Galleries, I wonder you don't drop into Hell! It would not surprise me, if I should see you drop down *now, this Minute*, into Hell." The ministers in the established churches were derided by the revivalists as "*Hirelings, Caterpillars, Daubers with untempered Mortar.*" Book learning was decried, and at New London, Davenport instituted a burning of books together with such vanities as necklaces, hoods, gowns, and wigs.[15]

The folk in the pews were seized by convulsions and faintings. Samuel Johnson, now safely ensconced within decorous Anglicanism reported of the revivalists that "their night meetings . . . looked like a very hell upon earth; some sighing, some groaning, some screeching and wringing their hands, the minister all the while, like a fiend tormenting them, till they would come to Christ."[16] Johnson felt half ashamed to derive a measure of satisfaction from the revulsion of those who came over to the Episcopal Church.

At Northampton in Edwards' own parish something much more alarming occurred. A man whom Edwards described as "a gentleman of more than common understanding, of strict morals, religious in his behavior, and an useful, honorable person in the town. . . . But . . . of a family . . . exceeding prone to the disease of melancholy," this man slit his throat, and a wave of suicidal inclination beset the community and many imagined voices saying, *Cut your own throat, now is a good opportunity.*"[17] The Great Awakening was in danger of becoming the great dementia.

Edwards set himself to discriminate. He found it very mysterious that so much good and so much bad should be mingled in the Church of God; that saving affection should be counterfeited by glistening appearances. He would not concede that physical manifestations discredit an experience. Why should not a sense of God's glory cause a body to faint? Mrs. Edwards had had faintings and her husband was persuaded of the genuineness of her piety. On the other hand, bodily convulsions are no proof of the operation of the Holy Spirit. Neither are amazing fears of hell, nor tumultuous joys to be considered infallible signs.[18] Nothing proceeding from the external senses can be a certain sign, whether it be of the ear, pleasant music, words of excellent signification, or of the eye, "as ideas of a visible beauty and glory, a shining light, and external glory of heaven, golden streets, walls and gates of precious stones, splendid palaces, glorious inhabitants shining forth as the sun, a most magnificent throne surrounded by angels and saints in shining ranks; or anything external, belonging to Jesus Christ," whether of his passion, the "blood trickling down; or his glorified state, with awful majesty, or ravishing beauty . . . in his countenance: . . . these things are no certain signs of grace."[19]

"The inheritance that Christ has purchased for the elect, is the Spirit of God; not in any extraordinary gifts, but in his vitally indwelling in the heart."[20] A sure sign is a sense of the transcendentally excellent and amiable nature of divine things as they are in themselves and without any reference to any benefit which they confer upon us. "The saint sees and feels plainly the union between his soul and God; it is so strong and lively, that he cannot doubt of it. And hence he is assured that he is a child . . . and cries boldly Abba Father."[21] If there be any signs beyond the intuitive assurance of sonship they lie in the region of disposition and behavior, for "the fruits of the Spirit [are] love, joy, peace, longsuffering, gentleness, . . . meekness," and the rest. "It is that charity, or divine love, which is pure, peaceable, gentle, easy to be intreated, full of mercy," which is "the most essential evidence of true godliness."[22] Humility, an absence of censoriousness, an eye for faults in oneself rather than in others, these are among the evidences of the working of the Spirit. There are no external manifestations which may be regarded as infallible signs of grace.[23] "The true saints have not such a spirit of discerning that they can certainly determine who are godly, and who are not[24]. . . . Doubtless it is the glorious prerogative of the omniscient God, as the great searcher of hearts, to be able well to separate between sheep and goats."[25]

What then became of the holy commonwealth? In his preoccupation with individual conversion Edwards appeared at times to have lost sight of the divine community. Then again he would unroll the scroll of God's plan for the ages in which America should have a unique place. The great revival was the prelude, but it had regenerated only a portion of the community and even ended on a note of doubt as to who the elect might be. If they were discernible by no external signs, the idea of the new plantation, the theocracy or government under the Lord God Jehovah, was incapable of realization, and if the sheep were quite indistinguishable from the goats the Church might in no way be set off from the world.

This Edwards would not suffer. Rather he would rally the Church and exclude the world. The Church should be the company of those who in their lives display a pattern of excellency even though short of perfection. The Church itself must consist of the twice born and the rest must be excluded from the Lord's Table. Only those persons should be admitted who could affirm:

"I hope I truly find in my heart a willingness to comply with all the commandments of God, which require me to give up myself wholly to him, and to serve him with my body and spirit, and do accordingly now promise to walk in a way of obedience to all the commandments of God, as long as I live." The children of the unregenerate should be denied baptism, and any guilty of a breach of the moral code should be disciplined. In other words the whole system of Solomon Stoddard—the Half Way Covenant, lax discipline, and the sacraments as saving ordinances—all were overthrown by his grandson.[26]

Unhappily Edwards fastened on a trivial incident and handled it indiscreetly.[27] Some youngsters were found behind a barn snickering over a manual of obstetrics. The names of those apprehended and of those suspected were publicly disclosed. Northampton seethed. Irritation because of the manner of discipline is understandable, but revulsion against revivalism apparently figured, since one leader of the opposition was the son of a suicide. The franchise was not involved because already extended. The demands of Edwards as to the Lord's Table were so minimal that commotion on that score appears incredible.

Yet a profound issue was at stake. Should the Church and the community continue to think of themselves as one? If so, would it be by reason of progressive relaxation of the standards of the Church? Edwards had desired to make them one by a universal conversion and had failed. More serious was the difficulty of even identifying the elect who constitute the kernel of the holy commonwealth. Yet he still thought of the saints as approximately recognizeable, and as distinct from the world. If then they could not rule the world, they would have to withdraw. The separation of Church and State inevitably followed. The abandonment of the ideal of a holy commonwealth might have followed had not Puritanism endeavored to conserve it in an altered context.

The preservation of the ideal became extremely difficult when the Church which should supply leadership was itself split into the New

Lights, as the children of the Awakening were called, and the Old Lights who deplored not only the extravagances, but also any attempt to modify the ancient ways. In the same community there came to be two Congregational churches of diverse persuasions. The New Haven green is witness to the schism. Center Church was Old Light. United Church resulted from the union of several New Light congregations. Milford likewise until recently had two contiguous Congregational churches, and so elsewhere.

Yale College was not immune to these convulsions. David Brainerd himself gave a foretaste of events to come. On his conversion he became censorious of those who knew no more than the old light, and when tutor Chauncey Whittelsey led some students in prayer, Brainerd commented, "He has no more grace than this chair." As a matter of fact Whittelsey appears to have been fully as ardent a seeker as Brainerd, but Whittelsey had had no convulsive experience. Brainerd's remark reached the authorities and in consequence he was expelled.[28] There was, however, a deeper reason. Without permission he had attended a meeting of Separatists. In other words a Yale student was giving countenance to the disruption of the churches. Brainerd tendered an apology for his "uncharitableness, presumption and insubordination," and might have been reinstated had he been willing to put in another year of study, but in the meantime he had been assigned to his mission to the Indians.[29]

A much more disturbing case for the college authorities was that of the Cleveland brothers who during vacation attended a Separatist New Light church. They also were present at a meeting conducted by a lay exhorter. For this they were expelled. There was sharp protest, particularly because the College was claiming jurisdiction over what had been done during a vacation. The Clevelands, moreover pointed out that in attending the separated New Light church in their home town, they were not separatists but were continuing their relation with that church in which they had been reared. President Clap chose to make no issue of this. He could concede the right to attend a New Light church. The offense was rather that on another occasion the Clevelands had sat under a lay exhorter. "This practice of setting up Lay-Exhorters . . . is without any Scripture Warrant, and is Subversive of the standing Order of a Learned Gospel Ministry, and naturally tends to introduce spiritual Pride, Enthusiasm, and all manner of Disorders into the Christian Church."[30] The Clevelands subsequently were granted their degrees.

The Great Awakening was thus bringing into question the chief purpose for which Yale had been established. Was a learned ministry necessary if Jonathan Edwards was right that the purpose of the minister is not to store the head but to stir the heart? For that task one does not need a mastery of ancient tongues and an acquaintance with classical literature. The Methodists were sweeping the land with lay preachers and New England was being invaded by exhorters unauthorized, untrained, and unrestrained. In all these movements Yale College saw a threat to its salient purpose, and when Whitefield visited this country a second time, the trustees would have none of him. In 1745 they declared: "It has always appeared to us, that you and other Itinerants have laid a Scheme to vilify and subvert our Colleges, and to introduce a Sett of Ministers into our Churches, by other Ways and Means of Education. In your Journal, p. 96. you say, 'As to the Universities, I believe it may be truly said, that the Light in them is now become Darkness . . .' "[31]

Yale was fighting no less for her own existence than for that very system which she had been founded to restore. Her concern was fully shared by the leaders of Church and State. The ministers in 1742 vigorously complained of the itinerant preachers to the Assembly which responded by forbidding even ordained ministers to preach outside of their own parishes save on express invitation from the incumbents. No minister should be settled except graduates of Harvard, Yale, or "some other allowed foreign Protestant college or university." And when the New Lights sought to take away the reproach of an untrained ministry by establishing at New London a school called "The Shepherds Tent," they were suppressed.[32]

At the same time this Puritan oligarchy was not impermeably obtuse. Though the first reaction to a thrust was invariably a counterthrust and concessions were grudgingly yielded only when impossible of denial, yet maturer reflection, plus the ineffectiveness of constraint, at length prompted reconsideration of the premises. In a society subject to continual change might not the essence of the holy plantation be better conserved by a more tolerant ecclesiastical structure? Where, in any case, did the real enemy lie, in the Baptists, the Quakers, and the New Lights, or as the century advanced, in the Deists and, the Unitarians? And if the latter constituted the genuine menace, might not an alliance with the former be expedient? Whatever the foe, a rupture of the standing order into Old Lights and New was plainly highly inexpedient. During the course of the eighteenth century such reflections reinforced by pressures from without produced a progressive removal of the restrictions upon dissenting religious bodies.

A few of the legislative milestones may be noted: in 1708 the year of the Saybrook Platform in which the churches tightened their own organization, the authority of the English Act of Toleration necessitated a grant of liberty of worship to sober dissenters in Connecticut. They still had to pay taxes, however, for the support of the establishment. Relief on this score was accorded to one group after another throughout the century, until in 1777 both Dissenters and Congregational Separatists were exempt from taxation provided their members registered themselves as belonging to and supporting nonestablished religious bodies. The standing order was therefore financed by taxes on Congregationalists and infidels. In 1784 the Saybrook Platform was deprived of any state support.[33]

Yale participated in all of these changes and the reason was not simply that the college reflected the life of the community. It was itself a replica of the community and the ferment without was matched by ferment within. At the time when the president and the Corporation might be adamant the tutors and the students would be agitating for change. The attempt of certain Seniors under Clap to reprint Locke's *A Letter Concerning Toleration* has already been noted.[34]

On the issue of the Old Lights and the New, Clap himself proved amenable. There were, as a matter of fact, gradations of light and Clap was of medium intensity. His readiness and the readiness of the students to be illumined to the level of the New Lights was a factor in the formation already mentioned of the college church as distinct from the First Church in New Haven where all the students hitherto had been required to worship. The pastor of that church, Mr. Noyes, was an old and antiquated Light, a devotee of decorum to whom unseemly enthusiasm was highly displeasing. He preached, as he said, for plain folk and tried neither to be learned nor moving. The students found him dull and tepid. To satisfy them, as well as to control the Episcopalians, Clap claimed the right of the College to have a church of its own, and after no little negotiation and friction with the First Church, Dr. Daggett of the New Lights was installed as minister and Professor of Divinity in 1757. When Whitefield, who had been rebuffed on his second visit, returned to the colony for a third time, President Clap invited him to preach in the college chapel.[35] Toward the end of the century Edwards the Younger, of the New Lights, pastor of the Separated or North Church in New Haven (now United Church), became a tutor to ministerial candidates in Yale College. The rift between the Old Lights and the New was thus healed.

CHAPTER IV

A Learned Ministry:
The Training in Yale College

The staff of Yale College during its first decades were like the men of Ezra and Nehemiah who carried sword and bow to withstand the machinations of Sanballat but spent most of their time laying bricks. The struggle against sectaries, who would wreck a learned ministry or against the Connecticut Assembly, which would interfere with the program, served only to safeguard the conditions under which the training of a competent ministry could go on.

Despite all the wrangles of New Lights and Old and of both with the Episcopalians, Yale was busy making learning the handmaid of religion. In this endeavor even the Episcopalians were not excluded. President Clap in 1766 boasted that Yale had prepared forty men for the ministry of the Episcopal Church.[1]

The nature of the training given a student in the College was conditioned by the preparation which he had received before arriving. A good grounding in the English Bible could be assumed. A striking testimonial to the educational value of the colonial practice of Bible reading in the home is given by Harriet Beecher Stowe:

"After breakfast grandfather conducted family prayers, commencing always by reading his chapter in the Bible. He read regularly through in course, as was the custom in those days, without note, comment, or explanation. Among the many insensible forces which formed the minds of New England children, was this constant, daily familiarity with the letter of the Bible. It was for the most part read twice a day in every family of any pretensions to respectability, and it was read as a reading-book in every common school,—in both cases without any attempt at explanation. Such parts as explained themselves were left to do so. Such as were beyond our knowledge were still read, and left to make what impression they would. For my part, I am impatient of the theory of those who think that nothing that is not understood makes any valuable impression on the mind of a child. I am certain that the constant contact of the Bible with my childish mind was a very great mental stimulant, as it certainly was a cause of a singular and vague pleasure. The wild, poetic parts of the prophecies, with their bold figures, vivid exclamations, and strange Oriental names and images, filled me with a quaint and solemn delight. Just as a child brought up under the shadow of the great cathedrals of the Old World, wandering into them daily, at morning, or eventide, beholding the many-colored windows flamboyant with strange legends of saints and angels, and neither understanding the legends, nor comprehending the architecture, is yet stilled and impressed, till the old minster grows into his growth and fashions his nature, so this wonderful old cathedral book insensibly wrought a sort of mystical poetry into the otherwise hard and sterile life of New England. Its passionate Oriental phrases, its quaint, pathetic stories, its wild, transcendent bursts of imagery, fixed an indelible mark in my imagination. Where Kedar and Tarshish and Pul and Lud, Chittim and the Isles, Dan and Beersheba, were, or what they were, I knew not, but they were fixed stations in my realm of cloud-land. I knew them as well as I knew my grandmother's rockingchair, yet the habit of hearing of them only in solemn tones, and in the readings of religious hours, gave to them a mysterious charm. I think no New Englander, brought up under the *régime* established by the Puritans, could really estimate how much of himself had actually been formed by this constant face-to-face intimacy with Hebrew literature. It is worthy of remark, too, that, although in details relating to human crime and vice, the Old Bible is the most plain-spoken book conceivable, it never violated the chastity of a child's mind, or stimulated an improper curiosity. I have been astonished in later years to learn the real meaning of passages to which, in family prayers, I listened with innocent gravity."[2]

After the Bible came the ancient languages. The degree of proficiency required on matriculation is curiously revealed by an entry in the diary of President Ezra Stiles under date of December 22, 1784. He recorded that he had "examined Miss Lucinda Foot, age 12, daughter of the Reverend Mr. Foot of Cheshire. She has learned the four orations against Cataline, the four first books of the Aeneid, and St. John's Gospel in Greek." He examined her not only on the portions prepared but at random elsewhere in Virgil, Tully, and the Greek New Testament, and in consequence gave her a parchment with a certification in his most approved Latin that he deemed her worthy to enter the freshman class of Yale College on every count save sex.[3] Had she been admitted it is not too much to say that the entire history of Yale would have been different.

Apart from such secular subjects as mathematics, geography, and natural science the curriculum retained the general features which had previously prevailed at Harvard and continued without essential modification at Yale throughout the eighteenth century. Ames, supplemented by Wollebius, was still basic for theology.[4] In ethics President Clap's treatise was added to Ames's *Conscience, with the Power and Cases Thereof.* Vincent's *Catechism* replaced the *Westminster.* Locke's *Essay Concerning Human Understanding* was the staple in philosophy. Edwards' *On the Will* was prescribed for a time, but then dropped.

A discipline by no means in lowly esteem was logic, for the New England minister was to be practiced in the art of driving his hearers to concede unwelcome truths by commencing with pleasant premises from which he would inexorably deduce unpalatable conclusions. The same art was used to confound the heretic and the unbeliever, so much so that when one of the clergy confronted the village atheist with the query "Do you admit your own existence?" rather than be ensnared, he snapped back "No."[5] Training in logic was given early. When the six year old granddaughter of the Rev. Nathanael Emmons came to him with a problem whether the moon is made of green cheese, he told her to work it out for herself. She returned announcing that she had it. "How?" asked he. "From the Bible," she answered. "But how?" "God," she replied, "made the moon before he made cows, therefore the moon was not made of green cheese."[6] Her grandfather's sermons were so fascinating for their logic that those who had grayed under his ministry rose in their seats rather than lose a word of the argument.[7]

What the students read outside of the prescribed courses admits of
no documentation. What was accessible and commended for their
reading can be determined with precision because in 1742 Rector Clap
published and printed a classified catalogue of the most valuable books
in the Library of Yale College. He made no pretense of completeness
but what he omitted can be reconstructed from the inventories of
previous gifts. Ezra Stiles in 1784 reconstructed the original deposit.[8]
Dummer supplied a complete list of the works he was sending from
England, a goodly portion of which are still extant. A Connecticut
farmer, John Davie, finding himself without the least premonition,
elevated to knighthood, returned to England and munificently played the
part of Sir John by donating to the Yale Library 169 volumes. The
manuscript list survives. A handsome collection was presented by Bishop
Berkeley. The original library has not been preserved in its entirety.
Some 260 volumes were assumed to have been lost in the fracas
attendant upon the attempt to prevent the transfer of the library from
Saybrook to New Haven. During the Revolution the entire collection
was dispersed and some never came back. But a very respectable portion
stands in the original order upon the shelves in the 1742 room in the
present Yale Library.[9]

Rector Clap expected the books to be an adjunct to education and in
the preface to his catalogue admonished: "And I would advise you,
my Pupils, to pursue a Regular Course of Academical Studies in some
Measure according to the Order of this Catalogue. And in the First
Year to Study principally the Tongues, Arithmetic and Algebra; the
Second, Logic, Rhetoric and Geometry; the Third, Mathematics and
Natural Philosophy; and the Fourth, Ethics and Divinity. Other less
principal Studies may be occasionally intermix't with these. Above all
have an Eye to the great End of all your Studies, which is to obtain the
Clearest Conceptions of Divine Things and to lead you to a Saving
Knowledge of GOD in his Son JESUS CHRIST."[10]

Since the library was assembled in rather haphazard fashion by miscellaneous gifts one is surprised to discover so great an accord with Yale's
dominant interests. Theology came first with philosophy as ancillary.

Theology included doctrine in the strict sense, Biblical studies with all the accessory linguistic disciplines, ethics comprising an interest in the study of man, whether in the present through travel and geography or in the past through history. The classics served both as drill in languages and as illustrative of the preparation for the Gospel among the heathen. After theology came natural science: optics, physics, astronomy, and medicine, with mathematics as an essential tool. Literature was but sparsely represented and curiously in this domain the fewest books have been preserved. Were they perhaps worn out by use?

Poetry appears in the works of Spenser, Chaucer, Pope, and Milton, among whom only Chaucer survives. Pope's *Homer* was there and Dryden's *Virgil*. Literary prose was represented by Addison, always a favorite model for the more elegant preachers. Plays and books of diversion included Shakespeare, Ben Jonson, and Don Quixote. Of these Ben Jonson only is extant. Beside them stood William Prynne's *Histrio-mastix*, or a *Scourge of Stage Players*.

The fine arts appeared in but a single work by an Italian Lomazzo, translated into English by Richard Haydock with the title A *Tracte Containing the Artes of Curious Paintinge, Carvinge & Buildinge* (Oxford, 1598).

Natural science was rich with Bacon, Boyle, Newton, and Harvey and reports of the Royal Society. A good deal of geography was ancient, Strabo and Ptolemy, but there was Heylyn's *Cosmographie* and recent maps. Histories covered the whole of Europe, Sir Walter Raleigh's *History of the World*, for example, with special treatises on the history of England, Scotland, Ireland, Asia, and America. Church history was copiously and impartially supplied through the *Magdeburg Centuries* for the Protestants and Baronius' *Annales Ecclesiastici* for the Catholics. The early church was covered by Eusebius, the *Historia Tripartita* and Sulpicius Severus; the popes up to the Renaissance by Platina. The Reformation in England was treated by Burnet and Strype. The Council of Trent and the Synod of Dort again did justice to the rival confessions. Biography ranged from Plutarch to Increase Mather. The classics were there in abundance. And here the only surprise is that the works of Cicero and Virgil are not extant. They may well have been eliminated by use.

In the field of theology proper, the marrow consisted of reformed divinity considerably augmented since 1701. But of the two characteristic movements of the eighteenth century, the Enlightenment and Pietism, the Yale Library in 1742 leaned much more heavily to the former than to the latter because the Great Awakening had not yet had time to exert its impact.

Protestant theology since the founding of the college had not grown more Lutheran. The only Lutheran item in fact was the *Augsburg Confession*. But the Library had become distinctly more Calvinist. The initial collection had had some of Calvin's commentaries but not his *Institutes*. The gap in the meantime had been filled three times over with two editions in Latin and one in English. The Puritan divines were represented in abundance: Ames copiously, together with Perkins, Preston, Trapp, and Charnok. There was the tolerant Independent John Owen, the teacher of Locke, and there was Henry Ainsworth, the Congregational exile in Holland, who was represented not only by his work on the Pentateuch but also by his *An Arrow against Idolatrie* (Amsterdam, 1640). The covenant theology appeared in a work of Dutch origin by Johann Braun, *Doctrina Foederum* (Amsterdam, 1692). William Perkins incidentally safeguarded this theology from any hint of meritoriousness by insisting that to "Give all diligence to make your election sure" means "Not with God . . . but to ourselves in our owne hearts and consciences." This in his *Cases of Conscience*.[11] A stout Puritanism is evident in Zachary Crofton's *The Fastening of St. Peter's Fetters by Seven Links, or Propositions. or, The Efficacy and Extent of the Solemn League and Covenant Asserted and Vindicated* (London, 1660). The claims of British Non-conformity were set forth in *Some Remarks on the Dialogue . . . wherein the Cause of Dissenters is Pleaded* (London, 1704). And the case for American Congregationalists was declared by Samuel Mather in his *An Apology for the Liberties of the Churches in New England: to Which is Prefixed, A Discourse Concerning Congregational Churches* (Boston, 1738). An entire collection of sermons preached before Parliament in the 1640's revealed the progressive development of Puritan opposition alike to Episcopacy and the Crown. The Puritan insistence on an educated ministry was espoused by Samuel Clarke in his *Golden Apples* where he asked "What are the best means to be used by magistrates in these seducing, and seduced times?" and answered, "They should encourage a godly, and learned Minister."[12]

The spirit of the Enlightenment displayed itself partly in the books on natural theology and natural morality, which are not of themselves to be equated with Deism. Take for example William Wollaston's *The Religion of Nature Delineated*, which is simply an elaboration of the traditional arguments for God from the necessity of a first cause and from the evidences of design. "The astonishing magnificence of the frame and constitution of the world," the variety of things and their uses "do all shew that there is some Almighty designer."[13] Such a substructure by no means precluded the superstructure of revealed religion. The same may be said in the realm of ethics with regard to the writings of the new natural law school, Grotius and Pufendorf, who in order to conserve the great medieval tradition of a universal morality, found themselves driven in an age of sectarianism to vindicate ethics on a secular basis. The design of none of these men was antireligious, though the effect of their effort might be to emancipate alike religion and morals from the authority of Christian revelation. More indicative of the new temper were the works seeking to bring religion into accord with reason, which to the Enlightenment meant little more than common sense. The library had for example Jonathan Dickenson's *Reasonableness of Christianity* (Boston, 1722), a work with the same title by John Locke, and an anonymous treatise entitled *Religion and Reason Adjusted and Accorded* (London, 1688).

In addition to those works which directly savored of the rationalism of the period there was a considerable body drawn from the tradition of humanism and latitudinarianism. The man who sired these tendencies in the age of the Renaissance was pre-eminently Erasmus of Rotterdam, and one is truly amazed to find in this Puritan library Erasmus more fully represented than Luther or Calvin. The father of the Reformation had but a single item. The progenitor of Puritanism had only the *Institutes* and a couple of Biblical commentaries. But the prince of the humanists appeared in twelve folio volumes fresh from the presses of Leyden. The Erasmian spirit of tolerance through a minimizing of the importance of the controverted themes found expression in a work of John Davenant, *Ad Fraternam Communionem* (Cambridge, England,

1640) in which he pleaded that the evangelical churches were not at variance in fundamentals. Chillingworth was there complete, and he it was who in his *The Religion of Protestants* relativized the whole concept of the fundamentals by declaring that that which is necessary to salvation for one man may not be essential for another.

Neoplatonism, a tradition often combined with Christianity but always fraught with peril because devoid of the Christian doctrines of the incarnation, the cross, and the resurrecton, was well represented. All the books needed to induct Jonathan Edwards into the system and thus modify New England Calvinism were already in the Yale Library: Plotinus and Jamblicus, the founders of the school, and of the Cambridge Platonists the three luminaries John Smith, Henry More, and Ralph Cudworth.

There were also works, some with a skeptical and some with a mystical tinge: Agrippa of Nettesheim, *On the Uncertainty of All the Learned Disciplines* (this in Latin), and Joseph Glanvill *The Vanity of Dogmatizing*. The very work from which originated the Socinian doctrine of the atonement stood on the library shelves; *The One Hundred and Ten Considerations* of Juan de Valdés, a Spaniard residing in the early years of the sixteenth century in the Spanish dependency of Naples. Valdés could discover no basis for the traditional doctrine of the atonement as an expiation or a payment of a debt. He assumed that God is ever ready to forgive and the only reason for the cross was not that God needed to be propitiated but that man supposed that He did. To remove man's scruple God suffered. This doctrine passed to the Socinians, and here in the Yale Library was Valdés in English dress translated by Nicholas Ferrer, a friend of George Herbert, and published at Cambridge in 1638.

More significant than the inclusion of such works was the actual temper of the library which, with remarkable catholicity, placed contraries side by side and left the student to form his own judgment. The attitude of strict conformity and repression which marked the Yale Corporation and the Connecticut Assembly was certainly not in evidence within the walls of the library. Here one found pro and con as to Christmas, a subject of deep concern to Puritans, who objected to the celebration of the nativity as a relic of popery—"Christ-mass"—and as an occasion for carnal jollification after the manner of the pagans. To show their contempt the Pilgrim Fathers had deliberately labored on Christmas day. John Davenport also objected that Christ cannot have been born on the twenty-fifth day of December for at that season shepherds would not have been in the field watching their flocks by night.[14] In line with this tradition the library had a book by Daniel Cawdry *Diatribe Triplex: or a Threefold Exercitation Concerning* 1) *Superstition.* 2) *Will-Worship.* 3) *Christmas Festivall.* But the library at the same time contained the sermons of Lancelot Andrewes (London, 1635) in which the meditations for "Christ-masse" occupied 169 pages.

One would expect blasts against Rome and they were not lacking. There was *The Protestant Almanack for the Year from the Incarnation of Jesus Christ, 1668 and from Our Deliverance from Popery, by Queen Elizabeth, 109,* which informed the reader that "February hath xxix. dayes" and quite irrelevantly added "It is a great question, whether the Scarlet Robes of the Cardinals, do signifie that they blush for shame of their own cruelties; or that they are double-dyed with the blood of Innocents."[15] Yet this same library had the *Summa* of St. Thomas Aquinas, the *Metaphysics* of Suarez and Fénelon's A *Demonstration of the Existence, Wisdom, and Omnipotence of God* (London, 1713).

For the Anglican Church there were those very works which had made Episcopalians out of Rector Timothy Cutler and tutor Samuel Johnson, and the books had not been removed after the defection of the tutors. Congregationalism of course received its vindication but there was no bigotry in a library which had not only Richard Hooker but even Archbishop Laud, if only his reply to a Jesuit. Sermons preached before Parliament stated the case against the king, but the library shelved his *Eikōn Basilikē* which made of him a martyr and well-nigh a saint. If nonconformity to the Church of England was justified there was also A *Third Defense of Ministerial Conformity ... in Answer to Mr. Calamy* (London, 1706),[16] and when one considers the Puritan aversion to the so-called Black Rubric in the Prayer Book, which allowed kneeling at the Lord's Supper, one senses a splendid sportsmanship in the inclusion of A *JUST APOLOGIE for the Gesture of Kneeling in the Act of Receiving the Lord's Supper* (London, 1629).[17]

The left-wing Protestant sects naturally were refuted, but in order that they might be refuted their works were made available. For the Quakers there was Barclay's *Apology* (Newport, R. I., 1729). Of George Fox there was *Gospel Truth Demonstrated* (London, 1706), and of William Penn and others *The Harmony of Divine and Heavenly Doctrines, Demonstrated in Sundry Declarations . . . Preached at Quaker Meetings in London* (London, 1696). This work was presented by that rampant revivalist James Davenport.

Though the library breathed more the temper of the Enlightenment than of Pietism, yet works of piety drawn from all confessions were not absent. There was the Anglican Jeremy Taylor's *The Rule and Exercises of Holy Living and Holy Dying* and Cardinal Bellarmine's *The Soul's Ascension to God* (London, 1705). There was a collection of prayers entitled *Enchiridion Precum* (London, 1707) and the hymns and other works of Isaac Watts. A precursor of German Pietism, Johann Arndt, appeared in his classic work on *True Christianity* (this in Latin). Jonathan Edwards' *Discourses* (Boston, 1738) were there including the sermon *The Excellency of Jesus Christ*. His only other work was the *Faithful Narrative* printed in London with a preface by Isaac Watts in 1737 and by him contributed to the Yale Library. But English Puritanism was itself not devoid of piety. Witness for example this excerpt from *David's Teares*: "Oh, God! faithful in thy promise, and fearful in thy revenge, my soule fixeth the eyes of her faith vpon thy Word, neuer so soon spoken, as sure to bee performed. Howsoever externall matters fall, I will never bee pulled from assurance in thy word: my soule shall alwayes confidently expect performance of thy promise: albeit thou seemest slow; albeit thou seemest altogether to abandon me."[18]

The Yale Library took cognizance of the Puritan concern for the Indian by the inclusion of several works devoted to Indian missions. There was *The Massachusetts Psalter . . . in Indian and English* (Boston, 1709), Cotton Mather's *India Christiana* (Boston, 1721), Experience Mayhew's *Indian Converts* (London, 1727), together with a manual entitled *The Knowledge and Practice of Christianity Made Easy . . . for the Indians* (London, 1741), in which this conversation is introduced:

"Indian. May I ask you one thing . . . Why did not that good Being whom you call your God, make all this known to us as well as to you?

"Missionary. I must tell you once for all, that we poor Creatures ought not to expect, the great God should give us an Account of everything he has thought fit to do."[19]

The practical aspects of the ministry were not neglected. There was John Edwards' *The Preacher* (London, 1705) and Burnet's A *Discourse of the Pastoral Care* (London, 1692). The character of the following tract is bespoken by its title: *Holy Oyle for the Lampes of the Sanctvarie or Scriptvre Phrases Alphabetically Disposed: For the vse and benefit of such as desire to speak the Language of Canaan, more especially the sonnes of the Prophets, who would attaine Elegancie and Sublimity of expressions* (London, 1630).[20]

Of Domesticall Duties by William Gouge was a fine exposition of the Puritan ethic of marriage where the stress was placed not on the remedy for sin nor the means of propagation, as in Catholic teaching, nor on romantic and passionate attachment as in the Troubadour tradition, but rather on companionability in the work of the Lord. The partners are enjoined to engage in prayer together:

"This latter doth especially concerne the husband, who is as a Priest unto his wife, and ought to be her mouth to God when they two are together: yet I doubt not, but that the wife may pray in the husband's presence when they two are alone, either for *triall* (that he may have knowledge of her abilitie and gift in that kinde) or for *helpe* (if the wife be much better able to performe that duty than the man is, as many wives are.)"[21]

The most glaring lack in the whole library was at the point of modern languages. There was one Italian dictionary, one book in Spanish, translations of the Bible into Dutch and Spanish, but nothing in German, although Arndt's *Vom Wahren Christenthum* was translated into Latin. There was not a book in French. Montaigne, Montesquieu, Fénelon, Descartes, and Du Pin were all done into English; otherwise they could scarcely have been read.

The study of all modern languages came but late to the American colleges. Harvard gave a course in 1735 but thereafter for the next forty-five years only intermittently. At Princeton Esther Burr recorded in her journal: "We have a French master in the house with us. He is learning the scholars French. Mr. Burr has a mind I should learn too but I have no time. A married woman has something more to care about than learning French, though if I had time I should be very fond of learning."[22] Esther Burr bore three babies and died at the age of twenty-seven without learning French. The venture soon lagged and Princeton did not have regular instruction until the beginning of the nineteenth century.

When in the 1780's the language became established at Harvard and at Columbia, the Yale trustees rejected the proposal of one of the alumni, himself a representative of Congress in Paris, that a course be instituted in the college.[23] Not until 1825 was French included as an elective in the third term of the junior year and then at the student's expense.[24]

The Yale Library was assembled in the spirit of that Christendom where Latin was a universal tongue. The other foreign language requisites were those needed by Biblical scholarship: Greek and Hebrew plus Aramaic and Syriac. The disintegration of Christendom had not yet imposed upon the scholar the task of acquiring some half-dozen tongues, with the result that the nonspecialist despairs and is content to know none save his own.

CHAPTER V

The Schools of the Prophets

During the eighteenth century ministerial candidates desiring further study sometimes continued at the college but more commonly spent a period of apprenticeship in the homes of resident parsons, themselves alumni of Yale and regarded as part of its graduate teaching staff. Here plainly Yale could not be equated with the campus at New Haven because the institution was so completely integrated with the entire community. Ministerial tutors were not selected by the College nor by the churches but were chosen by the students who often reined up at a parsonage door, unannounced, with a request for admission. When a tutor considered his candidate qualified he was recommended to a church. Following a call he was rigorously examined by neighboring churches, and if deemed qualified was ordained. Preference for tutors fell on men of the New Light persuasion, and this fact even more than the atmosphere of Yale accounts for the persistence of the unique combination of theological interest and evangelical temper.

These parsonage seminaries were popularly called "Schools of the Prophets." If the ministers who conducted them deserve a meed of recognition for devoting to students hours that might have been given to relaxation, the ministers' wives must not be forgotten for carrying the load of expanded households. Sometimes they had even to supervise the entire process in the absence of their husbands.[1]

The students for the time being became members of the family and sometimes for more than the time being. Not infrequently a young man left equipped not only with wisdom but also with a wife. This could not of course be expected in every instance, for even though the minister like the father of Jonathan Edwards produced sixty feet of daughters, he could not provide for all of his protégés if like Emmons he trained more than eighty. But each had his chance. There were no undue impediments. The Jonathan Edwards family required only that the girls be in by nine. A room was provided for male callers with heat provided lest temptation be offered to bundling. The students attended the Sunday evening catechizing of the children and each night shared in family prayers by candlelight.[2]

The theology inculcated by the ministerial tutors was Edwardean with progressive modifications. The three great teachers of preachers in the period after Edwards were Samuel Hopkins, Joseph Bellamy, Nathanael Emmons. The first two had been trained directly in the Edwards parsonage. Emmons came from the same vine if not the same vintage.

Paradoxically the point of departure for these Edwardeans was the divine goodness. Hopkins termed it "disinterested benevolence," a characteristic of God and also an attitude demanded of man whose love to God should proceed not from a consideration of benefits received but only from regard to God's excellency. We are to love God because He first loved us. We are to love Him because He is worthy to be loved. Nor should we cease to love were He to make of us an unwelcome disposition. One should indeed be willing to be damned for the glory of God as Moses requested that he might be blotted out from the book of life.

But this affirmation at once raised a serious question: If God were worthy to be loved would He so blot out anyone? God was claimed to be disinterested benevolence, and all that He does was said to be good and gracious, but as sovereign He is also ultimately the author of all that has come to pass. One must then inquire not simply why some are damned but why any should deserve to be damned, why God has created a world in which sin and misery exist.

The problem was not to be solved by diminishing God's accountability for what has come to pass. Emmons in particular wrestled with the problem of the fall of Adam. If God made him good, how was he capable of falling? The answer was that God must have wrought in Adam to make him fall, and with regard to our own sin Emmons rejected any transfer of guilt or any hereditary disposition. We sin, said he, for the same reason that Adam sinned because God impells us so to do.[3]

But if, then, God drives men to sin must not God be sinful? The only way out was to diminish the sinfulness of sin or at any rate to work it somehow into the fabric of good. Hopkins, in his sermon *Sin through Divine Interposition an Advantage to the Universe* answered that sin and misery are good in the sense that the universe is better with them than without them. He cited the sin of Joseph's brethren in selling him into Egypt, whereby in the providence of God they and their father's house and their people were saved subsequently from the famine. The explanation was not too satisfying because, since God was the subject of the inquiry, one could ask why He had allowed the famine. Bellamy was more penetrating when he appealed to the law that light cannot appear in its full brilliance without shade, nor virtue without vice. Justice cannot be displayed without punishment; nor mercy, if there be nothing to forgive. Would the universe have been so excellent had it been a sweet Elysium devoid of pain? Can even joy attain its full intensity if it be not release from dread and sorrow? Can the supreme quality of man be made evident other than through tragedy? With what astonishing luster and glory the mercy and grace of God shine forth in the death of Christ! If God aimed only at the happiness of His people, why did He not dispose Pharaoh to release them at once, and why did He detain them for forty years in the wilderness? What was His design in all this, if not to show forth all of His perfections that the whole earth might be full of His glory?[4]

Bellamy himself pushed objections to his own argument: "There are some calamities in this life, which God might be supposed to send upon his creatures for their good. . . . But what shall we say when God drowns a whole world, burns up several cities, and damns to all eternity millions of his creatures? yea, and all for nothing, when they deserved no ill at his hands, not the least! *Where is his justice now? Yea, where is his goodness?* . . . It is just as if a father, who has ten children, should tie up five every Monday morning, and whip them almost to death for nothing in the world but to make the rest love him, and be good and obedient children. And would they love him any the more for this? Yea, they could not but hate so cruel a tyrant."[5]

One answer was that God sent His Son to save fallen humanity. But then a new question arose: Why in that case are not all men saved? Judging by the way men behave here and now one may fairly assume that all are not saved. Yet God has made them such as they are and if He is absolute He must be finally responsible alike for their behavior and their destiny. Perhaps, however, the future may afford some alleviation. If God is both disinterested benevolence and infinite capacity surely He will not suffer Himself to be ultimately defeated by the recalcitrance of men. Neither Hopkins nor Bellamy could bring himself to a sharp break with the traditional view that some are irretrievably lost, but each was concerned to reduce the number of the damned. Christ's assertion that few are chosen, declared Hopkins, had reference only to his own time.[6] And Bellamy calculated that if all souls born in the past were damned and all in the future were saved, at the normal rate of population increase by the time of the millennium the proportion of saved to lost would be 17,000 to 1.[7] Pietism was attenuating Calvinism. An utterly disinterested benevolence on the part of man toward God and the neighbor was fast impelling God in the direction of universalism.

In the realm of church relations Hopkins, Bellamy, and Emmons were all vigorous proponents of the Edwardean contention that the Church should consist only of those who had had an experience of regeneration. The Lord's Supper should be denied to the tepid and baptism to their children. These followers of Edwards were responsible for the final collapse of the Half Way Covenant in New England. Another anomaly is here involved: they were struggling mightily to purify the Church, to maintain the full standards as to belief, emotional response, and behavior. But if God is absolute and man entirely dependent, how can man do anything either to improve himself or the Church? Emmons replied that the paradox lies in the New Testament itself: "Work out your own salvation with fear and trembling. For it is God which worketh in you both to will and to do of his good pleasure" (Philip. 2:12-13).[8] Oddly enough precisely because it is God who impels children to sin, their parents should surround them with the nurture and the admonition of the Lord.[9]

This concentration on elevating the standards of the Church and keeping pure her membership necessitated, as already noticed, the withdrawal of the Church from the community and by implication called for the separation of Church and State. One might infer that it carried with it also the abandonment of the ideal of the holy common-wealth, but perhaps paradoxically again such was not the case. Hopkins in particular and Bellamy also became staunch opponents of the slave trade. An extensive program of social reform was, however, precluded in this period primarily by circumstance. War is never conducive to reform and the late eighteenth century saw the French and Indian Wars, followed by the Revolution. Passion for the holy commonwealth was directed toward the fashioning of the American nation and only after the political question had been resolved could energies be directed to malignancies within the body politic.

Conceivably the inability to undertake at the moment any wholesale Christianizing of society prompted a transfer of hope for the holy commonwealth to the Messianic age. Hopkins wrote a treatise on the millennium in which he foretold an age of universal peace in the Church where all sectarian divisiveness would be healed and in the State where wars would cease and swords be beaten into plowshares. The Lord would bless His people with prosperity alike through the productivity of the soil and the advance of mechanization. The exact date could not precisely be determined. Yet it was to be observed that the fall of the Church occurred in A.D. 756 with the establishment of the temporal dominion of the popes. Add to this number the key figure from the book of Revelation, the number 1260, and one arrives at 1916 for the commencement of the blessed age of peace—just in the middle of the first World War.[10]

These teachers of preachers were all advocates of the plain style characteristic of the Puritans who scorned the meretricious embellish-ments with which the pulpit orators in England titillated a jaded aristocracy. The Puritan divines were addressing plain folk who one day weekly left their fields and shops to receive instruction in the ways of God with men. The only need was to take a text of Scripture and deduce from it by inexorable logic in numbered sequence the doctrinal truths latent therein. No need for an exordium for the truth itself should bear its own impact.

A glimpse at some of the tutors throws light both on their personalities and on their methods. Information with regard to Jonathan Edwards as a teacher is scant.[11] A little glimpse is afforded in a letter by his daughter Esther Edwards Burr, who after leaving home reconstructed a tutorial gathering. "Imagine now this eve Mr. Burr is at your house. Father is there and some others, and you all set in the middle room. Father has the talk, Mr. Burr has the laugh, Mr. Prince gets room to stick in a word once in a while, and the rest of you set and see and hear and make observations to yourselves. And when you go upstairs tell what you think. I wish I was there too."[12]

One might have supposed that Jonathan Edwards would have been indifferent to all of the craftsmanship of preaching, leaving gesture, tone, and words to take care of themselves. A fascinating passage from his manuscript *Miscellanies* reveals on the contrary that he considered such devices by no means to be scorned. Here is an entry under the word "tone":

"A tone is to be avoided in public, either in prayer or preaching, because it generally is distasteful; and a whining tone, that some use, is truly very ridiculous. But a melancholy musical tone doth really help in private, whether in private prayer, reading, or soliloquy; not because religion is a melancholy thing (for it is far from it), but because it stills the animal spirits and calms the mind and spirit for the most sedate thought, the clearest ideas, brightest apprehensions, and strongest reasonings, which are inconsistent with an unsteady motion of the animal spirits. Wherefore, this may be a rational account why a melancholy air doth really help religious thoughts; because the mind is not fit for such high, refined, and exhalted contemplation, except it be first reduced to the utmost calmness."[13]

Mrs. Edwards was no less influential with the students than her husband. She had charge of course of all the mundane arrangements of the household which came to include eleven children. Her husband's contribution was confined to cutting wood half an hour a day in winter— he did not even know how many milk kine they possessed. Mrs. Edwards ministered in addition to the spiritual condition of resident students especially during her husband's absences.

She was peculiarly able to assist the depressed because she had gone through a like state herself. In a vivid narrative she relates that she was melted and overcome by the sweet assurance that nothing could separate her from the love of God in Christ Jesus. She appeared to herself to float or swim in the bright, sweet beams of the love of Christ, like the motes swimming in the beams of the sun. She was brought into the Divine Being there to be swallowed up in God. Yet this could only be if all concern for self were dissipated. She strove for such a detachment from all that savored of self, that she could rejoice if some other evangelist reaped in Mr. Edwards' own parish a greater harvest than her

Samuel Hopkins

husband. She was so resigned that for God's glory she would be willing to die on the rack or at the stake or in darkness or horror. She overflowed in benevolence to all mankind and found it sweet that others should excel her in divine attainments. She would rejoice to follow the Negro servants into heaven.[14]

One can well believe that it was even more from Mrs. Edwards than from her husband that Samuel Hopkins derived his doctrine of God as "disinterested benevolence" and the insistence that men must be similarly devoid of self-concern in their dedication to God. Hopkins had had his religious awakening at Yale under the influence of Brainerd, who though but a sophomore had had the temerity to call upon this senior and to inquire as to his state of religion. Brainerd thought it impossible to be a Christian unless one's heart had been "sensibly and greatly affected by the character of Christ." Hopkins had already made a Christian profession and yet could claim no such experience. There followed acute distress until one evening "a new and wonderful scene opened to his view." He resolved on the ministry and having heard Mr. Edwards preach at Yale determined to train with him. In his diary

Hopkins records: "In the month of December, . . . being furnished with a horse, I set out for Northampton, with a view to live with Mr. Edwards, where I was an utter stranger. When I arrived there, Mr. Edwards was not at home; but I was received with great kindness by Mrs. Edwards and the family, and had encouragement that I might live there during the winter. . . . I was very gloomy, and was most of the time retired in my chamber. After some days, Mrs. Edwards came into my chamber, and said, As I was now become a member of the family for a season, she felt herself interested in my welfare; and, as she observed that I appeared gloomy and dejected, she hoped I would not think she intruded, by her desiring to know, and asking me what was the occasion of it, or to that purpose. I told her the freedom she used was agreeable to me. . . . I was in a christless, graceless state. . . . Upon which we entered into a free conversation; and . . . she told me that she had peculiar exercises in prayer respecting me, . . . that she trusted I should receive light and comfort, and doubted not that God intended yet to do great things by me."[15]

Jottings in Hopkins' diary have a distinctly Edwardean ring. He had been so sweetly visited that it "appeared something wonderfully great, and inexpressibly desirable, to be the instrument of bringing but one soul to the knowledge of this glorious God. . . ."[16]

As a teacher of students Hopkins was not the most popular of the New England divines, endowed with but few graces and not chatty. "His thoughts were in solid bullion and he had but little small change." Nevertheless he exerted a profound influence upon students. It was he who disabused Jonathan Edwards, Jr., of a scornful attitude toward the theology of his father and then passed the young man on for further training to Bellamy with the injunction to drill him in pronunciation.[17]

Not a few of the distinguished New England divines of the next generation owed the direction of their thinking to Hopkins. Odd perhaps that Unitarian William Ellery Channing the great opponent of Calvinism in the early nineteenth century, looked upon Hopkins with veneration for his struggle on the one hand to reconcile Calvinism with the essential truths of reason and on the other hand for initiating the revolutionary movement to mitigate Calvinism's harsher features. In Hopkins one sees the holy community deprived of its first earthly tabernacle, assuming new shape as an ideal of justice, humanity, and universal benevolence for all mankind.

Joseph Bellamy was a far more popular teacher than Hopkins. His books had greater grace of style and his pulpit discourse a more commanding eloquence. He was graduated from Yale at the age of sixteen, and at the age of eighteen was approved for ordination by the New Haven Association and in 1740 installed at the church at Bethlehem, Connecticut, where he remained for fifty years. During the Great Awakening he was often absent as an itinerant evangelist, but later resolved to confine himself to his own parish and to the task of educating ministers.

All biographers are agreed that no record and no descriptions can convey a sense of his power in the pulpit. But the testimony delivered at his funeral conveys some impression. "When the law was his theme, Mount Sinai was all in a smoke; the thunder and the lightning issued from his lips, and all was solemn as the grave. On the contrary, in the most melting strains, would he describe the sufferings of Christ, his matchless love for sinners, and, in persuasive eloquence, invite them to be reconciled to God. With what amazing terror would he represent the torments of the damned! And in what lively pictures, lay open the glories of heaven, and paint the joys of the paradise of God!"[18]

One who heard him declares that he would catch fire from his audience and burst into the most commanding eloquence. Once he was preaching on the text, "Cursed be he that confirmeth not all the words of this law to do them" (Deut. 27:26). He summoned to the platform the twelve tribes of Israel and apportioned them on Mount Ebal and Mount Gerizim, then demanded of each in turn whether it accepted for itself the curse. To each of the twelve was put the question and from each resounded the Amen. Then was described the immaculate holiness and justice of God in the infliction of punishment upon those who by disobedience incurred the curse. The Angel Gabriel was brought down from heaven to strip naked all who made excuse and drive them to find refuge in immediate flight to the atoning death of Christ whereby sin is pardoned and sinners saved.[19]

Bellamy's method of training his students was to set them questions covering the whole range of theology on which they were to write their dissertations. For reading he supplied them with works on both sides of a controversy. His library was said to have abounded chiefly in works to be refuted. It contained Barclay's *Apology* for the Quakers and three works by John Glas, the Sandemanian, together with unorthodox works on the Trinity. There was of course of goodly staple of Calvinist works from England, Scotland, and New England. The Biblical tools were poor.[20] Commonly the evenings were devoted to reading and discussion of papers by students. They had also opportunity to preach. Bellamy's comments stuck. To a boy whose sermon embraced the cosmos he remarked, "Do you ever expect to preach again?" He advised another that fish are caught by a wary approach and not by threshing the stream. Another sermon was compared to a field of buckwheat in luxuriant stalk but without grain.[21]

Another glimpse of Bellamy's tutorial activities is furnished in the memoir of the wife of the Reverend Cotton Mather Smith of Sharon, Connecticut. Incidentally the excerpt graphically discloses the role of the minister's wife in the training of students. Her husband was serving as chaplain at Fort Ticonderoga in 1775 and had left her to look after the household including the resident divinity students. She reported: "In common with many other well qualified Pastors my Husband had been in the habit of receiving into his family from time to time such young men as might wish, after leaving college, to fit themselves for the Gospel Ministry. At this time there were five such students in our house. My Husband provided for them by engaging his beloved friend, the Rev. Dr. Bellamy, of Bethlehem, to come and reside in our house, prosecute the education of the young theological students, supply the Sharon pulpit and attend to pastoral duties; a young friend of Dr. Bellamy engaging to perform like brotherly services for him in his parish. As Dr. Bellamy had two students of his own he brought them with him, which added to those already in our house made my family to consist of twenty-two persons besides servants.

"In our present state of peace and plenty [1795] this does not seem so very great a burden; but at that time when the exactions of the Mother Country had rendered it impossible for any but the wealthiest to import anything to eat or wear, and all had to be raised and manufactured at home, from bread stuffs, sugar and rum to the linen and woollen for our clothes and bedding, you may well imagine that my duties were not light, though I can say for myself that I never complained even in my inmost thoughts. . . . And besides, to tell the truth, I had no leisure for murmuring. I rose with the sun and all through the long day I had no time for aught but my work. So much did it press upon me that I could scarcely divert my thoughts from its demands even during the family prayers, which thing both amazed and displeased me, for during that hour, at least, I should have been sending all my thoughts to Heaven for the safety of my beloved Husband and the salvation of our hapless Country; instead of which I was often wondering whether Polly had remembered to set the sponge for the bread . . . or Billy had chopped light wood enough for the kindling, or dry hard wood enough to heat the big oven."

Mr. Bellamy on the Sabbath drew tears from those unused to weeping as he spoke of God's fatherly providence, and Mrs. Cotton Mather Smith went to bed more calm, for she had been no little disturbed by reason of Polly's mismanagement which would necessitate baking instead of washing on the following Monday. Mrs. Smith was up at three. By five the bread was ready to be molded, "and the hickory coals were lying in a great glowing mass on the oven bottom, casting a brilliant light over its vaulted top," reminding her of "Nebuchadnezzar's fiery furnace, seven times heated."[22]

The third great Edwardean theologian and teacher was Nathanael Emmons, even though he did not study directly under Edwards. In 1767, at the age of nineteen, he finished Yale and in 1769 was ordained by the South Hartford Association after having studied under Dr. Smalley. In 1773 he was installed at Wrentham, Massachusetts. Unexpectedly candidates came to him until in the course of fifty years he had prepared between eighty and ninety for the ministry. They found him addicted to study and so completely sedentary that his chair wore depressions in the hardwood floor. On principle, he would do no manual labor because the minister must be completely dedicated to his own task. When workmen besought Emmons to help gather in the hay before a storm, he answered, "I am not going to leave my work to do yours."[23]

He was in no way abstracted and negligent of his parish. He remarked, "The birth of every immortal soul is an event highly interesting to angels,"[24] and no less interesting to himself. To those who mourned he was the more consoling because of what he had borne himself. After three years of marriage he lost his first wife and shortly thereafter their two children on the same day. Then was he sorely tempted until he learned complete submission. The experience taught him that the hardest time is not the funeral, but the ensuing loneliness. Speaking comfort did not mean, however, the holding out of false hopes, least of all to him-

Nathanael Emmons

self, and when in 1840 his son Erastus died he preached as was the custom, on the following Sunday, a "fitting sermon" in which he freely confessed that he could not be confident of Erastus' state, since he had lived thoughtlessly and only on his deathbed believed himself to be reconciled to God. Such last-minute accommodations always appeared to the preacher to be of dubious validity. A few weeks later the minister was called upon to baptize a child named after his son. When he had pronounced the name Erastus, he was unable to finish.

He was never sure of his own salvation. At an age beyond ninety he was eager to get to heaven because he would like to look up Dr. Hopkins and the Apostle Paul, especially the Apostle Paul. "I believe that I shall be accepted," he added. "I shall be greatly disappointed if I am not."[25] He shared Edwards' opinion that parishioners other than the sick and the bereaved should be encouraged to come to the minister's study because here they could talk more freely than among their own families.

With Emmons the ministry was a rugged discipline. He was in bed by ten and always up before the sun. No wine, no liquor, and seldom coffee; but he was not dour. His humor was said to be, "not the mere crackling of thorns, . . . but the jubilee of reason."[26]

His sermons were said to be like a well-kept farm.[27] The suspense which he built up through proceeding from conceded premises to unpalatable conclusions by inexorable logic made hardened sermon tasters tingle with excitement.[28] But he was more than a logician. Like many another Puritan divine he would innocently glide into poetic prose as when he discoursed on Adam whose "habitation was Paradise and . . . [whose] heart was Heaven."[29]

His remarks to his students on preaching were pithy and wise:

"Style is like a window frame. There should be just enough sash to hold the pane."

"The most important requisites for an extemporaneous preacher are ignorance, impudence, and presumption."

"The close of a sermon should be like the approach of a ship to the wharf *with all sails standing.*"

"The secret of popular preaching is not to meddle with the consciences of your hearers."

"Better to leave the people longing than loathing."

Commenting on the sermon of one of his students, he said, "Your sermon was too much like Seekonk, plain, long, and level." Asked why young clergymen felt so small after talking with him, he answered, "Because they feel so big before."[30]

Emmons retired while he still had enough mind left to know that he should, and lived to be ninety-four. When in his latter days he walked through the streets dressed in the old style in a three-cornered hat, with bright buckles on his shoes and knees, and white locks flowing down his shoulders, the little boys gathered as if to see a general.[31]

CHAPTER VI

Revolution, Enlightenment, and
New Light Restored

On the Atlantic seaboard the last quarter of the eighteenth century was marked by the Revolutionary War and the formation of the United States. The holy commonwealth of the Puritans, if it were at all attainable, would now have to assume new contours. Moreover, established attitudes had been shaken and needed to be recast. First had come the problem of the legitimacy of resistance whether passive or active to the British crown ordained by God. If revolution were endorsed then the ethics of war might disquiet the sensitive conscience. The Revolution accomplished, there came the separation not only of the colonies but also of the churches from the mother country. The Anglican Church became the American Episcopal, tracing its succession from Scotland rather than from England. The separation of the Methodists from the Church of England was accelerated by the Revolution because when the Anglican Church declined to consecrate bishops for the Methodists overseas, John Wesley was prompted to take over himself. The Congregationalists, Presbyterians, and Quakers felt less of a rupture because they had been linked by no institutional ties. Yet the Congregationalists of New England had hoped that the lights on the candelabra in the wilderness would shine across the sea and prompt the English to emulate their migrant children. Now it was apparent that Americans would have to direct their efforts primarily to their own land.

A further consequence was that the churches in the New World increasingly lost their dominance in particular localities. The day was gone when Massachusetts could with cogency hang Quakers for their refusal to stay out of Massachusetts. They never had been hanged simply as Quakers but rather because they refused to stay banished. By the time of the Federal Constitution, of course, the hanging temper had passed. Likewise, the exclusion of any citizen of one state from another was no longer tenable. Free movement was facilitated and in consequence, religious minorities in every state increased and the appropriateness of the establishment of a single sect grew less and less apparent. Here was a factor reinforcing the logic of Edwardeanism with regard to the separation of Church and State.

The very situation of itself may account for the widespread dissent from all the churches on the part of the freethinkers—men like Ethan Allen and Tom Paine. To be sure, the elder Dwight laid the blame for the appalling upsurge of infidelity on the two wars. British officers, he believed, who had come over during the French and Indian Wars, and the French officers who assisted the Revolution, had insinuated ideas subversive of the old faith. Odd that the French were first hated as enemies and papists, and then feared as allies and infidels. Yale itself was at least mildly affected by the new currents. President Ezra Stiles, while no infidel, nor even a Deist, was a man of latitudinarian temper and expansive interests, a universal savant, much more concerned to encompass wide learning than to defend the tenets of a particular sect. The line might easily have run from Stiles to a Unitarian movement at Yale except for the grandson of Jonathan Edwards, the first Timothy Dwight, who brought Yale back to New Light revivalism, and routed the infidelity which he ascribed to the Revolution.

REVOLUTION: DAGGETT

The war swirled over Yale. The news of Lexington reached the college on a Friday night in April, 1775. The college broke up on Saturday. There was a resumption in June,[1] but during the war, closures were frequent because of "lack of regular commons."[2] The library was dispersed for safekeeping into private homes. Even to this day an occasional book turns up in an attic and is returned. Daggett resigned as president, though retaining his chair of divinity.

On July 4, 1779, the British landed a force of twenty-five hundred men at New Haven. Some one hundred students volunteered to fight a delaying or diverting action. One of their number relates the surprise of the company, as they were marching over West Bridge toward the enemy, to see "Dr. Daggett riding furiously by us on his old black mare, with his long fowling-piece in his hand." The students cheered heartily. Speedily dispersed, they heard the report that Daggett in the meantime from under the cover of bushes had fired his fowling-piece until routed out. The British commander, seeing but one man in a black coat, exclaimed, "What are you doing there, you old fool, firing on His Majesty's troops?"

"*Exercising the rights of war*," replied the professor of divinity.

"If I let you go this time, you rascal, will you ever fire again on the troops of His Majesty?"

"*Nothing more likely*," was the retort. Daggett was then marched at bayonet point through the hot sun over a detour of some five miles, since the bridge was out, from Westville to New Haven.[3] The exposure and fatigue were believed responsible for his death within the year.[4]

Among Yale ministers Daggett was by no means alone in his enthusiasm for the Revolution. The New Lights were more ardent than the Old, for the New were already rebels against the establishment, and the fervor of piety has been known on other occasions to feed the fever of patriotism. The Anglicans were for the most part Tory, for they could not readily reconcile loyalty to the Church of England with rebellion against the king, its head.

For all the clergy an ethical dilemma was posed by the war. Yale lay in the Calvinist tradition, which glided readily from the accepted Christian theory of just war into the mood of the crusade. The just war predicates that the end of war must be the restoration of peace after the vindication of justice. The war must be conducted under the auspices of government. The clergy should not participate because of their vocation. Force should be exercised resolutely but reluctantly and only against combatants. The crusade is a war for an idea. It may be conducted by the Church. The clergy may take part. The mood is exultant because the warfare is in the service of the Lord of Hosts. Any war of a theocracy tends to be a crusade, and the Calvinist colonies of New England oscillated between the two views, depending somewhat on the character of the enemy.

In the early period, war with the Dutch, who were fellow Europeans, fellow Christians, and fellow Protestants, was to be undertaken only if the violation of justice was abundantly manifest, as for instance if the Dutch incited and armed the Indians to prey upon the English.[5] War against the Indians fell into a different category. Since the Puritans were the New Israelites, by the same token the Indians were the Amalekites, "annoying this *Israel* in the Wilderness."[6] The conquest of ancient Canaan was the one example in all history of a war both predatory and just because commanded by the Lord God of Hosts. "By the immediate command of God" the Israelites made war on Canaan.[7] "God . . . gave charge to the *Israelites* to be the Executioners of his Vengeance upon the Canaanitish Nations; to make no Peace with them, 'til they were utterly destroyed from off the Earth."[8]

The French and Indian Wars assumed even more the quality of a crusade because the French were papists who had perfidiously butchered the Huguenots. "Our Nation is engaged in a *Just War* against a Proud, Haughty, Blasphemer, and Persecutor,"[9] said one of the Puritan divines. When Cape Breton fell, Thomas Prince, of the South Church in Boston, jubilated that an island important for the fishing trade and improved for thirty years by the prodigious labor of the French should thus fall into the hands of the English. "This is the Lord's doing! and it is marvelous in our eyes!"[10] The fall of Canada in 1760 produced paens of praise because the Lord of Hosts had routed the papists and the "aboriginals."[11]

Then came a war of a very different sort, against Protestants, against Englishmen, and against the very king of whom the colonials were the subjects. Revolution is always difficult to square with the formula of the just war, which by definition must be fought under the authority of the ruler. One way out is to declare that the ruler, as a persecutor of the true faith, has incurred the displeasure of the Lord and may be resisted by a crusade. Such came to be the theory of the English Puritans against Charles I, but in the early 1770's a religious issue was difficult to inject into the struggle. Or the ruler may be deemed a plain tyrant and by that token no longer a ruler, but in that case under what other ruler might the people resist him? The answer frequently was that the lead might be taken by inferior magistrates equated in England with Parliament, but this identification could not serve the revolutionists because Parliament was abetting the Crown.[12] The final recourse was the claim that the colonists had lapsed into the state of nature in which by compact they were able to form a new government. In this direction the thought of the clergy moved.

The Yale clerical contingent was prominent alike in personal example and in the formulation of ideas. Naphtali Daggett, whose attempt to be Horatio at the bridge has already been described, was one of the first to denounce the Stamp Act. "Where," said he, "are the mercenary Publicans who delight in Nothing so much as the dearest Blood of their Country? Will the Cries of your despairing, dying Brethren be Music pleasing to your Ears? If so, go on! bend the Knee to your Master Horseleach, and beg a Share in the Pillage of your Country."[13]

The Reverend Stephen Johnson of Lyme (Yale, 1743) averred: "By the essential, fundamental Constitution of the British Government, no Englishman may be Tax'd but by his own Consent, in Person, or by his Representative—Privileges extorted by the brave People of England from their Monarchs by slow Degrees, and the effusion of Rivers of Blood."[14] In a Fast Day sermon he declared that the violation of the compact releases the other party. Great Britain's abrogation of the charters put the colonies back into the state of nature and thereby freed them to set up whatever government they might choose after the manner of Rehoboam or of Holland in her late struggle for independence.[15]

Some of the Connecticut clergy not only served as chaplains but recruited and served with the troops. Jonathan Todd, of East Guilford, marched at the head of eighty-three of his townsmen. Benjamin Boardman, of Middle Haddam, and Eleazar May, of Haddam, each led one hundred. On a Sabbath morning Samuel Eells of North Branford after reading Washington's appeal for troops was himself elected captain of the company.[16] Clerical participation in war was characteristic of the crusade.

At the same time some of the clerical graduates of Yale were Anglican and Tory. The most distinguished was Samuel Seabury, who in 1776 became rector in the parish of Westchester, New York. He sided with the crown, and under the pseudonym of A. W. Farmer remonstrated with those who would forsake allegiance. Should it be over a tax on tea? "I, too, relish tea," said the rector, "but to pay this tax one would need only to sell the produce of a bushel of flaxseed once in THIRTY-THREE years. . . . Good God! can we look forward to the ruin, destruction, and desolation of the whole British Empire, without one relenting thought? Can we contemplate it with pleasure and promote it with all our might and vigour, and at the same time call ourselves *his Majesty's*

Samuel Seabury

most dutiful and loyal subjects?" Did not the farmers perceive that they were but exchanging one tyranny for another still worse? "You have blustered, and bellowed, and swaggered, and bragged, that no British Parliament should dispose of a penny of your money without your leave, and now you suffer yourselves to be *bullied* by a *Congress*, and *cowed* by a COMMITTEE. . . . Will you be instrumental in bringing the most abject slavery on yourselves? . . . Do as you please: but by HIM that made me, I will not.—No, if I must be enslaved, let it be by a KING at least, and not by a parcel of upstart lawless Committee-men. If I must be devoured, let me be devoured by the jaws of a lion, and not gnawed to death by rats and vermin."[17]

In consequence of the ensuing tensions, Seabury, being suspected of the authorship of the pamphlet, had to be hid in a chimney. He was then arrested and transported to New Haven on the charge of having refused to open his church for a Continental Fast Day. He retorted that his arrest was an infringement of the liberty of an Englishman and that to be transported for trial from the State of New York to the State of Connecticut was *"unjust, cruel, arbitrary, and tyrannical."* He was released and returned to his parish, but even after the Declaration of Independence he steadfastly refused in the conduct of divine worship to omit prayers for the King. To leave them out, he contended, would not only be a breach of duty but would be countenancing the rebellion.

When the King's forces invaded and then withdrew from his county, Seabury and his family went with them. The Colonials, on their return, consumed all the produce of his glebe and burned the pews in his church. During the Revolution Seabury served as a chaplain to the King's forces and also to a hospital in New York. At the close of the war the British commander, before evacuating the city of New York, gave the Loyalists an opportunity to seek refuge in British territory. Upward of twelve thousand are said to have migrated to Nova Scotia and the Bahamas, but not Samuel Seabury. He had bemoaned the rebellion, berated the Continental Congress, and refused to conduct the liturgy unchanged. Were he to return to Connecticut, he would unquestionably be subject to obloquy. No matter! The Church needed him. There were but fourteen priests in the state and many more were required. New priests then must be consecrated. New churches must be founded. And now that political separation was a fact, the Prayer Book must be revised; the petitions for the king removed, and new prayers inserted for new rulers. Seabury as a mere priest was not in a position to effect all of these changes. He sought, therefore, to transplant the episcopate to the United States. The convention of the clergy of Connecticut assembled and commissioned the Reverend Dr. Samuel Seabury to go to England and on their behalf to request for himself Episcopal consecration.

He addressed himself to the Bishop of London, to the Archbishop of York, and to the Archbishop of Canterbury, and these reverend dignitaries began to play battledore and shuttlecock with his petition. They pointed out that the King could not authorize omission of the prayers, only Parliament could do this. As for the episcopacy, they entirely agreed with Seabury that an Episcopal church without the episcopacy would be anomalous and unique, but they could not very well consecrate a bishop with the understanding that he would deliberately alter the Prayer Book. Thereupon Samuel Seabury, who before had so stoutly defended king and Parliament, now practically said botheration to king and Parliament, betook himself across the Tweed, and applied to the bishops of Scotland, who were nonjurors to the Hanoverian house in England. They thereupon, "in the name of the holy and undivided Trinity," heartily concurred in the plan of the clergy of Connecticut and advanced "the said Dr. Samuel Seabury to the high order of the Episcopate."

His return to Connecticut was not as tumultuous as might have been expected. Now that the connection with the crown had been severed, the victors no longer feared establishment of the Anglican Church. The Connecticut Assembly directly said, "Let a bishop come. He will stand on the same ground as the rest of the clergy!" The Americans moreover, had respect for a man of spirit. Dr. Samuel Seabury arrived as the first Episcopal bishop of this land.[18] At a Yale commencement he drove up in his carriage during the exercises and inquired if there were a seat for Bishop Seabury. President Dwight, relying on the Congregational contention that in the early church every pastor was a bishop, replied that there were some two hundred bishops present and Seabury might have a place among them.[19]

ENLIGHTENMENT: STILES

Even before independence was achieved, Yale resumed her labors. In 1779 Ezra Stiles, Old Light colleague of Hopkins at Newport, was elected president. He ruefully accepted, reflecting that the "diadem of a president is a crown of thorns."[20] An alumnus of the college, he was a tutor for six years, then a lawyer and a pastor. During his Yale days he had abundant opportunity to imbibe the spirit of Enlightenment in that collection of books whose temper he epitomized. But to say that of all the heads of the College he was the closest to the Enlightenment is only to point up how remote was the College and the whole Connecticut society from the shafts of Voltaire, the gibes of Tom Paine, or the decorous moralism of the English Deists. Ezra Stiles was an Old Light Calvinist, mellowed by the humanist tradition. He believed in freedom of inquiry and open access to all books, precisely because he shared the optimism of John Milton that truth is quite able to take care of herself. When President Clap declined the gift of books to the College library on the ground that some were deistical, Stiles remonstrated and sought to vindicate that free inquiry "for which Protestants have made so noble a stand. . . . it would be in vain to try to suppress it [this liberty] by hiding the deistical writings: the only way is, to come forth into the open field, and dispute the matter on even footing. The evidences of Revelation are, in my opinion, nearly as demonstrative as Newton's *Principia*, and these are the weapons to be used."[21]

Ezra Stiles

Stiles consorted with all and agreed with few. He was prompted in part by an insatiable curiosity which pried into the transit of Venus, the tails of comets, the structure of the eye as well as the peculiarities of religion. Before coming to Yale, in his pastorate at Newport, Rhode Island, he cultivated the Jews, attended the synagogue, learned Hebrew well enough to conduct a correspondence. His motive at the outset was simply to master the sacred language. For the same reason he acquired Syriac, believing the original of St. Matthew to have been in that tongue. Through these studies, having come to know and to like the Jews, he permitted himself a tentative optimism as to their ultimate salvation.[22]

Stiles visited the services of Baptists and even Quakers. He exchanged pulpits with his New Light colleague, Samuel Hopkins, and even attended Christmas services at the Moravian or Episcopal churches, saying that, although the day of the Lord's nativity was incapable of determination, nevertheless "on any day I can readily join with my fellow Christians in giving Thanks to God for his unspeakable Gift."[23] He decried the extravagances of the revivalists and yet was ready to have dinner with Mr. Whitefield, together with the ministers of the New Light church, the Baptist, the Episcopal and the Moravian, and in the home of a Quaker.[24] He was quite willing to enter into discussion with the Catholic priest, and delighted to read Thomas Aquinas, St. Bernard,[25] and Dionysius the Areopagite.[26]

But he was still very much of a Puritan in his own theology and in most of his tastes. He reported with apparent approval the distress of a Yale tutor—Stiles was then at Newport—that students had introduced dramatic exhibitions chiefly of a comic sort and were turning Yale into a Drury Lane.[27] Nor could he abide organs in churches. When one was installed in an Episcopal church at Providence, he remarked that it had come from a concert hall in Boston where it had been "promoting festivity, merriment, effeminacy, luxury, and midnight revellings," and now was being "used in the Worship of God."[28] One wonders, however, whether he may not have had an unconfessed nostalgia for an organ, since he records a dream in which he took some visitors to see the Yale Library and to his amazement discovered an organ installed in the sanctum. As he lifted the sumptuous covering, "the organ began to play spontaneously such bold and melodious notes as instantly awoke me."[29]

For all his basic Puritanism he was reproved by contemporaries as too broad and charitable, since he would neither excoriate the Arminians and Arians, nor would he rail against the New Light revivalists. He esteemed the solid integrity of the one and the holy zeal of the other. He frankly avowed his own attachment to the Presbyterian-Congregational system and lamented that so many coming to America left their Presbyterianism on the other side of the Atlantic. "But though," said he, "it be a glory to stand fast in the faith, it is a glory also to be 'Catholic and benevolent.' "[30] "It has given me some indignation," said he, "to see so little Charity among Christian sects."[31] When the New Lights in New Haven, after forty years of alienation from the Old Lights, declared themselves ready to share with them in the sacramental lecture, Stiles commented, "I wish them all well. May the God of Peace which brought again from the Dead our Lord Jesus Christ shed down balmy Love and sweet Peace into their Hearts and build them up in Union and Holiness to the heavenly Kingdom."[32]

His administration fostered among the students free discussion of a wide range of topics. In theology there was the ancient problem of whether foreknowledge necessitates predestination; in ethics, whether a lie is ever justifiable. The repeated debates on whether war is ever legitimate reveal perhaps an uneasiness of conscience in the New England mind where certainly no pacificism can be discovered prior to the nineteenth century. The legitimacy of polygamy was several times discussed. The problem was a hangover from the Reformation when the bigamy of the landgrave Philip of Hesse, the polygamy of the Muensterites, and the various proposals for the solution of the problem of Henry VIII had caused bigamy and polygamy to be thoroughly canvassed. A treatise on the subject by Theodore Beza was in the first Yale library. Another favorite topic was whether the flood of Noah covered the whole earth—a matter never conclusively settled. Some of the theological questions came directly out of the New Light controversy, whether an unregenerate person might enter upon the work of the ministry, whether sin might be regarded as an augmentation of the declarative glory of God. Certain topics were highly academic; for example, if a female should be admitted to public civil government. No doubt this was an echo of John Knox's *Blast against the Monstrous Regiment of Women.* Other topics were practical and pertinent: whether universal toleration would be good for the state, whether books should be subject to imprimaturs, whether the enslaving of Negroes be right, whether navigation on the Mississippi should be free, whether Shays' rebellion in Massachusetts was justified, whether Yale should admit to its corporation civilians along with the clergy. Clearly these young men were preparing themselves to take their places in a society still aspiring to be a holy plantation.[33]

Toward the end of his administration and the approach of the new century, Stiles began once more to sound the Ichabod note. The glory had again departed.[34] His quiet confidence that truth could take care of herself and that revelation was as secure as Newton's *Principia* perhaps fostered and certainly did not arrest among the students a devotion to the cult of the goddess of Reason and her high priest, Tom Paine. Lyman Beecher reported that most of the class before him—he came in 1793—were infidels, who called each other Voltaire, Rousseau, and D'Alembert.[35]

New Light Restored: Dwight

This astounding shift in the views of Yale undergraduates was due, according to Timothy Dwight, Stiles' successor, to the accompaniments of two wars. As already noted, he blamed the influence of British officers who came over to help fight the French, and then French officers who came to fight the British. "They perfectly knew," said Dwight, "how to insinuate the grossest sentiments in a delicate and inoffensive manner; to put arguments to flight with a sneer; to stifle conscience with a smile; and to overbear investigation by confronting it with the voice, and the authority of the great world. At the same time they were *the friends, and aids, of the American cause—nos très chers et très grand Amis, et Alliés.*"[36] How much more insidious were the French than the English who still believed in the Creator and conscience and allowed themselves to be reasoned with! Calvinists could get somewhere with that kind.

Accepting the presidency of Yale in 1795, Timothy Dwight was the man to discomfit these infidels. There was nothing of Ichabod about him. The churches of New England as compared with those of old England, said he, were flourishing, sound, and healthy. And as for the lost golden age, it was not quite so golden—heroic indeed, but stiff, overly rigid, intolerant as to trifles. The present generation was mellowed and kindlier to those of other persuasions[37]—meaning Baptists, Methodists, Quakers, and Episcopalians, but not the infidels, against whom all Evangelicals should present an unbroken phalanx.

He had many qualifications for leading in the fray, though one he lacked. A student said that, having been born before phrenology had discovered that bumps are requisite for greatness, he arrived with an unindented dome.[38] But for theology at any rate he was well equipped. On his mother's side he was an Edwards, and when mother and son discussed theology, neither could interrupt the flow of the other unless the speaker took time out for snuff. He inherited and accepted the Edwardean position and even some of the Hopkinsian refinements: divine sovereignty, human depravity, the freedom of the will, and the enthrallment of the inclinations, the ultimate responsibility of God for allowing evil, and at the same time the utterly disinterested benevolence of the Divine Ruler, and in matters practical a rejection of the Half Way Covenant. The cardinal tenets were all there. But there was a difference of tone which better spoke to the condition of a new time.

Dwight had appropriated much more than his grandfather of the new science, and when he rhapsodized over the excellency of God as displayed in His handiwork, the findings not only of Newton but of Herschel were evident. The sun, the moon, and the stars, said he, as they appear to the

Timothy Dwight the Elder

naked eye, have long disposed men to regard them as objects of religious adoration. "But, when the eye is permitted to look out of the window of Science into this vast field, it assumes an entirely new, and immensely nobler, character. Instead of a great splendid luminary, hung up in the heavens to communicate light, and warmth, to this world, and to measure the returns of day and night to its inhabitants, the Sun is seen by the eye of the Astronomer to be a vast world of itself; possessed of the wonderful power of emitting this equally wonderful element in immeasurable quantities to immeasurable distances; and the centre of many other worlds, which receive from this, their light and warmth, their motion, regularity, and harmony." In lyrical vein Dwight recalled the millions of stars hidden prior to Herschel from the eye of man. These stars are not "beautiful tapers, twinkling, merely for the gratification of mankind" but suns irradiating systems of worlds and all "sustained, regulated, and moved, by the hand of that Almighty Being . . . whose kingdom ruleth over all."[39]

Dwight was, however, not only an Edwards. He was also a Dwight and his father had not been a minister, but a man of affairs, a major, and a judge, a Puritan in his untarnished integrity. The Revolutionary War placed the elder Dwight in a frightful dilemma, for he sympathized with the Colonials but he had taken an oath to the Crown. A rebel he would not be, so sought to be neutral in a day when neutrality was not to be suffered. Therefore he resolved to migrate to the Mississippi. With two sons and other relatives he set sail for New Orleans, but perished in the wilderness.

In the meantime Timothy had been preparing for the leadership of the family which thereby fell to him. He had gone to Yale and there proved himself a high priest of what Harriet Beecher Stowe called "the golden calf of New England," namely, efficiency.[40] Dwight was a precursor of those experts who study manual processes to eliminate superfluous motions. He exercised himself in modes of handwriting to determine the most legible, swift, and easy strokes. He experimented on himself to find out the maximum amount of study the human constitution could endure. He drove Brother Ass as unsparingly as did David Brainerd. The result was a break in health and a permanent impairment of eyesight, so that later in life he could read only fifteen minutes at a time and for not more than two hours a day. Yet he had a genius for turning every reverse to advantage. A collapse in health occasioned a riding tour through New England, which not only restored his constitution but supplied the material for his most enduring literary work, *The Travels in New England*. The weakened eyesight led him to employ amanuenses, and to rely more upon conversation than books and upon memory than notes. He became a speaker of singular fluency and power.

In 1771 he became a tutor at Yale during the presidency of the ineffectual Dr. Daggett. Dwight, though only in his twenties, played the role of a modern dean. He was an innovator and introduced, at first informally, lectures on belles-lettres. He was himself a voluminous poet who aspired to do for the history of Israel what Homer and Virgil had done for Hellas and Rome. Then came the Revolutionary War and a chaplaincy on the colonial side, for unlike his father Timothy felt constrained by no oath. For him the war was a civil conflict not only because the Colonials were Englishmen but because the greatest acrimony lay between neighbors now divided into insurgents and loyalists both of whom raided cattle and burned fences and dwellings. After a year in the chaplaincy he was called home to take the place of his father. When at length he had set the family upon its feet he went into the ministry and eked out a meager stipend by teaching school on a coeducational basis. He held that girls should be trained because he expected them to preponderate in heaven.

Here then was a New Englander, voluminously read, widely traveled, broadly experienced, incorruptible in integrity and unassailable in ortho-doxy. This was the man called upon to assume the presidency of Yale in the depleted days after the Revolution when infidelity was rife in the College, membership in the church was scant, and candidates for the ministry were sparse. Dwight's explanation that it was all due to the ingratiating proselytism of British and French officers may be discounted because Deism was a universal phenomenon in that century, a reaction in part against dogmatism and in part a battle against established churches. One of the surest ways to have deflated infidels would have been for the standing order to relinquish all of its privileges. That was to come only somewhat later.

Dwight's method in the College was a head-on attack. When the seniors proposed for debate the question "Whether the Scriptures of the Old and New Testaments are the word of God," the president accepted the subject, heard the arguments, and then set out to flay the Philistines. In addresses and college sermons he smote the English and the French Deists with whom he had a firsthand acquaintance. He was not unfair to their arguments and when Tom Paine scoffed that if Satan had showed Jesus all the kingdoms of the world he ought to have discovered Amer-ica, Dwight replied that the word in Greek used for world comprised only the four tetrarchies of Palestine. And equally with Hume on mira-cles he was understanding and fair. But as to the aims and consequences of infidelity, he was scarcely just or dispassionate. Witness this perora-tion. "*What communion hath light with darkness? what concord hath Christ with Belial? or what part hath he that believeth with an Infidel?* From a connection with them what can you gain? What will you lose? Their neighbourhood is contagious; their friendship is a blast; their com-munion is death. Will you imbibe their principles? Will you copy their practices? Will you teach your children, that death is an eternal sleep? that the end sanctifies the means? that moral obligation is a dream? Religion a farce? and your Saviour the spurious offspring of pollution? . . .

Will you enroll your sons as conscripts for plunder and butchery? Will you make marriage the mockery of a register's office? Will you become the rulers of Sodom, and the people of Gomorrah? Shall your love to man vanish in a word, and evaporate on the tongue? . . . Will you enthrone a Goddess of Reason before the table of Christ? Will you burn your Bibles? Will you crucify anew your Redeemer? Will you deny your GOD?[41]

These words today might provoke a smile if not a sneer. They did not when delivered by Dwight, in part because his students for all their jaunty airs in the roles of Voltaire, Diderot, and D'Alembert had been brought up on the Scriptures and responded to words which plucked cherished strings. Furthermore, all descriptions of President Dwight agree that no word recorded from his pen faintly conveys the force of his person.

In 1802 the second Great Awakening was under way at Yale. It had already commenced in the churches. The mistakes of the first Awakening were avoided; there were no ravings, no swoonings. Illiterate itinerants were not encouraged, but settled ministers exchanged pulpits with one another. Hearts were quickened. Benjamin Silliman wrote to his mother, "Yale College is a little temple: prayer and praise seem to be the delight of the greater part of the students, while those who are still unfeeling are awed into respectful silence."[42]

Membership in the college church increased, and candidates for the ministry rose from the low mark of 5 per cent in 1792 to 31 per cent in 1805, approximately the average of the previous century.[43] Inasmuch as the peak of the first Great Awakening was not exceeded, one might interpret Dwight's success as not even the recovery of lost ground, but one must recall that the number of students going into the ministry was larger because the total enrollment was greater. Dwight gave himself unremittingly to the training of these ministerial candidates. He participated in their discussions and himself rendered judgments which an admiring student recorded and published. One sees again in these debates the concern for the contour of the holy commonwealth. Capital punishment, said President Dwight, should be exacted only of murderers. Prisons suffice for other offenders and prisons should be improved. Dueling is under no circumstances to be condoned. War on occasion has done some good but is a grave evil. Here are further questions and answers:

"Has Christianity benefited civilization?" "Indeed, yes! Behold how the Indians converted by Brainerd the very next year built a church and founded a school."

"Are the abilities of the sexes equal?" "In piety women excel and in ability they are fully the equal of men. The low quality of female instruction is disgraceful."

"Can the immortality of the soul be proved by the light of nature?" "No, but a strong probability can be established. For plainly even in this life there is no precise correlation between the soul and the body. Whenever was a nobler soul conjoined with a body more frail than in the case of Jonathan Edwards?"[44]

Whereas Dwight's interminable cantos on Canaan have achieved oblivion, his poem on his pastorate at Greenfield Hill is replete with evocative lines. He speaks of the church "with tidy neatness reputably gay."[45]

The Calvinist tradition with its near identification of the Church with the kingdom of God is apparent in Dwight's well-known hymn:

> I love thy kingdom, Lord,
>   The house of Thine abode,
> The church our blest Redeemer saved
>   With His own precious blood.
>
> I love Thy Church, O God:
>   Her walls before Thee stand,
> Dear as the apple of Thine eye,
>   And graven on Thy hand.
>
> For her my tears shall fall,
>   For her my prayers ascend;
> To her my cares and toils be given,
>   Till toils and cares shall end. . . .

To train men for service in a community dedicated to "God as governor" Dwight envisaged a genuine university with graduate schools for law, medicine, and divinity. He was, however, but a Moses suffered from Mount Nebo to view the promised land. His dream was to be realized only by his disciples and successors.

CHAPTER VII

The Divinity School[1]

Several considerations contributed to the establishment of the Divinity School in 1822. One was the separation of Church and State in 1818. The event is not to be exaggerated because there was not much left to separate. The franchise had long been universal and the Congregational churches were not exclusively supported by taxes because some had also endowments and pew rates. In any case on the eve of disestablishment the church rates were being paid only by Congregationalists and infidels because members of dissenting religious bodies could obtain exemption. The separation had chiefly symbolic value. It meant that ministers lost their wigs and buckles, that the last prop was removed from the old theocracy. And it is not without significance that Yale College was founded when the first prop went and the Divinity School as the last was removed. The loss of prerogatives was met by an increase in prerequisites.

Wholly apart from this situation a divinity school would have come, because this was the era of professional schools whether of medicine, law, or divinity. Yale was not the first to establish a divinity school, the sequence being Andover, 1808; Princeton, 1812; Harvard, 1815; Bangor, 1816; Auburn, 1818; General, 1819; and Yale, 1822. The primary reason for these foundations was the inadequacy of the apprenticeship system. Parish ministers were too busy to conduct schools. Such labors entailed neglect of their flocks, not to mention their wives. Ministerial libraries were inadequate.[2] Hence students found it increasingly expedient to continue for a time in college. The founding of the Yale Divinity School came in response to a request from fifteen such students that they be recognized as a special group and that they be accorded additional instruction. Funds came from the churches for a new professorship in theology, and some members of the existing faculty were assigned to divinity. In no sense was this move intended as a withdrawal of theological education from the college. Physically speaking there was no withdrawal. The theological students continued to reside on the campus and

Racing to morning prayers

to vie with the undergraduates in dressing while racing to morning prayers. Professors served both the Divinity School and the college. The real meaning of the new step was a closer affiliation of theological education with university instruction. The apprenticeship system had been replaced by a professional school.

Again, the second Great Awakening created a new need by increasing both the demand for and the supply of ministerial candidates in numbers exceeding the capacity of the former "Schools of the Prophets." Yale was called upon to supply the West—Yale rather than Harvard, where the Unitarian defection occasioned a shrinking constituency. During the eighteenth century both Yale and Harvard had been New England institutions, Yale supplying the southern portion and Harvard the northern, though with overlapping. In 1774 Ezra Stiles estimated that in all New England there were five hundred Congregational ministers of whom three-fifths were trained at Harvard and two-fifths at Yale. Princeton trained less than a dozen. Yale supplied over 80 per cent of the Congregational churches in Connecticut. But her range did not go beyond Vermont![3] However, in the period from 1825 to 1860, one-fourth of the Yale Divinity School graduates settled west of the Hudson.

The increasing denominational spread likewise rendered inappropriate the training of all of the students in the surrounding Congregational parsonages. Because of the plan of union with the Presbyterians, only two-thirds of the students in this period were Congregationalists, and nearly one-seventh joint Presbyterian-Congregational. Of the 649 students, twenty-six were Episcopalian, nine Baptist, and thirteen from various denominations.

Of all the factors immediately operative in the founding of the Divinity School, none was more potent than a new form of thinking called the New Haven theology, which will be described in the next chapter. This chapter is devoted to sketches of the first faculty of the Divinity School and of those men in the college and the pulpit of Center Church who exerted a preponderant influence on the minds of the divinity students.

THEOLOGY: NATHANIEL W. TAYLOR[4]

The most outstanding individual was Nathaniel W. Taylor, the first incumbent of the new chair of Theology. In 1800 at the age of fourteen he rode his grandfather's best pacer down the Derby road to enter college. For four years he was Dwight's amanuensis, and from Dwight received his first comfort in the midst of religious distress, through a sermon on the text, "A bruised reed he will not break." Young Taylor was hesitant to confide in the great man and Dwight, sensing his diffidence, opened up and the tears coursed as he spoke of his own hopes of salvation. What a contrast to the flamboyant Dwight tilting against infidelity!

When Taylor was invited to the pastorate of Center Church, he was prone to decline on the score of inadequacy. Dwight stepped in. Taylor objected that he could not meet the demands, "not without a miracle." Dwight answered, "You do not know what you can do. . . . I have no fears of the issue, and I know much better what *you* can do, than you know yourself."[5] "Pope Dwight" was right.

Leonard Bacon described Taylor's preaching: "Those solid and massive discourses, full of linked and twisted logic, yet giving out at every point sharp flashes of electric fire. . . . Those sermons of his, which have been heard by so many thousands, especially in times of religious awakening—

those strong and terrible appeals to the conscience of the soul unreconciled to God—those magnificent and more than Miltonic portrait-
ures of God's government—those expostulations in the name of Infinite
Pity—those thunderings and lightnings from eternity—these, in the deep
heavy tones of that trumpet voice, and with the impressive flashes of
that eye through which the soul looked out from beneath the 'dome of
thought'—these live in our remembrance. . . . It was in times of religious

Nathaniel W. Taylor

awakening and revival that he loved to preach. His favorite sermons were
composed under such excitements; and to his own mind every one of
them was redolent with blessed memories of success. All his theology
was shaped and framed with reference to the doctrine and work of the
conversion of sinners to God. If he could have had his choice, he would
have said, 'Let me die in a time of religious revival.' "6

In 1822 Taylor was induced to leave Center Church and by special
appointment to become the first professor in the newly constituted
Divinity School. He was inducted after having subscribed to the Saybrook Platform.

Taylor was described by his pupil Theodore Thornton Munger, later
pastor of United Church, as marked by a massive head, hair falling in
heavy locks over the shoulders, lustrous eyes betokening descent from
beautiful women. After lecturing for an hour he would give the students
a chance and would invariably worst them by his invincible logic.
Though unconvinced they enjoyed defeat for the pleasure he derived

from victory. In addition to logic there was pathos. His voice would tremble and tears would start. Who could resist "logic and tears"? His class met in a room where the windows rattled and heat was supplied only by a gaseous stove. He would tighten his cloak and remark, "Money enough for breaking glass in the laboratory, but not a penny for theology," a rueful reference to the appropriations for the flasks of Benjamin Silliman. The two men were firm friends with peripheral differences. Silliman reproached Taylor for smoking tobacco and Taylor labored with Silliman for contradicting the Bible as to creation. In his bearing Taylor was dignified, in attire immaculate. "You would not have liked," said he, "to have seen President Day wearing butternut trousers." But Taylor was not aloof toward students and when Munger one day saw him waiting for someone on the Green, the young man was amazed to find that he was the person for whom the great man was lingering.[7]

HOMILETICS: ELEAZAR T. FITCH

The chair of Homiletics was filled from 1822 until 1852 by Eleazar T. Fitch. He retained his post as preacher to the college, in which capacity he delivered a series of doctrinal sermons on a four-year cycle. Repetition was tedious to the faculty who were denied the mercy of graduation, and their testimony as to the waning of his creative powers may perhaps be discounted. Some students were irked because Fitch retained the "plain style" of sermons, didactic in content and minutely divided into numbered heads and subheads, so that an undergraduate complained of being subjected to mathematics not only during the week but also on the Sabbath. Dwight the Younger, who reported this, commented that for himself in sermons he preferred mathematics to athletics. Fitch was excessively diffident and never had the courage to preach without a manuscript, thereby giving rise to the yarn that when some undergraduates broke the windows of his residence, he rushed out exclaiming, "Boys!—Boys!—I have left my manuscript in my study. Come back at eleven tomorrow and I will read you what I have to say."

Yet when visitors supplied the college pulpit, the students were of the opinion that their regular preacher was superior.[8] One recorded that though Fitch would begin in a half-embarrassed manner, fumbling the

Bible and pinching the pulpit cushion, he would at times burst into "fervid eloquence, and his face would glow and his hand tremble . . . until with a half-cough and a pinch at the cushion," he lapsed into "his strong but treadmill argumentation."[9] Another hearer testified that students profited even from discourses beyond their ken and that admiration prompted imitation even of his "hems."[10]

James Hadley, commenting in his diary on Fitch's preaching, struggled

Eleazar T. Fitch

to be fair: "Dr. Fitch in the afternoon—quite heavy—I or he. . . . Dr. Fitch in forenoon, on what subject I am utterly unable to say. Unimpressiveness and evanescence about his writing. . . . Baccalaureate. . . . How a man can contrive to be so unimpressive on such an occasion is more that I can understand! . . . It is a great fault of Dr. Fitch's sermons that he often carries on a skillful fencing bout against an antagonist whom he does not bring out before the audience, so that his finest thrusts and strokes appear like mere pantomime. The afternoon sermon, 'On Consecration to God,' I was so unfortunate as not to hear. I was bodily present in the Chapel, but spiritually with Daniel in the den of lions."[11]

Fitch's supreme excellence would appear to have lain in the reading of hymns. He was himself an accomplished musician and even the composer of a popular song entitled "Take Heed," giving advice to a maiden to beware of blind Cupid. He would read hymns with exquisite lyrical expression in which there was more music than in the singing which followed. Fitch revised the hymn book. There had been several attempts before both by Dwight the Elder and Joel Barlow but Fitch was so far from satisfied that he simply would not read the stanza:

> So Samson when his hair was lost,
> Met the Philistine to his cost;
> Shook his vain limbs with sad surprise,
> Made feeble fight and lost his eyes.

Of his prayers it is said that they gave "a tremulous sense of the august Presence invoked."[12]

His sermons, if diffident in manner, certainly were not timid in content. For the baccalaureate in 1826, he had the temerity of a Puritan in taking as his theme the transitoriness of this mortal life.[13] On a pleasant June day, his young hearers may have thought the subject unseasonable. But when one now reflects that every man then present has long since been dead, it does not appear so unrealistic.

PRACTICAL THEOLOGY: CHAUNCEY A. GOODRICH

Chauncey A. Goodrich, like Fitch, came from the college faculty to the Divinity School, though at a much later date. From 1817 to 1839 he was professor of Rhetoric in the college and incidentally took over from his father-in-law, Noah Webster, the successive revisions of his dictionary. In 1839 Goodrich became professor of Practical Theology in the Divinity School. His career illustrates the very intimate relations between the School of Divinity and the college, for during the period while only on the college staff, he became in 1829 the editor of the *Christian Quarterly Spectator*, the organ of the New Haven theology. After his transfer to the Divinity School he was even more active in his pastoral ministry to the undergraduates, and more effective because he no longer stood in a disciplinary relationship. Dwight the Younger said that no student of the years from 1840 to 1858 would ever forget the voluntary Sunday evening services invariably addressed by Professor Goodrich.[14] Only by inference can one reconstruct a picture of his personal ministrations because he is himself the historian of the revivals in Yale College and for that reason has omitted reference to the central figure. One is entitled to read much into the following account of the revival of 1831:

"The spring of that year," said he, "will long be remembered as one of the most remarkable seasons of refreshing from on high, which has

ever been experienced at this College. . . . The whole college stood waiting in solemn expectation, to see the arm of the Lord revealed. Within
the compass of the next week, the long-sought influence of the Spirit
came, not with rapid and overwhelming power, as in the revival of
1802, but rather like the 'still small voice,' before which the prophet
wrapped his face in his mantle as he stood upon the mount. It spread
silently and slowly throughout the whole institution. The number under

Chauncey A. Goodrich

conviction of sin was never very great at any one time, but as these were
led by divine grace to put their trust in the Redeemer, others were
brought forward in their place, through the prayers and the labors of the
people of God; until at last there were comparatively few rooms left,
where the cry was not heard 'What shall I do to be saved?' . . . Many,
indeed, of those who were awakened, afterwards yielded to the fatal
delusion of putting off repentance to a more convenient season; but
before the end of the term nearly one-half of the impenitent in College,
were hopefully brought into the kingdom of God. As the fruits of this
revival, seventy-four were added at a subsequent period to the college
church, and not far from thirty to other churches."[15]

A little glimpse into his instructions on sermonizing is afforded by an
entry in Hadley's diary. A sermon on temptation, an exposition of the
story of Joseph and Potiphar's wife, seemed to the fellow students too
lush in the depiction of the blandishments of the seductress. "Goodrich
agreed in those criticisms; not so I."[16]

Goodrich the revivalist was also one of the most ardent social reformers
on the faculty. Notice will be taken in another chapter of his antislavery
and missionary zeal.

SACRED LANGUAGES: JOSIAH WILLARD GIBBS

Josiah Willard Gibbs was the most scholarly and the most tentatively minded member of the staff. James Hadley said of him that he held "even his own opinions in some sort as provisional, until a greater weight of adverse argument should require their surrender."[17] Goodrich and Taylor were thoroughly impatient with Gibbs' readiness to hold all

Josiah Willard Gibbs

conclusions in abeyance. Taylor exclaimed half jocosely and half testily, "I would rather have ten settled opinions, and nine of them wrong, than to be like my brother Gibbs with none of the ten settled." In 1824 Gibbs was called to the faculty of the Divinity School to teach the sacred languages, Greek and Hebrew. He was eminently a philologian who sensed ahead of other Americans that philology is a science to be painstakingly pursued in order that language may become a more precise instrument of thought. The lesser breed delighted to mock and related that when Gibbs and Stuart became heated in a debate with regard to a vowel point in the Hebrew, one of them brushed his handkerchief over the page and the point disappeared.[18]

Student notes on Gibbs' lectures and published articles reveal a man perhaps more undeviatingly committed to truth than his friend Taylor, who somewhat grandiloquently proclaimed that he would follow truth if it took him over Niagara. He might have added, "only if the current is swift." Gibbs' loyalty was to truth as the object of a quest. His temper is well revealed by his handling of the discrepancy between the Gospel of John and the Synoptics as to the date of the crucifixion. Gibbs enumerated seven possible explanations. Only the fourth and the seventh to his mind were worthy of consideration. Each of these had the merit of harmonizing the accounts. As between the two, "I cannot make up my mind."[19] A modern scholar would feel that Gibbs posited much in assuming that a correct solution must of necessity reconcile the divergence. A better example of his rigorous honesty is to be found in an article evaluating Catholic criticisms of Protestant translations of the Scriptures. Catholics object that Protestants in many instances have substituted the word "image" for the word "idol." Gibbs pronounced the Catholics right. They contend that "congregation" has been used in place of "church," and "repentance" has displaced "penance"—here Protestants, he said, are right. But Catholics were justified in complaining that the word "dissension" had been substituted for "schism," and "sect" for "heresy"—whereas Protestants have properly replaced the word "Catholic" by the term "general." Plainly Gibbs did not care where the ax fell. The only thing he would not do for his students was to think for them vicariously.

THE COLLEGE PRESIDENTS: DAY AND WOOLSEY

The College faculty before the Civil War must receive attention as a formative influence on the minds of the theological students partly because they had commonly received their earlier training in the College and partly because the whole community was so small and so contiguous. The first president after Dwight was Day in 1817. His first name was Jeremiah, and the students thought he looked the part. He was more addicted to prudence than his predecessor, and was so reserved that when he told his eighteen-year-old daughter, about to leave for the winter, that she would be missed, such an unwonted declaration of affection threw the lass into tears. His wisdom was in such repute that twenty-five years after his death the college treasurer thought to settle a debate on the relative merits of corner lots by an appeal to his authority. Day insisted on resigning in 1846 at the age of seventy-three, saying to those who protested, "You had better let me resign now, when I have the intelligence to do so." He lived for another twenty-one years.[21] The range of his interests is revealed in the titles of two of his publications: *Calculation of Longitude of Yale College from the Solar Eclipse of*

September 17, 1811, and *An Inquiry Respecting the Self-Determining Power of the Will* (1838).

His successor, Theodore Dwight Woolsey, served from 1846 to 1871. He hesitated to accept the presidency because he believed ordination to be prerequisite and doubted his own readiness. Yet he was ordained and inaugurated on the same occasion. He was the scholar, slightly stooped with an abstracted air, a finely chiseled face, eyes of profundity.[22]

Theodore Dwight Woolsey

Thus he muses in bronze on the Old College Campus where now and then an irreverent undergraduate will toss a hat upon his sculptured head.

THE COLLEGE FACULTY: HADLEY AND SILLIMAN

Of the undergraduate faculty the omission of any may be invidious, but two alone will be mentioned because they appear betimes in these pages, Hadley and Silliman. The diary of the former has already been quoted. He was professor of Greek and so proficient that he could hear an entire recitation without opening the book.[23] His comments on the persons of the period are priceless. Religious concern and intellectual bafflement appear in the entries about his Bible teaching. The prophecy of Zacharias he considered hard and the story of the Magi difficult to believe. "Strauss' objections very forcible." The prayers interspersed throughout the diary disclose an earnest spirituality.

Benjamin Silliman was professor of Chemistry and Natural Science. He was a devout Christian, one of a long line of Yale scientists who have not sensed a conflict between science and religion. At the age of eighty-two, Silliman declared his gratitude that by God's forbearance and blessing he had been privileged through the explanation of natural science to exhibit the works of the Creator. "Science and religion," he affirmed, ". . . form two distinct volumes of revelation."[24]

PASTOR OF CENTER CHURCH: MOSES STUART

At the time when the Divinity School was on the site of Battell Chapel and the churches on the Green were but within the kick of a football, the pastors were influential in forming the student mind. In the late eighteenth century Jonathan Edwards, Jr., the pastor of the North Church, now called the United Church, was the more outstanding. He was also a tutor in the College. His activity in the antislavery cause will be noted later. In the first half of the nineteenth century the pastors of Center Church moved to the fore—Moses Stuart, Nathaniel W. Taylor, and Leonard Bacon. Taylor has already been mentioned; a word then on Stuart and Bacon.

Moses Stuart was the man reputed to have debated with Gibbs over the Hebrew vowel point which turned out to be only a flyspeck. The two men were very similar, but Stuart was a public speaker and writer with much more capacity to dramatize his subject and to make the ministers and the churches see its relevance. Stuart owed something perhaps to his training for the law. He was on the point of taking up a practice when invited to a tutorial position at Yale. Here under the influence of Dwight he became interested alike in theology and in religion. The upshot was his ordination. During a period of disability on the part of the aged Dr. Dana at Center Church, Stuart was asked to supply and did so with such eminent favor that Dr. Dana was nudged into retirement and Stuart at the age of twenty-six became his successor. This was in 1806. Then commenced the second Great Awakening in Center Church. Two hundred new members were admitted into full communion. After but four years Stuart was then called to the chair of Hebrew at the Andover Theological Seminary. Center Church was loath to give him up, as Greenfield Hill had been to relinquish Dwight. At this time Dwight himself interposed and protested to Andover that Stuart could not be spared, to which came the rejoinder, "We do not want a man who can be spared."

In an earlier day he would never have been invited to such a post, because he knew almost no Hebrew. The study of the tongue had fallen, into sorry disrepute from which the pedantic quotation from the sacred tongue in the public discourses of President Stiles had not rescued it. But Andover knew, as well as Yale, that it is quite possible to train up a professor of anything if only he be able and sufficiently young. Stuart was then thirty.

He had to create his own tools. First in manuscript Stuart began

Moses Stuart

circulating a Hebrew grammar, then set up in his own home a printing press and imported Hebrew characters with which in 1813 he brought out the first respectable grammar of Hebrew in the English tongue. The press must have been a trial to his wife with five children to keep out of his boxes of Hebrew type. Besides she had to subdue the brood all through the mornings while he studied at home. She believed that he had a special mission from the Lord and conveyed to the children that Father was doing a great work on the Bible. They were somewhat puzzled, for they supposed that God had long since taken care of the Bible. But they surmised that their father had been named Moses because he had received some additional assignment from on high.[25]

Wrestling with Hebrew soon brought the awareness that the resources of world scholarship must be tapped, notably the literature of Germany. Stuart set himself to the acquisition of this new tongue. He could scarcely have learned it in college, for Yale was still quite provincial as to the modern languages. Not until 1825 could a student take French and not until ten years later Spanish. Only in the 1840's was German offered.[26] Stuart, by his own example and by his translations, did much to put America into touch with continental scholarship. He would order cases of books from abroad and tensely await their arrival by sailing vessel, each day scanning the small gilt vane on the Seminary chapel to see whether the wind was favorable for the incoming ship.[27]

At Andover Stuart was a campus figure. Oliver Wendell Holmes described him as "tall, lean, with . . . great solemnity and impressiveness of voice and manner, he was my early model of a classic orator. His air was Roman, his neck long and bare like Cicero's, and his toga—that is, his broad cloth cloak—was carried on his arm, whatever might have been the weather, with such a statuelike, rigid grace that he might have been turned into marble where he stood, and looked noble by the side of the antiques in the Vatican."[28]

Having become a teacher, Stuart was commonly in the pew on the Sabbath. His daughter describes him during the sermon, "He was the most attentive and the most restless listener. To keep still seemed to be a physical impossibility to him. If the sermon was poor, he shrugged and moved his large, white hands. His face was pitiable. If it was good, no one doubted his appreciation. At an apt remark he would draw his red handkerchief across his mouth. If he dissented, no words could have expressed his dissent more sharply than his looks."[29]

In the classroom Stuart was tart, jocose, and exhilarating. A student recalled his thin angular figure, modulated voice and vehement gesticulation, the flashes of electric fire which for one who had once heard him would still spark from the dingy pages of his printed works.[30]

Edwards A. Park, sire of a distinguished family in the academic world, declared that not a man in Stuart's classes but would have fasted a day rather than miss one of his lectures.[31]

His greatest memorial is to be found not so much in what he did as in what he inspired. Over one hundred of his students became missionaries and transferred to other languages the philological methods acquired from him. "Judson [translated the scriptures into] Burmese, Gordon Hall and Newell in Mahratta. Winslow and Spaulding in Tamul, Thurston and Bingham in Hawaiian, Goodell into Armeno-Turkish, Temple and King in modern Greek, Byington, Kingsbury and Wright in Choctaw, Worcester in Cherokee, Dwight and Riggs in modern Armenian, Bridgman in Chinese, Schauffler in Hebrew-Spanish,

Jones in Siamese, Perkins in modern Syriac, Hall in Ojibway, Grout in Zulu, Bryant in Grebo, and Walker into Mpongwe. . . . Something bordering upon the romantic is there, that while he, in solitary toil, was gathering from all the dialects of the East whatever could elucidate the inspired Scriptures, his reward was to come when men trained by his wisdom, and inspired with his enthusiasm, carried his name and influence back to the Acropolis at Athens, to the isles of the Aegean, the valley of the Nile, to Jerusalem and Damascus, the Tigris and Euphrates, to Ararat and Mesopotamia, and to the remoter lands beyond the Ganges.[32]

SUCCESSOR TO MOSES STUART: LEONARD BACON[33]

Leonard Bacon was the son of a Congregational home missionary, David Bacon, who with his family had gone out to the Western Reserve impelled by the example of his namesake, David Brainerd. To this second David physical hardships, financial worries, and misunderstandings with the Board brought an early death. His son Leonard might have taken up his father's labors had he not felt constrained through a sense of responsibility to his mother and the other children to accept in 1825 the pastorate of Center Church. He was only twenty-three. The assignment was exacting, two sermons a Sunday, a meditation during the week and never a vacation. When Senator Hillhouse gently suggested that his sermons were not up to the standards of his predecessors, Bacon answered, "They shall be made worthy." Yet he never felt he was equal to Taylor and Stuart. The saying became current, "as dull as Dr. Bacon when he has only the Gospel to preach." This may, however, have been a tribute because he displayed overwhelming power when roused by moral indignation. The address which he gave before the American Board on the subject of slavery was declared to be "one of the grandest exhibitions of power ever made by an American Divine. Condensed, stringent, and acute,—it had also a broad and lofty sweep of view and a simple, nervous, massive dignity of style, which placed it in the same class with Webster's political and juridical efforts."

Because Leonard Bacon was so devastating in controversy, he gained the reputation of being primarily a warrior. "Dr. Bacon's idea of heaven," it was said, "was a great debate in which Dr. Bacon had the floor." His wit was mordent and his sarcasm devasting. He would refer to his opponent's "devout and prayerful calumny." But if he was called "the fighting parson," he was really a militant mediator. He spoke of himself as being constantly "in a state of betweenity." He was a mediator between factions in Congregationalism, and in no little measure the credit is his for averting a split in the Congregational churches of Connecticut over the Taylor-Tyler controversy. On the slavery question he labored desperately to avert a rupture with the South. In the temperance crusade he strove for moderation. His role in these reformatory efforts will be described later. If at times he seemed aggressive, there was never any self-display. When he received an honorary D.D., he went downtown by back streets to avoid being called "Doctor." Leonine in appearance, with a shaggy mane above his massive brow, a patriarchal beard in place of a necktie, he yet breathed such benignity that a child, seeing him in his latter days on the platform of Center Church, supposed that he was God. Even the more sophisticated could have mistaken him for Father Christmas.

Bacon was a Puritan, given to that introspection which characterized the diaries of the period. Consider these lines written when he was twenty-one:

> My life speeds on. Magnificent designs,
> And vain abortive efforts; splendid hopes,
> And bitter disappointments fill the round
> Of all my circling years.

In an earlier generation he might have sought his solace in wrestling with the immutable decrees, or considering whether sin is an ultimate advantage to the universe or discussing whether man has natural or also moral ability. But Bacon was weary of metaphysics. He retained the Puritan fury of laboring for the glory of God and threw himself without stint into all the reformatory activities of his day. He was active in several missionary societies, an education society, an antislavery society, a tract society, not to mention the associations and assemblies of the Congregational and Presbyterian Churches. Here was a new type of Congregationalist, the ecclesiastical statesman.

He sought to invigorate his generation, as Cotton Mather had done in the *Magna Moralia*, by portraying the Golden Age of Congregational beginnings. His *Genesis of the New England Churches*, coupled with his

Historical Discourses, mark the beginning of scientific historiography of the American church.

His hymn for the bicentenniary of New Haven in 1833 makes of history a testament of devotion:

> O God, beneath thy guiding hand
>   Our exiled fathers crossed the sea,
> And when they trod the wintry strand
>   With prayer and psalm they worshipped thee.
>
> . . . .
>
> Laws, freedom, truth and faith in God
>   Came with those exiles o'er the waves,
> And where their pilgrim feet have trod
>   The God they trusted guards their graves.
>
> And here thy name, O God of love,
>   Their children's children shall adore
> Till these eternal hills remove
>   And spring adorns the earth no more.

CHAPTER VIII

The New Haven Theology

THE TAYLOR-TYLER CONTROVERSY

Yale Divinity School was established in part to sponsor the New Haven theology whose chief architects were three members of the first faculty, Taylor, Fitch, and Goodrich. It was a little difficult for some of the next generation to understand precisely what the New Haven theology was all about but at the time the strife out of which it grew was acrimonious. Leonard Bacon thought the differences were no greater than that between the names of the chief protagonists, Taylor and Tyler. But Bacon, one must recall, was an irenical statesman concerned to avert disruption by minimizing the controversy. At the peak feeling ran so high that Taylor was deemed magnanimous to have visited a chieftain in the other camp on his deathbed and with a tear and a kiss to have proved the bond of friendship unbroken. The theological differences admit a fairly clear formulation, even though they may appear inconsequential to a generation for which all Calvinists have come to look alike. Even at the time Tyler was willing to concede that Taylor's words were less objectionable than his spirit.

The New Haven theology was more a temper than a creed, a temper of critical conformity and filial dissent. No traditional credo was left untested and untouched. The freedom which Jonathan Edwards had exercised toward his grandfather, in the belief that the old gentleman had he lived would have been of the same mind, actuated a succession of theologians who considered themselves Edwardeans while proving, and revising the views of President Edwards.

They were all wrestling with the same problem: how to reconcile the sovereignty of God and the freedom of man. Either God is sovereign, absolute, all-knowing, and all-powerful or else He is not the one and only God. On the other hand, if man is not a free agent, moral responsibility can be conserved only by magnificent sophistry. The New Haven theology unflinchingly refused to make God anything less than God and man anything short of accountable. The emphasis oscillated between the horns. The New Lights, Bellamy, Hopkins, and Emmons, were called the Consistent Calvinists because they pushed to the uttermost the logic of divine sovereignty even to the point of making God ultimately the author of evil. Those of the Old Light or Old Calvinist persuasion were more moralistic and the New Haven school at this point was in their succession, but the New Lights had been the great revivalists and the Second Great Awakening was a renewal of their tradition with its insistence on man's native corruption and the necessity for a drastic regeneration through an act of the omnipotent God.

In meeting these problems Taylor and his colleagues were confronted by a new generation tinctured with the Enlightenment, whether represented by Deists at Yale or Unitarians at Harvard. The Enlightenment had insisted that religion be subject to reason in a more far-reaching sense than that of logical deduction from Biblical data. The Bible itself must be tested by the rules of internal consistency and conformity to universal experience. Moreover, God must be conceived as exemplifying that morality which He demands of man, actually a combination of Stoicism and the Sermon on the Mount. In meeting this new generation the New Haven theologians were able to avail themselves of a philosophy then on the way toward regnancy among all the schools of the seaboard. It came from Scotland and is commonly called Scottish Realism. Basically it was an affirmation of confidence in man, his ability to know and his capacity to do. This philosophy originated as a refutation of skepticism. Hume, assuming that reality consists of matter and mind, had argued that mind could never really know matter because what we experience is only a mental construct set up by the mind in response to an external stimulus. To this, Reid of the Scottish school replied that in contact with reality there is an immediacy of apprehension in which to be sure the mind is active through intuitive perception. Hume had also sought to undermine belief in miracles on the ground that miracles posit divine causation, but causation lies beyond our ken, since we experience only sequence and not actual causation, as when we see one billiard ball move *after* being hit by another. To this the reply was that Hume did not act upon his own assumptions and was not so skeptical of causation as to allow himself to be trampled to death by a runaway horse through failure to get out of the way. The appeal was thus to the trustworthiness of unreflective responses. Scottish Realism was called the philosophy of "common sense," because the universal reactions of healthy individuals—the diseased, of course, do not count—may be regarded as sound and for that reason the universal feeling that man is a free and responsible agent is correct.[1]

These assumptions when appropriated by the New Haven school meant an abandonment of the philosophy of Jonathan Edwards and at certain points a modification of his theology.[2] Taylor applied to the Bible itself the test of "common sense," since God cannot be guilty of absurdity. The philosophical idealism of Edwards was replaced by a dualism of mind and matter. His contention was rejected that we all are as integrally related to Adam as to our own past selves because each moment of our lives is related to every other only through a continuous re-creation on the part of God. Taylor held instead that God has brought into being autonomous individuals. Edwards' view that all knowledge is sensation communicated to us by God was replaced by the view that in sensation the mind is active. A mere impact from without produces no sensation in one asleep. This being so, preparation for salvation includes more than waiting for God to supply a sensation. As to the will, Taylor broke with Edwards and asserted that choice is not predetermined by prior motives. If motives conflict the will may fasten upon the inferior and invest it with such strength that it becomes dominant. There is thus genuine choice. Plainly the Augustinian strain in the Edwardean theology was diminished and Taylor even went so far as to say that as a theologian any clergyman in New England was superior to St. Augustine.[3] The Neoplatonic element in Edwardean thought was eliminated in favor of a stark Hebrew moralism. There was no streak of mysticism in Taylor, no tendency to regard evil as mere negation, nor to say that for this reason sin might be regarded as an ultimate advantage to the universe.

The Hopkinsian theodicy plainly had to go. A skeptic taunted: "Sin exists,—Could God have prevented it? If he could, and did not, where is his benevolence? If he could not, where is his omnipotence? Who can answer this?"[4] Taylor could, and his answer was emphatically not that sin through divine interposition is an advantage to the universe. One may say that God had to permit sin in order to make possible an unconstrained virtue, but it would have been vastly better if man had not availed himself of the permission actually to sin.[5] "But," demanded Tyler, "does not this mean that God is a disappointed and unhappy being, who is obliged to look with everlasting regret and sorrow upon the defeat of his designs, that he is forever engaged in fruitless efforts to render all his moral creatures holy and happy?"[6]

In other words, God has failed. This, according to Tyler, was the subversive deduction to be drawn from Taylor's principle and it is hard to see how Taylor could escape from the dilemma unless he wished to posit an ultimate triumph of God in the future through universalism. But he was no more ready to do that than had been the Edwardeans of the preceding generation. He would neither attenuate sin nor the consequences of sin to all eternity.

Everything that Taylor was saying thus far won the endorsement of the Unitarians and they, quite as much as Tyler, were ready to claim that Taylor had departed from historic Calvinism and Edwardeanism. But this Taylor roundly denied. Edwardeanism, he pointed out, admitted of variety and he was not to be read out for divergence on certain points so long as he retained the essentials, and the essential was total depravity —taught by Scripture, confirmed by experience. Scripture asserts that "in Adam all died," and the inference was that in Adam all sinned. This point gave Taylor immense difficulty. He did not believe in the solidarity of all mankind with Adam as taught by Jonathan Edwards. He did not believe that the sin of Adam was imputed to his descendants. Dwight had already given that up. Taylor did not believe in hereditary biological corruption. This would make total depravity something physical. He did not believe that God impels us to sin as He impelled Adam. In that case, God would be the author of sin. But how then are we related to Adam? Apparently only in this, that we are constituted like him, but even so there is a difference. Adam was innocent for a time, whereas we sin as soon as we can. Perhaps the explanation is that Adam started life all grown up. Plainly Taylor could not make it all come out even.[7]

But on one point he was unshaken—total depravity. Precisely what did this mean? It did not mean, according to Taylor, that man is devoid of any good. The natural man is entirely capable of justice, honor, and magnanimity. The point is that until we are quickened by grace the ruling motive of our lives will not be disinterested love for God. As soon as we are able to act at all we shall sin by operating from lower motives. Are children then sinful when born? No, not until they actually sin. And how soon will they sin? Taylor admitted that he did not know.[8] To opponents he appeared to have gone over to the Philistines. He insisted that he was still guarding the ark of the Lord, because of the view that man is corrupt in his ruling motives and will so remain until reborn.

Does it then follow, he was asked, that man really is not free? Taylor answered with the familiar but specious distinction between foreknowledge and foreordination. His slogan was "certainty with power to the contrary"[9] but if there is genuine power to the contrary how can there be certainty? And if there is certainty, where is the power to the contrary? Taylor was still an Edwardean in his inability to extricate himself from this dilemma. But then who can?

The one thing plain was this—man is corrupt. He needs to be converted. He can be converted. He is able to respond to God's pleas. Even the natural man may be impelled by lower motives toward the good and the preacher is warranted in appealing to self-love, which is not selfishness but regard for the true welfare of the self. Taylor and Edwards were at one in their entreaties to sinful man to lay hold of the proffered grace of God. Taylor cannonaded on "the reason, the conscience, the will, and heart of those unreconciled to God."[10] "Is it credible," demanded Taylor, "that God commands instant action on pain of eternal death, and then . . . cuts the sinews of all action, that he uses the language of hope and contradicts it with the language of despair? Such chicanery might disgrace an earthly monarch who would tantalize his subjects in the ruin and wretchedness of guilt. But does it mar the administration of the Eternal's throne? God forbid." Taylor freely conceded, in fact he stoutly affirmed, the doctrine of grace and the complete dependence of man upon God for assistance, but at the same time "no sinner ever was, . . . or ever will be converted in this state of inaction." Does the sinner know that grace will be supplied? He does not. Is it then not irrational to attempt to act when he does not know whether he will have the power? Of course, but what human act can be rational? To decline to act is to take the responsibility for going to hell, because there is ample warrant for the belief that one *may* go to heaven.[11]

This was the point of that ringing *Concio ad Clerum*, or address to the clergy, namely, that if man fail to act he incurs responsibility. "Glad would he be, to escape the guilt of it. Oh—could he persuade himself that the fault is not his own,—this would wake up peace in his guilty bosom. Could he believe that God is bound to convert and save him; or even that he could make it certain that God will do it—this would allay his fears—this would stamp a bow on the cloud that thickens, and darkens, and thunders damnation on his guilty path. But his guilt is all his own, and a Just God may leave him to his choice. He is going on to a wretched eternity, the self-made victim of its woes. Amid sabbaths and bibles, the intercessions of saints, the songs of angels, the intreaties of God's ambassadors, the accents of redeeming love, and the blood that speaketh peace, he presses on to death. God beseeching with tenderness and terror—Jesus telling him he died once and could die again to save him—mercy weeping over him day and night— heaven lifting up its everlasting gates—hell burning, and sending up its smoke of torment, and the weeping and the wailing and the gnashing of teeth, within his hearing—and onward still he goes—See the infatuated mortal! —Fellow sinner,—IT IS YOU.

"Bowels of divine compassion—length, breadth, height, depth of Jesus' love—Spirit of all grace, save him—save him—or he dies forever."[12]

THE FERMENT OF THE BEECHERS

The spokesman of the New Haven theology outside of New Haven was Lyman Beecher of Litchfield, Connecticut, who looked upon himself as a Calvinist commissioned to deliver the despondent from the sloughs of high Calvinism. Son of a blacksmith, he had in large part paid his way through Yale College by trundling watermelons and cantaloupes in a wheelbarrow across the Green for his fellow students, including Moses Stuart.[13] While in college Beecher had fallen into a sullen religious state from which only the sermons of Dwight had aroused him. The reading of Brainerd's journal had thrown him into a protracted hypochondria, and Edwards' *On the Affections*, though overwhelming, was in his judgment "to common minds most entangling." Yet in after years Beecher could write his own son at Yale "after the Bible, read Edwards."[14] Light broke for Lyman Beecher in no sudden blaze but only by degrees.

Beecher and Taylor first met in the study of President Dwight. Taylor was the younger by eleven years and at that time was Dwight's amanuensis. One day arriving ahead of the President, Taylor found waiting a plain man whom he took to be a farmer come to arrange for the winter's supply of potatoes. When Dwight came in, he heartily greeted the uncouth-looking visitor and introduced him as Mr. Beecher. Taylor wondered if he was the Beecher who had attracted notice through a sermon against dueling. He was. When Beecher was afterwards reminded of the meeting, he said, "Ah, yes, we took hold of hands in Dr. Dwight's study, and we never let go."[15]

They were allies in harvests and heresies and rivals in gardening. Beecher was gleeful that at Litchfield, through the use of cold frames, he could produce cucumbers ahead of Taylor.[16] On every visit to New Haven he made at once for the house on the corner of Temple and Wall and went up the back stairs to Taylor's study. Because fresh sea food was impossible in those days in distant Litchfield, the Taylors always served Beecher clams, lobsters, or fish. Once he turned up unannounced in the middle of the afternoon. Nathaniel Taylor happened to be away. Mrs. Taylor, having consigned the children to the maid, had settled down to entertain guests for tea, when in strode Beecher carrying a shad which he had purchased at the market on the Green. "Mr. Beecher," said Mrs. Taylor, "you shall have that fish for your *breakfast*." But Beecher without a word went to the woodshed, cleaned and dressed the fish himself, and in the kitchen kindled a fire, cooked the shad, and had it for supper.[17] After Taylor was dead and Beecher was failing, his children sometimes rallied his memory by asking, "surely you remember Dr. Taylor." "Oh, yes, yes, Taylor, Taylor a part of me."[18]

Both men were revivalists and theologians, but with a difference. Taylor would hardly have said when he came to wear bifocals that the upper half was for shooting pigeons and the lower for metaphysics.[19] Beecher used scarcely the lower for metaphysics. "I have always been going at full speed,"[20] said he. Emotionally he was mercurial. In

Lyman Beecher

the evening he might gather the family about him to bemoan his approaching demise, and in the morning roust them early out of bed to go fishing.[21] In religion a gleam was almost bound to be followed by gloom. His distinction is that he recognized more than others the possibility of a physical basis for such ups and downs. In prescribing for the despondent he would sometimes recommend a cessation for weeks from religious devotions in favor of a course of muscular exercises.[22] On receiving word that his son in Philadelphia had suffered a collapse, Beecher wrestled for an hour to compress concerned affection into a telegram and produced this: "Ease up. Rest—sleep—exercise. Cold water—rub. No tobacco. —Father."[23]

Yet Beecher never went to the length of turning Christianity into a health cult. He was as fervent a revivalist as any and used the full arsenal of Calvinist appeals. In his first parish he reported that his people reminded him of hens half asleep on a roost, who, when a candle is passed before them, open first one eye and then the other. But after Beecher preached on divine election, "There was not an eye in the whole church but what glistened like cold stars on a winter's night.[24]

He was always a war horse who sniffed the battle from afar and talked often of wringing his opponents' necks and hanging them from their own gallows.[25] But his fighting was that of a sportsman who after a match would shake hands and dine with his opponent. After battling for the standing order, when it was once definitely doomed, he manfully conceded that the Church did better to rely on voluntary effort than on wigs, shoe buckles, cock hats and gold canes.[26] And he promptly formed an alliance with his former foes against the Unitarians. He regarded himself still as a Calvinist and protested that he was removing no foundations.[27] His subversiveness was to be found less in theology than in his practical, activist, and optimist bent.

When he went out to Cincinnati he joined the Presbyterians in accord with the Plan of Union which west of the Hudson united the denominations in a scheme popularly called "Presbygational." The Presbyterians of the Old Side were speedily disconcerted by discovering that the incorporation of the Congregationalists in the Midwest meant an accretion to the ranks of the New Side. There were heresy trials; Beecher was tried. He was accused of wrecking the Westminster Confession and the Saybrook Platform. He answered that he subscribed to both, but there must be some latitude of interpretation. This was the old Congregational position that creeds are for "substance of doctrine." "The attempt," said he, "of universal and exact conformity must split the Church into small and consequently feeble and impotent departments."[28] A statement of faith on the part of the church is legitimate, but to him who subscribes it can mean only what he understands it to mean. Beecher then went on to affirm roundly that man enjoys freedom of choice and is morally responsible, but then he fell back on the old Edwardean distinction between natural and moral ability. Edwards had said that a devoted son is physically able to kill his parents but simply could never bring himself to do it. He has natural ability but moral inability. The question then comes to be whether the motives determine the will or the will is able to create the motives. Beecher left this question alone. He was acquitted, but in a few years the growing strength of his party caused the separation of the Old Side and the New Side Prebyterians.

The Congregational churches avoided a schism, but a dissenting theological seminary was established, later to be known as the Hartford

Seminary Foundation. The president was the great opponent of the New Haven school, Bennet Tyler. This division of seminaries has often been regarded as a calamity and repeated overtures throughout the years have been made looking toward reunion. The opponents of the move are today vindicated by the size and roles of the two institutions. If such numbers were now to be combined both seminaries would lose the touch of intimacy. Moreover, after the initial controversies have subsided, separate foundations not infrequently discover other and adequate reasons for a continuance of their independent ways. Hartford, for example, has reached out beyond the confines of Congregationalism to provide leadership for many of the left-wing Protestant sects, such as the Schwenckfelders, the Quakers, the Brethren, and the Mennonites.

The rift, which came at the moment of the founding of the Yale Divinity School, has been both the first and the last. Whereas other theological institutions have been rent by subsequent conflicts, Yale preserved her unity and connection with the churches. The slavery issue caused a secession from Lane Seminary to Oberlin. The doctrine of future probation severed Andover from the Congregational constituency and produced a decline until the entire senior class was able to marry the daughter of President McGiffert of Union. The seminary, after being closed for a time, was revived in conjunction with Newton. The storm over higher criticism occasioned friction between Union Theological Seminary and the supporting Presbyterian body and Fundamentalism led to a minor schism at Princeton. Yale has never, since the beginning, experienced a rupture of the bond within herself or with the churches. This is no occasion to glory, for there is no particular nobility in waiting to endorse unpopular positions until after some other seminary has succumbed in the first assault. But there is perhaps a historic vocation in the role of an institution sufficiently in advance of its constituency to exert a pull and not too far ahead to occasion a snap.

The older Calvinism underwent continuous modification from three directions: Biblical criticism, natural science, and personal religion. The Biblical scholars looked upon theology as a science to be built up from the Scriptures, rather than as a system to be deduced from metaphysical premises. The Bible was not merely the touchstone but the rock from which Moses struck the stream, and the Bible must be interpreted with the aid of linguistic tools in accord with the principles of historical investigation. Moses Stuart affirmed his loyalty to "the Word of God, the ultimate and supreme authority; and to perfect freedom of the human mind in the interpretation of that word, accountable to none but its author."[29] This was a declaration of independence for the Biblical scholar, but if he were the one to declare the mind of the Lord then some answers would have to wait. The tentativeness of Gibbs profoundly irritated Nathaniel W. Taylor, who could not cannonade with powder not yet quite dry. Even worse, these Biblical scholars were approaching a consensus at the point of some very upsetting conclusions. Genesis, they were coming to see, was not a literary unit and the sources out of which it was composed were in a measure discrepant. The Germans were already advancing this view. Professor Gibbs commented, "Our theologians, English and American have been very reluctant to admit this theory. But we do not see how the truth of it can well be denied. . . . It is not a question to be decided by appeals to popular impressions, but by a candid examination of all the facts."[30] Moses Stuart accepted from Eichorn the multiple source theory of Genesis while retaining the Mosaic authorship but only by making of Moses essentially a redactor.

The effect of such methods was bound to be a degree of tentativeness in theology until the Biblical data could be gathered. The churches were uneasy when they found Yale students denying the accepted meaning of certain texts. Systematic theology was giving way to Biblical theology and the faithful might well feel insecure if final answers to ultimate questions must await the verdict of historical experts.

The second impact came from natural science which during the eighteenth century had occasioned no conflict with religion, because the physics and the astronomy of Newton and Kepler were deemed merely to exhibit more amazingly the marvelous works of the Creator. But in the nineteenth century chemistry and more particularly geology and biology caused great upheavals. The conflicts were not too convulsive at Yale because the scientists were men of deep piety. For example, Benjamin Silliman. One of his students, Leonard Bacon, testified that since hearing Silliman's lectures "I have never seen a pebble by the wayside without some thought, distinct or indistinct, of the ocean in which it was rounded, and the geological eras through which it has come to us."[31] Another student, however, confessed to disquiet. S. G. Goodrich recorded that before hearing Silliman he had confused chemistry with the diablerie of Friar Bacon and upon entering the professor's lecture room and observing "a furnace, an anvil, a sink, crucibles, flasks, retorts, receivers, spatulas, a heap of charcoal, a bed of sand, thermometers, pyrometers, barometers, hydrometers, and an array of other ometers . . . I began to feel a strange sort of bewilderment, . . . [only increased by] an odor . . . which seemed to me to breathe of that pit which is nameless as well as bottomless. . . . At last the lecturer began. I was immediately attracted by his bland manner and beautiful speech. All my horrors passed instantly away. . . . [But] what a general upsetting of all old-fashioned ideas of creation was this! . . . Earth, that stable, old-fashioned footstool of man and his Maker, was resolved into at least fifty ingredients."[32]

If chemistry was disquieting, how much more was geology, which lay also within the province of Professor Silliman. He was acutely aware of the discrepancy between the Mosaic account of the creation and the geologic ages. The two might be reconciled, said he, by regarding the six days as six periods of extended duration. They could not, in any case, have been days of twenty-four hours before the sun was created. At the same time, we must concede that Moses presumably did not have the full facts in mind. He wrote in remote antiquity before the age of science. "Most of the facts which geology has developed were unknown to him." He told the story "with the same understanding with which it is commonly received."[33]

This was quite too much for Nathaniel Taylor. When Silliman informed him that the wall of the Grove Street Cemetery contained fossils millions of years old, Taylor rebutted, "God *can* create fossils in stone, and you can't prove that he didn't."[34]

Moses Stuart was scornful of the harmonistic proposal that Moses was speaking not of days but of eras. That, said Stuart, is not what Moses meant. The word "yom" in Hebrew means a day of twenty-four hours. The meaning of Hebrew cannot be ascertained by cracking rocks. Rather, roots must be examined, Hebrew roots. Modern science may pass judgment on whether Moses was right but not upon what Moses meant to say, and when he said "morning and evening the first day," he meant twelve hours. How else would his readers have understood him? "I say to geology, God speed. I would only ask patience in arriving at final conclusions. The surface of the whole earth must first be examined, and I would insist that the conclusions which geology feels entitled to draw should not be forced upon Moses."[35] The sturdy integrity of Stuart in refusing to save the accuracy of Moses by allegory and his mandate to geology to pass judgment after all the evidence was in meant the end of the Mosaic cosmology.

The third assault upon high Calvinism came from personal religion: a rebellion of the heart against the immutable decrees. One may well wonder why it had not come sooner. The eighteenth century offers abundant examples of those who were lacerated by doubts as to fate of loved ones dying prior to conversion. Yet resignation was the response esteemed and sought. Why now should resignation have turned to insurrection? Sociological causes were suggested by Harriet Beecher Stowe, daughter of Lyman Beecher. "In old New England," said she, "when the colonies were under the crown, God was conceived as an arbitrary despot. But after the rise of the republic God assumed a more democratic mien."[36] This observation, even if it be not valid, is highly interesting as a sociological explanation of religious change. It would never have occurred to Jonathan Edwards.

Change there was.[37] The farm moved to the factory. Church and State were separate. The aristocracy in general was not to be identified by wigs. Among the clergy the bewigged had become dewigged. Whereas

Eleazar Wheelock, 1711-1779
founder of Dartmouth

Joel Hawes, 1789-1867
Congregational minister at Hartford

the eighteenth-century divines wore seried curls from crown to shoulder, those of the nineteenth century displayed unruly spikes of native hair. Harriet Beecher Stowe regaled her generation with quaint stories of old New England already enveloped in the haze of bygone days.

No change exceeded that effected by the railroad. Easier travel ended the isolation of Connecticut, bringing contact with Boston's Unitarians and Transcendentalists. Coincidently the improvement in ocean travel facilitated a closer acquaintance with Europe. Harriet Beecher Stowe succumbed to the seductions of Florence and Fiesole. She compared the majesty of the pealing organ in gothic shrines with the plaintive melancholy of New England's fugues.[38] She went even so far as to suggest that Protestantism and Catholicism are but variant forms of Christianity conditioned by time, place, and tradition. In her novel *The Minister's Wooing* she tells of a New England lass whose lover was reported lost at sea. A bachelor minister then paid suit and was accepted. The wife of the French Ambassador, a Catholic of course, visiting the village and coming to know the lass, remarked that in France such a one would have become a nun, but in New England she would resignedly marry a minister and bring up a parsonage brood. One solution seemed as valid as the other. Relativity had invaded the citadel of the saints.

Intercommunication with other religious bodies had early shaken some of the assumptions of Lyman Beecher. His first wife, Roxana Foote, was a daughter of Tyre and Sidon who brought Melkart into the temple of Jehovah. She was an Episcopalian, and had never had that convulsive experience in religion which New England regarded as normative. She could not remember when she had not gone to God in prayer. In retrospect her husband declared that if anyone in the world ever exhibited disinterestedness it was she.[39] But at the time of their engagement he felt that a Hopkinsian conversion on the part of them both was a necessary prerequisite for successful marriage. They must be utterly disinterested, ready in their devotion to God to suffer anything and yield anything for His glory. The supreme test for Lyman was whether he would be willing to give up Roxana.[40] To her he put the stock question of readiness to be damned for the glory of God. "Is it possible," she answered, "that . . . when I pray with agonizing importunity that God will have mercy upon me, I can yet be willing that my prayer should be rejected?"[41]

In after years when Beecher heard ardent converts proclaiming readiness to be damned for the glory of God he would exclaim, "Be damned then if you want to be."[42]

The second Mrs. Beecher, Harriet Porter, was tinctured with Bostonian liberalism and when her husband attempted to read to her Edwards' sermon on *Sinners in the Hands of an Angry God*, she rose with flushed cheeks and swept out of the room with the words, "Dr. Beecher, I shall not listen to another word of that slander on my Heavenly Father!"[43]

Quite conceivably the relativity induced by interchange provided the oxygen in which grief formerly stifled now flared into passionate rebellion. The daughters of the Beechers, Catherine and Harriet, were the ones who headed the insurrection of the heart.

Catherine was Lyman's first born, the companion of his walks, his literary pursuits, his theology, and his religion. She was wooed by Professor Alexander Metcalf Fisher, the prodigy of New England, at twenty-three professor of mathematics and physics at Yale University. He was also a musician and a poet. His portrait by Samuel F. B. Morse hangs in the rotunda of Woolsey Hall. The face is finely chiseled, the eyes deep and brilliant. Fisher shared poems and piano playing with Catherine. They were engaged. Then he was commissioned by Yale University to make a scientific tour of the universities of Europe. The ship on which he sailed was wrecked off the coast of Ireland. There was but one survivor, and it was not he.

To Lyman Beecher fell the task of breaking the news to his daughter. It was all the harder because Fisher was not converted. The father strained his theology to the uttermost to comfort his child, "I can only say that many did and will indulge the hope that he was pious." Catherine wanted more than hope. Her father went a step further. "That God is influenced in His sovereign determinations by the conduct of sinners, I believe—and that there is more reason to hope for one whose whole life has been an example of excellence than for one who has spent all his days in vice and sin." Catherine wanted more than hope.

At first she wrote rebelliously to her brother, saying that God would have to clear Himself before He could offer her a revelation. After a year or two, grown more mellow, but not less assertive, she declared in a book that "any man who sincerely and habitually loves his Maker, so as to make it the chief object and effort to discover His will and obey it, will secure eternal happiness."[44] She could not believe that children are born incapable of obedience and then held responsible for disobedience. She affirmed that we have control even over our emotions. The word reached the continent of Europe that in America a woman had refuted Edwards on the will, at which a German theologian exclaimed, "Vat, a voman, refute Edwards on de vill! God forgive Christopher Columbus for discovering such a country."[45]

When Catherine visited in the family of Nathaniel Taylor, the little girls resented her because she engaged their father in conversation during the hour which would have been theirs. They did not know that Catherine was battling for the soul of Alexander Fisher.[46]

Sister Harriet was both nostalgic and rebellious toward a faith, for her, irrevocably gone. The Edwardean distinction of natural ability and moral inability, marshaled so triumphantly by her father to vindicate his orthodoxy before the presbytery, was gently satirized by one of her village characters. "Our state and condition by nature was just like this," says he. "We was clear down in a well fifty feet deep, and the sides all round nothin' but glare ice; but we was under immediate obligations to get out, 'cause we was free, voluntary agents. But nobody ever had got out, and nobody would, unless the Lord reached down and took 'em. And whether He would or not nobody could tell; it was all sovereignty. . . . There wa'n't one in a hundred,—not one in a thousand,—not one in ten thousand,—that would be saved. Lordy massy, says I to myself, ef that's so they're any of 'em welcome to my chance."[47]

When these words were penned, Harriet had grown mellow and was able to write with a touch of amusement. It had not been always so. She had lost a child in infancy from the cholera and a son aged sixteen by drowning, both prior to conversion. The problem of their fate is the theme of *The Minister's Wooing* where young James is lost at sea unregenerate. Calvinism's high spirit of resignation enabled "strong spirits," she says, to walk, "palm-crowned, with victorious hymns, along these sublime paths, [while] feebler and more sensitive ones lay along the tracks bleeding away in lifelong despair. Fearful to them were the shadows that lay over the cradle and the grave. The mother clasped her babe to her bosom, and looked with shuddering to the awful coming trial of free agency, with its terrible responsibilities and risks; and, as she thought of the infinite chances against her beloved, almost wished it might die in infancy. But when the stroke of death came, and some young, thoughtless head was laid suddenly low, who can say what silent anguish of loving hearts sounded the dread depths of eternity with the awful question, Where?

"In no other time or place of Christendom have so fearful issues been presented to the mind. . . . The clear logic and intense individualism of New England deepened the problems of the Augustinian faith. . . . The individual entered eternity alone, as if he had no interceding relation in the universe."[48] The news that James was lost benumbed his sweetheart and crazed his mother, until the Negro mammy, Candace, took the mother on her lap and rocked her as a babe. " 'Honey, darlin', ye ain't right,—dar's a drefful mistake somwhar,' she said. 'Why, de Lord ain't like what ye tink,—He *loves* ye, honey! Why, jes' fel how *I* loves ye, —poor ole black Candace,—an' I ain't better 'n Him as made me! Who was it wore de crown o' thorns, lamb?—who was it sweat great drops o' blood?—who was it said, "Father, forgive dem"? Say, honey!—wasn't it de Lord dat made ye? Dar, dar, now ye'r' cryin'!—cry away, and ease yer poor little heart. He died for Mass'r Jim,—loved him and died for him,—jes' give up his sweet, precious body and soul for him on de cross! Laws, jes' leave him in Jesus's hands! Why, honey, dar's de very print o' de nails in his hands now! . . . Don't ye 'member how He looked on his mother, when she stood faintin' an' tremblin' under de cross, jes' like you? He knows all about mothers' hearts; He won't break yours. It was jes' 'cause He know'd we'd come into straits like dis yer, dat He went through all dese tings,—Him, de Lord o' Glory! Is dis Him you was a-talkin' about?—Him you can't love? Look at Him, an' see ef you can't. Look an' see what He is!—don't ask no questions, and don't go to no reasonin's,—jes' look at *Him,* hangin' dar, so sweet and patient, on de cross! All dey could do couldn't stop his lovin' 'em; He prayed for 'em wid all de breath He had. Dar's a God you can love, ain't dar?' "[49]

CHAPTER IX

Coming to Terms

HORACE BUSHNELL

If the Beechers might conceivably have been influenced in their theological thinking by changes in their society even more might this have been true of Horace Bushnell,[1] who in college had worn homespun. In his boyhood the old Sabbath was still in vogue. He recalled a Saturday afternoon at Preston, Connecticut, when the family sent him to a farmer for apples, but the good man refused to supply the lad lest he be unable to reach home with his burden before the first star introduced the Sabbath day.[2] Bushnell lived through the adjustment of Hartford to the introduction of the railroad. To the businessmen who were in consternation lest it destroy the prosperity of their city hitherto dependent upon the river, he pointed out that the flourishing state of their already famous banks and insurance companies depended not on the river but on the enterprise of the citizens.[3]

Such a man might easily have been thinking new thoughts for the reason that he lived in a new world. But he had been thinking new thoughts prior to the outward changes. While yet a student he was in ferment and at Yale Divinity School was recognized as being at once the best and the most disconcerting of pupils. His innovations illustrate again the battle of the generations. He later described the New England fathers as "provincial, grappling manfully enough with a few speculative questions . . . phosphorescing bravely" in the gloom but unacquainted with the sunlight of the great Christian tradition.[4] Bushnell like the Beechers was prompted to deviations from the New England tradition chiefly through acquaintance with other and older traditions. In diverging from his own immediate background he looked upon himself not as an innovator but as a restorer of that wider and more primitive Christian heritage from which New England had departed, yet he did not feel himself so far removed from Connecticut Congregationalism as to be deterred from seeking ordination, nor did the Ministerial Association find any reason to reject him. He was ordained to a church in Hartford

Horace Bushnell

and there remained for the better part of his life. From Hartford he was to exert a greater influence over the mind of the Yale Divinity School than that of any formal member of the faculty. In the present school a professorship and a dormitory appropriately bear his name.

Early in his ministry Bushnell came to realize that he was maturing views which would disquiet his colleagues. He wondered whether his wife, a lineal descendant of John Davenport, would be willing to share with him in pulling away from the ancestral moorings. To her he wrote in 1839: "I have been thinking lately that I *must* write and publish the whole truth on these subjects as God has permitted me to see it. I have withheld till my views are well matured; and to withhold longer, I fear, is a want of that moral courage which animated Luther and every other man who has been a true soldier of Christ. Then, thinking of such men lately, I have often had self-reproaches which were very unpleasant. Has my dear wife any of Luther's spirit? Will she enter into the hazards and reproaches and perhaps privations, which lie in this encounter for the truth? Strange, you will say, that I should be talking, in the same letter, of doing more for my family and of endangering all their worldly comforts. But I am under just these contending impulses. However, in what way shall I do more for my family than to connect their history with the truth of Christ? How more, for example, for our dear boy than to give him the name and example of a father who left him his fortunes, rough and hard as they were, in the field of truth?"[5]

His fears were not fantastic, for had the Association been able to muster three members of his own congregation willing to prefer charges of heresy against him, he could have been brought to trial. Instead, his congregation withdrew from the Association rather than subject him to the possibility of prosecution.

Radical he appeared. Basically he was a mediator. There were three movements of his day with which he felt impelled to come to terms. The first was Unitarianism, the second natural science in the form of geology, and the third Transcendentalism. The first and the last centered in Boston. The new geology was regnant at Yale.

Unitarianism was a complex movement. It involved a higher appraisal of man than did consistent Calvinism. At this point, Nathaniel W. Taylor had already made a marked accommodation. There was also the picture of God. Both Bellamy and Taylor had acutely felt the problem, but were averse to a drastic solution. Now, Channing, the Unitarian, was bringing the Calvinist God under severe indictment with no apologies for presumption. Has not God, he inquired, endowed man with moral capacity, and must not man use that capacity to pass judgment upon the character of God? If any human parent, he argued, were to imitate the heavenly Father and bring children into the world "totally depraved and then to pursue them with endless punishment, we should charge him with a cruelty not surpassed in the annals of the world . . . [what] rectitude [is there] in consigning to everlasting misery beings who have come guilty and impotent from his hand?"[6] Bushnell in his reply frankly confessed that he did not know what would be the ultimate fate of the wicked. Perhaps they may "shrink to . . . intensified littleness and fiendishness, eaten [away] . . . by the malice of evil."[7] This suggests that the penalty is not imposed, but is inherent in the very character of evil.

The Unitarians objected also to the Edwardean interpretation of the death of Christ, a theory derived from the jurist Grotius who said that

God as a moral judge cannot forgive sin without satisfaction, but man's sin is so enormous and his capacity so frail that he cannot render due satisfaction. Hence God has Himself paid the penalty by substituting His Son for sinful man. To this the Unitarians objected that there is no justice in punishing the innocent in place of the guilty. How is justice to be satisfied by substitution? Bushnell answered, "Quite right." There is no substitution. Christ did not become blind for the blind and lame for the lame. In civil law there is not substitution. Bushnell affirmed that the death of Christ was vicarious but not substitutionary; vicarious in the sense that love projects itself into the suffering of another, enters fully by feeling into grief and pain and even sin. Christ was so burdened by our maladies that he "bore the disgust of their loathsome decays, felt their pains over again, in the tenderness of his more than human sensibility."[8] "Love is a principle essentially vicarious in its own nature, identifying the subject with others, so as to suffer their adversities and pains, and taking on itself the burden of their evils. It does not come in officiously and abruptly, and propose to be substituted in some formal and literal way that overturns all the moral relations of law and desert, but it clings to the evil and lost man as in feeling, afflicted for him, burdened by his ill deserts, incapacities and pains, encountering gladly any loss or suffering for his sake."[9]

Nor are we to suppose that Christ represents compassion, whereas God exercises stern justice. "Nay, there is a cross in God before the wood is seen on Calvary; hid in God's own virtue itself, struggling on heavily in burdened feeling through all the previous ages, and struggling on heavily now even in the throne [throes?] of the worlds. This, too, exactly is the cross that our Christ crucified reveals and sets before us. Let us come then not to wood alone, not to the nails, not to the vinegar and gall, not to the writhing body of Jesus, but to the very feeling of our God and there take shelter."[10]

The doctrine of the Unitarians which was deemed most significant and which gave them their name was that of the unity of God to the exclusion of triune diversity. On this subject the Edwardeans themselves at certain points had skirted on dubious fringes. The view of Edwards rested on the Neoplatonic theory of the necessary self-diffusion within the very being of God, a theory neither novel nor unorthodox but no longer appealing to men like Nathaniel W. Taylor who had dropped the Neo-platonism of Edwards. Moses Stuart, who was among the first to fire on the Fort Sumter of the Unitarians, at the same time frankly diverged from Edwards and indeed from the whole tradition of Trinitarian thought in flatly denying the generation of the Son. "The fathers in general," said he, "nurtured in the bosom of heathenism and emanation philosophy . . . do not appear to have apprehended anything repulsive in the doctrine of generation as to the divine nature. I am unable to agree with them here. The pure and spiritual and immutable nature of God . . . is so deeply impressed upon me that I feel an instinctive repulsion to any approximation toward such an idea of the Godhead as interferes with these essential predicates."[11]

Even more subversive was Stuart when he translated and published an essay of Schleiermacher in which he declared that the trinitarian formula applies only to God as revealed and not as ultimate being.[12] This was the disavowal of metaphysics further developed by the Ritschlians. Bushnell with similar presuppositions declared himself unable to subscribe to any theory of the Trinity current in New England.[13] "Who, now," he inquired, "is God thus existing in himself? He dwells in eternal silence, without parts, above time. . . . Does He, then, reason? No; for to reason . . . as deducing one thing from another, implies a want of knowledge. . . . Does He inquire? No; for He knows all things already. Does He remember? Never; for to remember is to call up what was out of mind. . . . Where then is God? by what searching shall we find Him out? . . . What, then, shall we say; what conception form of God as simply existing in Himself, and as yet unrevealed? Only, that He is the Absolute Being—the Infinite—the I Am that I am, giving no sign that He is, other than that He is."[14] God is pavilioned in darkness.[15] He cannot be revealed as the infinite and absolute. Of God unrevealed we can say almost nothing.[16]

Further, said Bushnell, one cannot assert that God is three persons in one substance. All such statements are but analogies, and the Unitarians, who refuse to call God, Son and Spirit, are quite as much at fault in calling him Father because Father also is a figure of speech.[17] Nevertheless, the doctrine of the Trinity is not to be rejected. For it is not a description of God's ultimate being but only of the modes of His self-disclosure. He makes Himself known to us as Father, He makes Himself known to us as Son, He makes Himself known to us as Spirit. This is not modalism, for it does not pretend to know whether God is one, acting in three different modes. It is simply an instrumental trinity, viewed from the angle of man who himself can testify to the three ways in which he has experienced the Great Mystery.[18]

Bushnell complained likewise that the current New England view, conceived of God in static rather than in dynamic terms. The Trinity was pictured as a triangle lying on a single plane with unaltering equations of the three and the one. This, he contended, is to forget the tradition of Catholic Christianity in accord with which the Trinity is also generative. The Son is begotten of the Father, and the Spirit proceeds from the Father and from the Son. Bushnell was returning to the Neoplatonic aspect of the Trinitarian doctrine, which makes the Trinity a process of limited self-diffusion within the being of God. Bushnell was likewise reverting to Edwards over the heads of his disciples. Bushnell complained of his own contemporaries that they were so rabidly opposed to the Unitarians as to be ready to subscribe to anything that had three in it, even to the point of tritheism.[19]

The second great adjustment of Bushnell to current thought lay in his unreserved appropriation of the new geology from which Taylor had shrunk. At Yale the scientists Benjamin Sillman and his son-in-law and successor Dana were the great harmonists, and Moses Stuart, the theologian, was the great obstructionist to their pious endeavors. We have noted his insistence that all the geologic evidence must be in before too confident assertions were advanced. This was not an unreasonable demand, because geologic theory was in flux. A battle was going on between the Vulcanists, who ascribed the earth's crust largely to the igneous, and the Neptunists, who stressed the aqueous. The Neptunists emitted more heat because the Vulcanists threatened to exclude the flood as a prime factor in geological formations. In the end the flood receded because it could not explain the successive layers. Yet one ingredient of the flood theory was retained, namely, that of catastrophe. Buckland in England, whose work was widely known in America, posited a succession of disasters each of which destroyed all of the preceding forms of life.[20]

The same theory was espoused in America by a graduate of the Yale

Divinity School and a pupil of Benjamin Silliman, Edward Hitchcock, a Congregational minister and later a professor and president of Amherst College. Hitchcock was troubled to explain how the Apostle Paul could have been right in saying that death entered with Adam when actually whole eras of life had been extinguished before man arrived. The most plausible explanation was that God, anticipating the sin of Adam, had introduced death in advance.[21] The more serious problem still remained of how to square the successive eras with the account of creation in Genesis. The equation of the six days with the six eras was reefed on the stubborn insistence of Moses Stuart that the Hebrew word "day" meant simply twenty-four hours. The theory of Buckland and Hitchcock presented a new difficulty.[22] There might indeed have been six catastrophes, but Genesis chronicles cumulative not successive creations. Bushnell, cognizant of these difficulties, frankly consigned Genesis to mythology.[23]

Having done so, he was able to discover in the successive creations and disasters the outworking of a stupendous plan of God, who throughout incredible ages has been bringing into being and wiping out the inorganic and the organic, the whole creation groaning and travailing in the long foreshadowing of the redemption of the sons of God.[24]

"How magnificent also," mused Bushnell, "is the whole course of geology, or the geologic eras and changes, taken as related to the future great catastrophe of man, and the new-creating, supernatural grace of his redemption. It is as if, standing on some high summit, we could see the great primordial world rolling down through gulfs and fiery cataclysms, where all the living races die; thence to emerge, again and again, when the Almighty fiat calls it forth, a new creation, covered with fresh populations; passing thus, through a kind of geologic eternity, in so many chapters of deaths, and of darting, frisking, singing life; inaugurating so many successive geologic mornings, over the smoothed graves of the previous extinct races; and preluding in this manner the strange world history of sin and redemption, wherein all the grandest issues of existence lie. This whole tossing, rending, recomposing process, that we call geology, symbolizes evidently, as in highest reason it should, the grand spiritual catastrophe, and Christian new-creation of man. . . . What we see, is the beginning conversing with the end, and Eternal Forethought reaching across the tottering mountains and boiling seas, to unite beginning and end together. So that we may hear the grinding layers of rocks singing harshly—

> Of man's first disobedience and the fruit
> Of that forbidden tree—

and all the long eras of desolation, and refitted bloom and beauty, represented in the registers of the world, are but the epic in stone, of man's great history, before the time."[25]

The third contemporary movement with which Bushnell came to terms was Transcendentalism, the American version of the Romantic Movement, and quite as much of a thistle in the pillow of the Unitarians as of the Calvinists. The Transcendentalists reproached Unitarianism and Calvinism alike as cold and logic chopping. Samuel Taylor Coleridge, the high priest of the Romantic Movement, shifted from logic to feeling. In his *Aids to Reflection* he declared that whatever "finds me" in the Scriptures is true for "whatever finds me bears witness of itself that it has proceeded from a holy spirit."[26] The key to the Bible is not logic but imagination, passion, emotion. In the same vein Bushnell averred that if the logic-chopping theologians of New England were to find themselves in the presence of Moses' burning bush they would analyze the flame and put out the fire.[27] To receive inspiration from the Bible we must leave off ratiocination and lay ourselves open to that which transcends the thought of man. "If we take all these old books of story, biography, and prophecy and join ourselves to these old hymns of worship, we seem to be insphered among God's very thoughts,—let in deep into the discerning of them. And we are lifted by the swell of a certain deific undertone in them, which is the Eternal Mind heaving up through, in great inspirations and tides of thought that have no human measures."[28] Therefore, "the poets are the true metaphysicians."[29]

This being so, precise theological formulations become impossible. Doubly so because language itself is not a precise instrument. Bushnell had rediscovered the Platonic doctrine that words themselves are "but the image and shadows of divine things," mythological and symbolic. This view was reinforced by the philological studies of Professor Gibbs and his demonstration of the processes whereby words acquire meanings and undergo transformations, and particularly his contention that all abstract terms are but "faded metaphors."[30] Bushnell went so far as to assert that the root of his own heresy was his theory of language.[31] Abstract ideas cannot be adequately conveyed by words because words originate from the concrete, but to speak of an abstract idea as crooked or straight is to invest it with a quality of which it is incapable. For that reason the most satisfactory mode of description consists in the piling up of adjectives that one image may supplement another and even in employing antithetical metaphors because paradox best exhibits the inner quality of truth.[32] Notably in the field of religion language is inadequate because religion is not a dogmatic proposition, but a response to ultimate reality in terms of wonder, awe, and reverence.

Bushnell, thus vibrating to the divine, considered the formulation of Christian truth in the propositions of a creed to be shockingly irreverent.[33] The Apostle Paul elaborated no minutely articulated scheme of theology. He was a seer emitting fire, a vehement soul possessed with Christ, never dreaming that he would one day be regarded as the first professor of Christian dogmatics.[34] Because of the infirmities of language all creeds and catechisms should be held in a certain "spirit of accommodation." Yet, despite his disparagement of creeds, Bushnell did not sympathize with the Unitarian rejection of them. "I have been readier to accept as great a number as fell in my way, for when they are subjected to the deepest chemistry of thought . . . they become, thereupon, so elastic, and run so freely into each other, that one seldom need have any difficulty in accepting as many as are offered him." Bushnell was pleased with the Saybrook Platform because it permitted subscription either to its own articles or to those of the Church of England or to the Westminster Confession or to the Savoy Declaration.[35] One can understand why Professor Chauncey Goodrich came out with an article entitled "What Does Mr. Bushnell Mean?"[36]

Bushnell felt that since the life of religion centers in feeling, the cultivation of religion calls for response to all that may induce feeling. In company with his generation he turned not only to the word of Scripture but to that other scroll of God, the page of nature. There was no radical departure here from Calvinism. For did not Edwards feel the majesty in the thunder? The Romantic Movement, however, stressed the immanence of God "whose dwelling is the light of setting suns." Emerson warbled about nature relucent with divinity: "There is a property in the horizon which no man has but he whose eye can integrate all the parts, that is, the poet." For him "the leafless trees become spires of flame in the sunset, with the blue east for their back-ground, and the stars of the dead calices of flowers, and every withered stem and stubble rimed with frost, contribute something to the mute music."[37] Similarly Bushnell burst into the poetry of prose at the sight of a ship "like a spirit rushing through outer darkness and dashing the brimstone fires about along its path."[38]

Even more majestic in the essay on *Religious Music* is the description of God's mountain symphony. "I have heard some fine music, as men are wont to speak—the play of orchestras, the anthems of choirs, the voices of song that moved admiring nations. But in the lofty passes of the Alps I heard a music overhead from God's cloudy orchestra—the giant peaks of rock and ice, curtained in by the driving mist, and only dimly visible athwart the sky through its folds—such as mocks all sounds our lower worlds of art can ever hope to raise. I stood . . . calling to them, in the loudest shouts I could raise, even till my power was spent, and listening in compulsory trance to their reply. I heard them roll it up through their cloudy worlds of snow, sifting out the harsh qualities that were tearing in it as demon screams of sin; holding on upon it as if it were a hymn they were fining to the ear of the great Creator, and sending it round and round in long reduplications of sweetness, minute after minute; till finally receding and rising, it trembled, as it were, among the quick gratulations of angels, and fell into the silence of the pure empyrean. I had never any conception before of what is meant by *quality* in sound. . . . I had never such a sense of purity, or of what a simple sound may tell of purity, by its own pure quality. And I can truly affirm that the experience of that hour has consciously made me better able to think of God ever since—better able to worship. All other sounds are gone—the sounds of yesterday heard in the silence of enchanted multitudes are gone; but that is with me still, and, I hope, will never cease to ring in my spirit till I go down to the slumber of silence itself."[39]

If then nature is thus suffused with God, the line between the natural and the supernatural is attenuated and miracle cannot any longer be viewed as an occasional and erratic injection of the supernatural into the natural. Bushnell defined the natural as that which comes to pass from within itself and the supernatural as that which acts upon the natural from without. The law of gravitation is natural. The lifting of an arm, which for a moment suspends that law, is supernatural. If then every instance of the exercise of man's creative will is supernatural, why should not God also be capable of the supernatural?[40]

The supernatural order, whether exercised by man or by God, does not abrogate the natural. The law of gravitation is not extinguished because man can lift an arm; neither are miracles suspensions of the laws of nature, and no a priori ground exists which precludes their possibility. Whether a particular miracle occurred is a matter of evidence. By this token post-Biblical miracles are not excluded. Bushnell conceded their possibility while skeptical as to their actuality. The Biblical miracles, whether of the virgin birth or of the resurrection, created for him no conflict between science and religion.[41]

The doctrine of the divine immanence, which attenuated the distinction between the natural and the supernatural, diminished also the cleavage between the natural man and the redeemed. Bushnell rebelled against the view that a child is born so depraved as to be alienated from God and to be in need of a drastic upheaval. Wordsworth pictured the child as "trailing clouds of glory," and as attended at first by the vision splendid until it fades into the light of common day. Bushnell would not glorify childhood as superior to adulthood, but he did feel that every child is born into the family of God and should never think of itself as alien. There is no need for the convulsive experience deemed necessary by the previous generation. For that reason Bushnell was skeptical of revivals. If Christian nurture did its proper work, said he, there would be no need for revivals. They are a confession of failure.

In support of his position he cited the attitude of the Old Lights, who deprecated religious convulsions. Yet he satisfied neither the Old Lights nor the New, for what he wanted was the experience without the convulsion, whereas the Old Lights felt that he who was born in Boston need not be born again, and the New Lights insisted that the experience must be preceded by an intense sense of alienation from God. Bushnell never went so far as to deny that there is the possibility of alienation, but it is no more evident, said he, in the child than in the adult. Alienation occurs all along and so also must reconciliation, for the grace of God is as available to the young as to the mature, and with God's help the child need not sink into a slough either of sin or of despondency.[42] These views were developed in successive editions of his great work *Christian Nurture* (1847, 1860, 1867, 1872, 1876) which has given the title to the Horace Bushnell chair of Christian Nurture in the Yale Divinity School.

On account of this position Bushnell was considered dubious, but Leonard Bacon pronounced the verdict when he said, "Brother Bushnell is essentially sound," and so he was, and he became essentially sounder. In later life he pruned some of the excrescences of youthful exuberance and returned more nearly to the central affirmations of the Calvinist tradition. The emergence of evolutionary thought which he rejected made him perceive that the line between the natural and the supernatural could be too far blurred, for if man belongs wholly to nature, will he not be one with the animals, and like them, subject to mortality? This problem was destined to engage more particularly the generation after Bushnell, yet he was sufficiently alerted to recoil from the unguarded statements of his earlier years.

Then, too, he was always so basically Calvinist, so clear sighted and tough minded that he could not dismiss sin by defining it in Neoplatonic terms as merely the negation of good, as simply disharmony or misdirection. "Is it then given us, . . . to look over the sad inventory of the world's history, the corruptions of truth and religion, the bloody persecutions, the massacres of the good, the revolutions against oppressions and oppressors, and the combinations of power to crush them, . . . caste, slavery, and the slave trade, piracy and war, tramping in blood over desolated cities and empires—can we look on these and have it as our soft impeachment to say, that they are only the misdirections of discordant causes in human nature?"[43]

No inevitable law of progress is validated either by the course of life on the prehuman level or by the history of man. One might almost discover rather a law of deterioration, for great civilizations have disintegrated and succumbed, whereas a barbarous people has never emerged into a civilization by any simple process of development. American culture filled Bushnell with no rhapsodies of optimism. The transplanting of any people, he felt, is bound to occasion a decline in morals. Witness the enormities practiced in Massachusetts after the Pequot War and the western migrations again breaking down restraints. The Mexican War appeared to him to be an instance of bowie-knife civilization.[44]

Bushnell argued that not only is there sin but even original sin, not in the Edwardean sense of continuous creations in accord with an all-embracing pattern nor in Taylor's sense that all men are created like Adam, but in the sense of a sociological solidarity of mankind. "Under these physiological terms of propagation, society falls or goes down as a unit, and evil becomes, in a sense, organic in the earth,"[45] the more so because Bushnell believed in the inheritance of acquired characteristics.[46] An individual, said he, cannot be held directly accountable for sins which he has not committed, yet the pressures upon him are such that sin appears to be predetermined.[47] This essential reversion to Calvinism threw Bushnell back on the old question as to how, if evil were a reality, God could be both good and all-powerful. Bushnell quite agreed with Taylor that God had to allow the possibility of evil in order to insure the possibility of unconstrained virtue, and also that God would vastly have preferred man not to have availed himself of this liberty to commit actual sin.[48] Was then God frustrated as Tyler had claimed? Bushnell gave the answer from which Taylor had shrunk: "Nothing which [God] could have done by omnipotence, no silent peace of compulsion, no unconsenting order of things, made fast by His absolute will, could have given any such impression of His greatness and glory, as this loosening of the possibility of evil, *in the purpose finally to turn it about . . . and transform it* by his goodness and patience."[49] Bushnell at last had taken that step from which the New England divines had steadily recoiled of positing in the end a universal victory to God.

He left no doubt that the victory would be of God rather than of man. In fact the picture of man came to be as somber as that of Edwards and therefore the need of a drastic rebirth was reaffirmed.[50] The probing of his own heart had taught him that he might easily have consented to the crucifixion of his Lord.[51] The integrity of man's soul has lapsed, the silver chord of harmony is broken. The will is as impotent to restore the primal order as to marshal the birds into squadrons amid the tempests of the air. Only God can restore the crystalline unity.[52]

The inescapable conclusion is that after all man does need the radical upheaval demanded by the earlier New Englanders whose only mistake was to posit the necessity of a uniform and universal experience. Some but not all may need convulsions.[53] Bushnell was anticipating William James' *Varieties of Religious Experience*, but by no means was he beatifying the complacent because the respectable may still need that drastic upheaval which consists "in the changing of one's reigning love."[54] Not for everyone is religion "a fireball shot from the moon,"[55] but for some it must be.

How then shall the change be brought to pass? By means not essentially different from those of Edwards. Having looked upon ourselves, we must contemplate the excellency of Christ. The main difference is that the fear of hell is supplanted by the pang of conscience.

For those then who are moved by the miracle of the cross, for those who are transformed in their ruling affections, for those who are made new, what then is in store? The answer of Bushnell gathers up the strands of earlier New England aspiration. With Edwards he saw the goal of the individual's ascent in union with the divine. When a "soul . . . is in peace with itself, it becomes an instrument in tune . . . discoursing heavenly music in its thoughts and chanting melodies of bliss, even in its dreams. We may even say . . . that when a soul is in this harmony, no fires of calamity, no pains of outward torment can, for one moment, break the sovereign spell of its joy. . . . [*such a soul*] *partakes a divine nature, it is become a kind of divine creature.*"[56]

As for the destiny of man, the new astronomy caused Bushnell to project the consummation beyond even the millennial reign of Christ on earth to some time-transcending sphere where the inanimate and the animate, where men and the denisons of far-flung worlds, should discover their unities in joint praise of the Omnipotent.[57]

CHAPTER X

New Occasions Teach New Duties

In the early nineteenth century the changes taking place in the structure of society confronted the churches with new responsibilities and necessitated new techniques. The aspiration of Calvinism for a holy community had not been diminished but rather unfettered through the growing insistence on God's benevolence and man's capacity. The Enlightenment had brought reinforcement with its humanitarianism as had also the Evangelical revival with its concern for the lowliest human soul. The world was at peace; the time was propitious for reform. So it was in England in the nineteenth century and so it was in the States. Hope was high. Hopkins and Bellamy panted like the hart for the millennium, and Beecher was forever puffing for progress. Later the Civil War, itself in some measure the result of the preceding great crusade, retarded reform but the decades up to the war were marked by a very ferment of crusading efforts, some directed toward the realization of the Church's constructive program in the new society and some toward the correction of abuses long present but aggravated by the changes of the industrial revolution. There was an increasingly sensitive social conscience in America.

The secularization of education called for a new program of religious training for youth. The opening up of the West laid upon the churches the responsibility for home missions. The emergence of the United States as an independent nation brought an awakening sense of obligation to other peoples through foreign missions. At the same time social abuses cried for correction at home. The shooting of Alexander Hamilton prompted a campaign against dueling. The increased consumption of hard liquors called for elimination or more drastic measures of control. The invention of the cotton gin, with new profits to be derived from slavery in the South, led to an all-out attack on the institution of slavery.

One might have expected the churches of the Calvinist tradition to look to the State to implement all of these reforms, but at the time of the separation of Church and State in Connecticut in 1818 the State was in the hands of the "ruff scuff," and since the Congregational Church was actually flourishing on its own the inclination was to ignore the State and rely on voluntary effort. When this effort proved inadequate, the earlier Calvinist attitude reasserted itself, the more so because the separation of Church and State in this country was unique. It was not motivated by hostility to religion or to the Church but partly by the realization of invidiousness in favor to one church in a land of sects and partly by the resolve of the Church to maintain her own standards undiluted by mingling with the entire populace. The separation was friendly. The State was not hostile to the Church nor the Church aloof from the State.

One principle became clear: the State needs the Church because the State cannot enforce reforms lacking in popular support. The social task of the Church then is to mold the public mind. To this end à new technique was introduced largely through the sponsorship of church leaders. It consisted in the formation of societies, one for each specific reform; one society to free the Negroes, one to educate the Negroes, one to repatriate the Negroes. All who favored a particular objective could unite, however much they might diverge on other points. Among the advantages of this strategy was the surmounting of confessional differences. Methodists, Baptists, Episcopalians, Quakers, Sandemanians, Millerites and what not could all unite against John Barleycorn. Even infidels might be enlisted. Therefore, these societies cannot be denominated as Christian, without qualification, yet their constituency and leadership were prevailingly among the churches, obviously in the case of the missionary and Sunday School societies. In all of these endeavors the Yale contingent played no inconspicuous part.

EDUCATION IN RELIGION

The progressive secularization of education presented the churches with a problem of devising new means for religious instruction of the young. Throughout the eighteenth century children learned spelling and religion concomitantly through *The New-England Primer*. The alphabet was mastered with the aid of rhyming couplets of Biblical content. For the letter "A" the children recited: "In Adam's fall we sinned all." For "P": "Peter deny'd His Lord and cry'd." For "Q": "Queen Esther sues and saves the *Jews*." The *Primer* included the Lord's Prayer, the Apostles' Creed, the Ten Commandments, the names of the books of the Bible, and an account of the burning of the Protestant John Rogers in the sight of his wife and ten or eleven children—John having been for some time in prison was not sure of the count. There was the Assembly Catechism and sometimes also John Cotton's *Milk for Babes Drawn Out of the Breasts of Both Testaments*. Prayers and some of the hymns of Isaac Watts followed. An occasional edition had this delectable "Song for the Lord's Day Morning":

> This is the Day when Christ arose
> So early from the Dead;
> Why should I keep my Eye-lids clos'd
> And Waste my Hours on Bed?[1]

Little by little a more secular tone invaded the *Primer*. For the letter "W": the couplet "Whales in the sea God's voice obey" gave way to: "By Washington great deeds were done."[2] In 1801 Noah Webster of New Haven brought out a revision in which the letter "A" was represented no longer by Adam but by Apple Pie.[3] More drastic was Webster's *Elementary Primer* in 1831, which set itself the sole task of teaching spelling with no ancillary purpose of inculcating religion. Watts' hymns were replaced by "I Like Pussy" and "Twinkle, Twinkle, Little Star." There was nothing against religion, but a spelling book should teach spelling. If religion is to be taught, write another book.

That assignment was undertaken by Josiah Willard Gibbs, who compiled *Selections from the Holy Scriptures; Intended as Sabbath Exercises for Children*.[4] The passages were culled judiciously from the Psalms and elucidated by notes sometimes of a critical character; as for example, that

David could not have written *all* of the 51st Psalm, which prayed for the rebuilding of Jerusalem, evidently after the destruction. Gibbs announced another book of moral extracts which apparently never appeared.

His labors were in accord with a movement well underway, the Sunday School. It had been commenced in England without the approval of

THE PIOUS GIRL AND HER SWEARING FATHER.

I SHALL SOON BE TEN YEARS OLD.

" Ah, there's old Sylvester," said Mary to her eldest sister, Pauline, as they were going to school; " he looks as if he meant to tell us one of his grave stories."

" Don't laugh at him," said Pauline; you know

THE
TEACHER'S OFFERING,
OR,
Sunday Scholar's Magazine.

No. 9.   SEPTEMBER, 1825.   VOL. 2.

THE HISTORY OF SUSAN GREEN;

On sunday the 17th of December, 1826, (this very winter,) three boys belonging to a town in the state of New York, were drowned in the Champlain river near Rouse's Point.

the ecclesiastical authorities, hence outside of the Church but on an interdenominational basis. In Connecticut the ecclesiastical pillars were favorable and wisely appropriated the interdenominational feature. The Connecticut Sunday School Union was organized in 1825 and included along with the Congregationalists, the Baptists, Methodists, and Episcopalians. The president of the Union was Nathaniel W. Taylor; one of the vice-presidents was Timothy Dwight, a son of the president of Yale; among the managers appears the name of Leonard Bacon. After two years New Haven reported a maximum attendance in Sunday Schools of 369 in the summer and 348 in the winter. "There are twenty-seven male and thirty-five female teachers all of whom are hopefully pious." So great was the popularity of the schools that a saucy little girl who defied her mistress was brought to terms only by the threat to tell her Sunday School teacher. After the turn of the half century, New Haven had between two and three thousand scholars. The Catholics borrowed the plan and established two schools. "Great comfort and pleasure" were expressed by a Protestant reporter that "even *there*" children were "kept quiet for a while on the Sabbath."

The instruction consisted chiefly in memorization. The annual report derived great satisfaction from the achievement of 150 scholars who in a year had committed to memory 36,570 verses of Scripture, 50,052 answers in the Catechism and 7,740 verses of hymns. Today such methods are held in high derision, though it might not be amiss if adults could recite more than the Lord's Prayer.

An effort was made to provide religious literature for youth in the form of a journal started in 1823 by the New Haven Sabbath School Union with the title *The Teacher's Offering*. Biblical tales were retold with simplicity and somewhat modernized illustrations. Woodcuts enforced the brevity of life, the merits of precocious piety, calamities visited upon Sabbath breakers, and the blessings attending the devout. In 1857 an eminent divine pronounced, "The Sunday schools, the most potent agent of civilization existing in the world."[5]

MISSIONS

The winning of the stranger within and without the gates had long been regarded by the founding fathers of New England as incumbent upon the Church. Missions to the Indians had been continuous, and the examples of Edwards and Brainerd had never been forgotten at Yale. The Great Awakenings and the theology of Samuel Hopkins gave a new impetus to missionary endeavor at home and abroad. Hopkins' calculation that the millennium would come in 1866 supplied an urgent reason for a great ingathering while yet there was time. His doctrine of God's universal benevolence meant that every creature should be invited, and the demand for disinterestedness in the service of God impelled men to brave all the hardships of perilous voyages, rugged living in inhospitable climes, and the antipathy of unfriendly peoples. No medieval saints and no Jesuit missionaries outdid the endurance of these Protestant pioneers.[6]

At first Yale felt a greater concern for the Indians and the West than for the foreign field. The Missionary Society of Connecticut, organized in 1798, declared as its purpose "to Christianize the heathen in North America and to support and promote Christian knowledge in the new settlements within the United States."[7] Nathaniel W. Taylor grew less enthusiastic even about the West, because of the need to insure the triumph of his theology by planting his students in New England. But Lyman Beecher felt that the New Haven Theology was very nicely taking care of itself. He went West, headed Lane Seminary in Cincinnati, and from there issued a rousing plea for help. At first the dictum of Jonathan Edwards that the millennium would commence in America had seemed to him chimerical, "but all providencial developments since, and all existing signs of the times, lend corroboration to it. But if it is by the march of revolution and civil liberty, that the way of the Lord is to be prepared, where shall the central energy be found, and from what nation shall the renovating power go forth? What nation is blessed with such experimental knowledge of free institutions, with such facilities and resources of communication, obstructed by so few obstacles, as our own? . . . But if this nation is, in the providence of God, destined to lead the way in the moral and political emancipation of the world, it is time she understood her high calling, and were harnessed for the work. . . .

"It is equally plain that the religious and political destiny of our nation is to be decided in the West." The West, then, must have colleges, the West must have teachers, and if we do not hurry, added Beecher, the Catholics will get there first.[8]

The West must have more than touring evangelists whose method, said one critic, is "like trying to burn a pile of green buckeye logs by lighting shavings under them. At the moment of the missionary's departure, the shavings are burning brightly. No sooner is he gone than the flash is over, leaving only charred logs."[9]

The students of the Yale Divinity School were responsive to the need. A Society of Inquiry was formed with monthly meetings to listen to papers about home and foreign missions. Out of this society came the formation of the Illinois Band. The declaration of purpose received cordial endorsement from President Day and Professors Taylor and Gibbs. It read:

Believing in the entire alienation of the natural heart from God, in the necessity of the influences of the Holy Spirit for its renovation, and that these influences are not to be expected without the use of means; deeply impressed also with the destitute condition of the Western section of our country . . . and believing that evangelical religion and education must go hand in hand . . . we the undersigned hereby express our readiness to go to the State of Illinois for the purpose of establishing a Seminary of learning. . . .

Theron Baldwin, John F. Brooks, Mason Grosvenor, Elisha Jenny, William Kirby, Julian M. Sturtevant, Asa Turner, Jr.
Theological Department Yale College, Feb. 21, 1829.

Julian Sturtevant became the founder and first president of Illinois College.[10]

Asa Turner is called the father of Congregationalism in Iowa. Here is his advice to new recruits: "Come prepared to expect small things, rough things. Lay aside all your dandy whims boys learn in college, and take a few lessons of your grandmothers, before you come. Get clothes, firm, durable, something that will go through the hazel brush without tearing. Don't be afraid of a good hard hand, or of a tanned face. If you keep free from a hard heart, you will do well. Get wives of old Puritan stamp, such as honored the distaff and the loom, those who can pail a cow, and churn the butter, and be proud of a jean dress or a checked apron.

"Tell those two or three who think of leading out a sister this fall, we will try to find homes as good as Keokuk, the high chief and his lady live in, and my wife will have the kettle of mush and the johnnycake ready by some cold night in November."[11]

Professor Goodrich actively assisted the Basel Mission with its head-quarters in Switzerland, a unique undertaking in that the missionaries sent by this board to the West of the United States affiliated with the church dominant in the area, with the result that missionaries operating under one society were attached to several denominations.[12]

Foreign missions enlisted interest earlier at Andover than at Yale, yet Yale at one point gave an impetus to Andover. In 1809 a Hawaiian named Obookiah was brought by a sea captain to New Haven. The lad desired to stay and receive instruction. E. W. Dwight undertook to teach him to speak and read English, saying when the boy stumbled, "Try Obookiah, it is *very easy.*" Obookiah evened the score because he was able to fill his cupped hands with water and bring all of it without spilling to his lips. When Dwight vainly tried, Obookiah would say, "Try, Mr. Dwight, it is *very easy.*" The interest aroused by the con-version of Obookiah led to the founding of a foreign missions school at Cornwall to prepare Hawaiians and American Indians to work among their own peoples. The early death of Obookiah prevented his return, but a period spent at Andover prompted the mission of Hiram Bingham to the Sandwich Islands.[13]

In 1836 Yale began connections with missions in China. In that year Jay Robert Morrison asked Professor Gibbs to serve as the Correspond-ing Secretary of a "Society for the Diffusion of Useful Knowledge in China." In 1845 the directing committee included President Jeremiah Day, Benjamin Silliman, Chauncey A. Goodrich, as well as Gibbs.

In 1837 Gibbs received a letter from E. L. Bridgmann of Canton, pleading for a dissemination in the West of knowledge about China. A letter of 1845 from S. W. Bonney reported on the mission in Hong Kong. The island appeared to be "a most eligible location," because under English protection. "There are 20,000 Chinese on the island. I know of nothing to prevent a large supply of scholars, unless the 'Light of Reason' (His Excellency Toon Kwong) should think that the light of Revelation is too dazzling for his dear children and forbid them to have intercourse with the 'Outside barbarians.' Even in that case they would probably disobey and remain with us as some boys have already done contrary to their parents' wishes and *orders.*"

In 1845 William A. Macy went out from the Divinity School with the hearty commendation of his professors. In 1858 he wrote from Shanghai to Professor Gibbs, "I see that your son is now just graduating: it is hard for me to realize that this is the case. Cannot you give him up to the exigencies of this land? Will not he come to apply the advantages in point of education which he has enjoyed to the promotion of the cause of Jesus among this people? I say these things on the supposition that he is a member of Christ's true Church: I know not, but I infer that a child trained up by a faithful mother now in glory must have heeded her instructions enforced and sanctified by her removal."[14]

This son was Professor Josiah Willard Gibbs, Yale's famed physicist, the luster of whose name has made that of his father almost forgotten.

ATTACK ON DUELING

Not only the instruction of the young and the conversion of the heathen devolved as duties upon the Christian community but also the reformation of morals. One of the evils attacked was dueling. When Alexander Hamilton fell before the pistol of Aaron Burr, the grandson of Jonathan Edwards, in 1805 Burr's cousin, President Dwight of Yale, stigmatized dueling as trivial, absurd, and a violation of the laws of man and God.[15] Lyman Beecher emptied the vials of prophetic wrath in a sermon: "Duelling is a great national sin. With the exception of a small section of the union, the whole land is defiled with blood. From the lakes of the North, to the plains of Georgia, is heard the voice of lamentation and woe; the cries of the widow and fatherless. This work of desolation is performed often, by men in office; by the appointed guardians of life and liberty. On the floor of Congress, challenges have been threatened, if not actually given, and thus powder and ball have been introduced as the auxiliaries of deliberation and argument. Oh, tell it not in Gath, publish it not in the streets of Askelon! Alas! it is too late to conceal our infamy. The sun hath shined on guilt, and the eye of God with brighter beams surveyed the whole. He hath surveyed, and He will punish. His quiver is full of arrows, His sword impatient of confinement. Ten thousand plagues stand ready to execute His wrath. . . .

"Be not deceived—The greater our present mercies and seeming security, the greater is the guilt of our rebellion, and the more certain, swift and awful, will be our calamity. We are murderers, a nation of murderers, while we tolerate and reward the perpetrators of the crime. And shall I not visit for these things, saith the Lord?—Shall not my soul be avenged on such a nation as this?"[16]

This sermon was committed to a messenger for transmission to the printer. Part of the journey was by water. Becoming overwarm from rowing, the messenger shed his pea jacket and heard something splash. It was the sermon. The beach was combed in vain. A month later, as Beecher was sawing wood, he saw a man running toward him swinging something and grinning so that his teeth showed at fifteen rods. The sermon, wrapped in leather, had washed high on a thicket and remained legible. When Henry Clay the duelist was running for President, that sermon was distributed to the number of forty thousand copies and contributed to his defeat.[17]

One would suppose that if dueling is bad, war is worse. Disillusionment in the wake of the War of 1812 prompted the formation of societies directed toward peace. Some Yale men may have participated, but none of the Yale coterie was prominent and active in this cause, which is rather the more remarkable because the American Peace Society was not pacificist. Unitarian Harvard, with its greater confidence in the perfectability of man, was much readier to espouse this cause than was orthodox Yale.

The Temperance Campaign

The case was different with regard to temperance. The campaign in Connecticut was launched by the crusading Lyman Beecher.

There were, of course, coincident efforts in the neighboring states. The virulence of the crusade and the drastic measures adopted exceeded anything in previous Christian history. The prevailing attitude of all of the churches toward alcoholic beverages had been until the latter part of the eighteenth century one of moderation rather than of total abstinence.[18] Even the monastic orders of the Catholic Church did not demand abstinence. St. Benedict allowed his monks a generous libation of wine each day, and the Benedictines became famous for their vintages. The Reformation brought no change. Luther indeed railed at his Germans as guzzling swine and recommended that the princes command all of their subjects to get drunk because such is the perversity of human nature that they would then all be sober.[19] But Luther did not propose total abstinence and felt bereft if unable to obtain his nightly glass of beer. The more somber Calvin did not disdain a gift of wine, and John Knox, sometimes called the father of English Puritanism, had his wine cellar. The Puritans, while upbraiding the unseemly imbibing of the Cavaliers, were not themselves complete abstainers. In colonial New England drinking in taverns was normal and regulated. Minors, apprentices, and servants together with habitual inebriates were not to be served.

The great change alike in drinking and in abstinence occurred in the eighteenth century. The reasons appear to have been two: first, the industrial revolution with the introduction of distilled liquors and the growth of a business concerned to push consumption; secondly, the Evangelical Revival with its quickening of conscience and kindling of reformatory zeal. In eighteenth-century New England rum, made from the sugar cane of the West Indies, became the staple of commerce and a source of government revenue. Rum financed the fur trade with the Indians; rum was the medium of the slave trade—two hundred and fifty gallons a head. Rum debauched the people who no longer drank cider. Weddings and funerals were the occasions of indulgence. Houses, barns, bridges could not be successfully constructed without a "warming." The Continental Congress supplied grog to the armies of the Revolution. Even ecclesiastical gatherings, ordinations, and meetings of the associations were marked by guzzling at church expense. In 1721 the house of the rector of Yale College was financed by grants from the Legislature providing for the purpose one year's revenue from the annual income in rum.[20]

In England excessive drinking was also evident. Vigorous protests began with the Methodists. John Wesley saw how the industrial revolution had debased the worker by drudgery and debauched him by grog. Wesley demanded total abstinence from all of the members of his society. But for some time the rules did not carry over to the American frontier.

A new impetus came from the findings of an American Quaker, Benjamin Rush, of Philadelphia, a physician, who took care to record the mischievous effects of alcohol on the American soldiers during the

Revolution. His tract, combining scientific investigation with religious ardor, enjoyed a wide popularity. It came into the hands of Lyman Beecher.

He was greatly exercised over what he witnessed at ordinations where the sideboards carried all the liquors in vogue. The clergy formed queues, and if none became positively drunk the hilarity and jocose conversation were in excess of the seemly. The General Association of Connecticut was disturbed and appointed a committee, which at the next meeting at Sharon in June, 1812, reported that intemperance was increasing most alarmingly, but after prayerful inquiry they offered no remedy. "The blood started through my heart when I heard this," records Beecher, "and I arose instanter." His remonstrance led to the establishment of a new committee of which he was the chairman. Its report called upon the churches to provide no more liquor for ecclesiastical gatherings. The laity were exhorted to consider ardent spirits no part of hospitable entertainment. Families should desist, and employers should not supply their workers. Dr. Dwight expressed some apprehension lest his young friends "transcend the sanction of public sentiment." But with his peculiar smile he added that were they disposed, he would not hinder.[21] Indeed he supplied a tract in which he urged all those addicted to intoxication to abstain absolutely, and all those not in peculiar danger to guard themselves scrupulously.[22]

Dwight's stand was really nothing more than the traditional injunction to temperance. Beecher was demanding that everyone abstain absolutely from hard liquors. He did not as yet include the soft.

The response was heartening. The Association not only issued the recommendation to the churches but also requested the State Treasurer not to serve "ardent spirits or wine at the customary public entertainment of the clergy at the general election." Another request was sent to the Fellows of Yale College "that they should use their endeavors to prevent in future the provision of either ardent spirits or wine at the customary public entertainments at Commencement."[23]

At the Yale Commencement in 1812 a society was formed for the reformation of morals. Later in 1829 the Connecticut Temperance Society was organized with Jeremiah Day of Yale as president. There was a local chapter, also, in Yale College.[24] Leonard Bacon threw his bulk into the fray in a tract entitled *Total Abstinence from Ardent Spirits.*[25] The term "ardent," was commonly applied only to hard liquors. The claim, said he, is made that alcohol is one of the bounties of providence and must be good for something. So is arsenic—good for killing rats—and alcohol is good for producing inflammable gas. Consider the ravages wrought by alcohol. In New Haven with a population of ten thousand, thirty die annually from drink. The money expended in two years would more than construct a new Farmington Canal. (The reference is to the waterway which linked New Haven with Hartford. Heralded as a great feat of engineering, it was not in use more than ten years because superseded by the railroad.)

Bacon was presumably talking only of hard liquors; but when in practice inebriates proved incapable of maintaining sobriety on the soft, these, too, were put under the ban. The pledge was made more inclusive. "So here we pledge perpetual hate to all that can intoxicate."[26] One society had two levels of membership: the names of some were marked with the letters "O.P." for "old pledge"; others with a "T" for total. Hence they came to be known as "T-Totalers."[27] In their support Beecher declared that beer differs from ardent spirits only in that it does not rasp with so keen a file; and wine, said he, is no remedy for intemperance.

So rigid a demand posed a serious problem for Protestants, since the Bible enjoins only sobriety and does not interdict the use of wine. The reformers made the opportune discovery that the Biblical Hebrew and Greek have several words for drinks made from juices. Some of these were assumed to have been unfermented and hence commended. At first Moses Stuart was as adamant against this wresting of Scripture as he had been on the six days of creation but subsequently suffered his reformatory zeal to impair his exegetical integrity.[28]

In the meantime the ardor of the reform began to wane. A new upsurge came through the formation of a temperance society consisting only of reformed drunkards. One of the most dramatic was John B. Gough, a pale, pensive youth who disarmed his hearers by disclaiming any rhetorical art and then thrilled them with the horrible, dissolved them with the tender, and enchanted them with the beautiful. One day Gough lapsed. He explained that an acquaintance had given him a drugged soda. The temperance reformers believed him. The ungodly scoffed.[29] In 1851 he lectured on temperance in the Yale College chapel. James Hadley recorded in his diary that he considered the man a charlatan, but was later impressed.[30]

Thus far the reformers had been loath to appeal to the State, but their feeble success posed the question whether mere exhortation would suffice. In 1838 Leonard Bacon surveyed the results of the temperance reform up to that date.[31]

Certain gains, he said, were to be recorded. The distillery had been closed for lack of patronage. Ardent spirits were now served by only two out of the four Congregational churches, only one Methodist, no Baptist, and but two or three Episcopal. Yet in many respects the changes were not salutary. Under the restraint of family life, drinking in homes was replaced by drinking in grog shops. There were fourteen such in New Haven on Church Street between Chapel and Crown. A visitor to New Haven marveled that such dens should thrive under the eaves of a New England college. There were grog shops connected with fish and meat markets open even on Sundays. Despite the reform New Haven had still thirty deaths a year from drink. What then could be done? Enforce the old tavern laws, was Bacon's answer, whereby liquor was served as a part of general entertainment and only to the mature and the controlled. At the time only one drink shop in New Haven was a licensed tavern. One was licensed but not a tavern, and the rest were oyster shops, groceries, confectioneries, and some even mere cellars. Bacon's view came to the ears of the grocers, who composed a spirited protest no whit inferior in florid eloquence to any composition of the pillars of society.

Too long they had "endured, without a murmur, the taunts, the abuse, the scoffs, the insults, and the unrelenting persecutions of such Pharisaical hypocrites." Therefore they were resolved to "test the constitutionality of the license laws."

Bacon retorted: "You tell us that the laws which interfere with your operations are unconstitutional. Unconstitutional! Do you tell us that the State of Connecticut has no constitutional power to protect herself against one of the deadliest of social evils—no power to regulate her own internal police—no power to punish crimes committed within her own jurisdiction?"

Government regulation, then, of some sort was necessary. There were those who argued that the measures proposed by Bacon would not suffice. So long as liquors were distilled, so long as an industry was seeking to promote consumption, persons addicted to alcoholism could never be secure. Therefore, prohibition! Due to the efforts of Neal Dow, a Maine Quaker, who as mayor of Portland first dried up that city, the Maine Liquor Law was enacted in 1851. Other states followed. Moses Stuart applauded.[32]

The sequel we all know. Today the prevailing practice of serving alcoholic beverages at university functions sets the Divinity School apart but even in the churches the recoil from an abortive experiment has occasioned a trend toward the mores of earlier New England. There is this, however, to be added, that Yale recognizes alcoholism as one of the major social problems of our age and the Institute of Applied Physiology devotes to it major attention.

CHAPTER XI

Mine Eyes Have Seen the Coming

The problem which most deeply agitated New England in the first half of the nineteenth century was that of slavery. The institution had long been established. The slaves in New England were Indians, later the Negroes. Slaves scarcely differed as to their treatment from indentured servants. The greatest sin in New England had been not so much slave holding as slave trading. The situation is well illustrated by what Samuel Hopkins discovered at Newport, Rhode Island, when he became pastor there just before the Revolution. Newport was a seaport of some ten thousand inhabitants, so much the mart of New England that a London merchant is reported to have addressed a letter to "New York near Newport." The prosperity of this coastal town rested on the slave trade. Of the 202 ships engaged in delivering Africans to Charleston, 59 were owned in Rhode Island, and of the 17,048 Negroes taken to that port during the four years from 1804 to 1808, the Rhode Islanders carried 6,238 and of these the Newport slavers accounted for 3,488. In other words, the South employed the slaves, the North supplied them.

Hopkins was smitten. His God was a God of benevolence and should His children traffic in men? Hopkins reproached himself because he had once owned a slave and sold him for a hundred dollars. Though the money was long since spent and he in penury, Hopkins scraped the sum together and gave it to a missionary society. He was quite alone in disquieting the complacency of Newport, for the Quakers, having emancipated all slaves of their own, had grown torpid as to troubling the consciences of others. Hopkins stood before his congregation of opulent ship owners.[1] He had few graces with which to insinuate an unpalatable word. He was ungainly with a monotonous drawling voice which in his later years sounded like a cracked bell.[2] But one thing he had—even his opponents called him "Old Sincerity." He began with cold fact and ruthless logic. "By drink we have incited the Africans to war upon each other that the captives might be sold into slavery. They are herded together, examined as to soundness, branded with a hot iron, manacled in the holds of ships, and transported to the West Indies. Thirty out of every hundred die in transit, which means 30,000 murdered every year. Families are separated, the infirm, feeble, and females with child must work with the rest and if they fall behind, suffer the lash. Such is the oppression that they do not increase by propagation and replacement is by new importation."

An imaginary objector says that it is impossible to free all slaves at once and under the present circumstances. "Suppose," replies Hopkins, "our children were slaves in Algiers and there were not a family in the American colonies which did not have some relatives in captivity. And why are we not as much affected by the slavery of the blacks? If one of our boys is impressed into the king's ship, how do his parents grieve!" The objector interposes, "If free, the blacks would be worse off." Answer: "I grant that slavery debases, but because we have reduced them to abject misery shall we continue therein?"[3]

Hopkins alienated many of the wealthy members of his congregation, but others were convicted of guilt. His words rallied the flagging who had not bowed the knee to Baal. Moses Brown, the Quaker of Providence, promptly corresponded with him and in New York and Philadelphia societies already organized for the abolition of the slave rejoiced over his efforts.

The zeal of Hopkins reached out to his ministerial colleagues as he sought to impress antislavery principles on Bellamy, himself the owner of a slave whom he deemed so contented as not to wish emancipation. Hopkins asked whether Bellamy would grant freedom if it were desired. Bellamy promised. The slave was called. Hopkins inquired: "Have you a good master?" "O, yes, very very good!" "Are you happy in your present condition?" "Yes, very happy." "Would you be *more* happy if you were free?" "O, yes, massa—me would be much more happy."

Bellamy broke in: "From this moment you are free."[4]

At the time when Hopkins was pastor of the New Light Church in Newport Ezra Stiles was pastor of the Old Light Church. His awakening as to slavery came when a parishioner inquired whether Stiles would like to share in a slaving expedition on the coast of Guinea. He contributed a small keg of rum and was rewarded with a little blackamoor. The lad was given the name "Newport" and for short was called "Newp." He speedily adapted himself to the new home. Once, after he had learned to talk, Stiles found him alone in the kitchen and in tears. Asked the reason the boy answered that he was thinking of his father and mother from whom he had been stolen. Stiles wilted. He could not now return the lad but released him at once. "Newp" elected, as a free man, to stay with the family and accompanied them to Yale. When Mrs. Stiles was dying, she confided her husband and children to the care of "Newp," and the children in turn, after the president's death, for thirty years assumed responsibility for the old servant.[5]

The Beechers were seared by slavery through the experience of the first Mrs. Beecher's sister, Mary Foote. Lyman called her "a beautiful creature, one of the most fascinating human beings I ever saw. Her smile no man could resist." Lyman was a good judge of how much a man could resist. When Mary was but seventeen, she was passionately wooed by Mr. Hubbard, son of the Episcopal rector in New Haven. This Mr. Hubbard was a merchant in the West Indies. When Mary, as his wife, joined him in Havana, she discovered that he had there already a family of mulattoes. "What she saw and heard of slavery filled her with constant horror and loathing. She has said that she has often sat by her window in the tropical night, when all was still, and wished that the island might sink in the ocean, with all its sin and misery, and that she might sink with it."[6]

In the first phase of the campaign against slavery the objectives of the New England reformers were two: the abolition of the slave trade and the emancipation of the slaves in their own area. In 1791 Jonathan Edwards, Jr. in New Haven came out with a denunciation of the slave trade as vehement as that of Hopkins at Newport. Edwards calculated that the trade occasioned one hundred thousand deaths a year. Slavery, he said, violates the golden rule. How would we feel if our children were kidnaped for perpetual and cruel bondage in Africa? Slavery conflicts with the principle that all men are "created free and equal." If any fear that the system is too entrenched for change, let them recall that thirty years ago scarcely a voice was raised in protest whereas today the further importation of slaves is prohibited by law from New Hampshire to Virginia.[7] The real question was one of enforcement.

As for the slaves already in bondage, in 1784 Connecticut passed a Gradual Emancipation Act whereby children born of slaves after that year could not be held for more than twenty-five years.[8] The Connecticut Anti-slavery Society, founded in 1790 under the presidency of Ezra Stiles, had as its objective to insure to those "groaning under the iron hand of slavery" all the benefits "of the wise and humane laws of our country." In other words the Gradual Emancipation Act was not to be evaded. Among the signers were Jonathan Edwards, Jr., Benjamin Trumbull, John Trumbull, Chauncey Goodrich, Noah Webster, Theodore Dwight, and Thomas Seymour.[9] The result of this and similar measures was the eradication of slavery during the course of the century. In 1756 in Connecticut there were no free Negroes and 3,634 slaves, whereas in 1850 there were 7,693 free Negroes and no slaves.[10]

With the slave trade prohibited by law and actual slavery rapidly diminishing in New England the problem shifted to the country as a whole and the North felt constrained to extend its own reforms to the South. There were but two ways in which this could be done. One was with the consent of the Southern slaveholders. The other was without their consent, through war. A third option for the North was to preserve her own rectitude by secession. The Union in that case would be dissolved, and slavery would not be abolished in the South.

The Yale contingent was well nigh to a man for emancipation by consent. War would be an appalling expedient. The division of the country might assuage the Northern conscience, but it would not emancipate the Southern slaves. This being the case, the agitation must be conducted in a temper apt to disarm and enlist the Southern slave owner. He must be sympathetically approached and with an understanding of his problem.

Nathaniel W. Taylor was so very understanding that for long he could not endorse abolitionist sentiment. While he was presiding over the meetings of the Rhetorical Society of the Divinity School in 1842, the question came up, "Does the greatest good of the greatest number justify the· continuance of slavery at the South?" The Society discussed the question with warmth for two and one-half hours and declined to vote. Taylor insisted, but the men replied that they did not know. The question was revived in 1848 when the president voted "yes" and the Society sustained him. In 1851 the question was whether slavery in this country has been on the whole an evil. The president gave a negative vote. The Society did not sustain him but was about equally divided. "At a late hour the Society adjourned," records the secretary. The hour was just after ten-thirty.[11]

Moses Stuart at Andover was reckoned among the reactionaries, though as a matter of fact he desired emancipation. The question was as to the means. When William Lloyd Garrison brought to America an English abolitionist orator, Andover Seminary refused him permission to speak in the chapel. A hall was secured in the town. Stuart urged the students not to attend. "I warn you on the peril of your souls not to go to that meeting tonight." The students took a chance on their souls.[12]

Goodrich, Fitch, and Gibbs were readier to press reforms, but of all the Yale family the outstanding exponent of decisiveness coupled with moderation was Leonard Bacon. He was flanked by Benjamin Silliman and Lyman Beecher.

The moderates believed "the consent of the South . . . [to be] indispensable to any plan for the abolition of slavery."[13] Consent could be won only through understanding and respect, and respect was warranted because the slaveholders in the South were not to be compared with the raiders of Africa. Take for example the case of a Presbyterian minister who had inherited slaves whom he would gladly emancipate if they would but leave. There were good reasons for their reluctance since the lot of the free Negro was difficult.

Was it wise, then, to set Negroes free in a society where they would be subject to so much discrimination? In New Haven they were segregated in an area between State Street and the Quinnipiac. The river bank was called New Liberia and was a den of vice. In 1828 the Negroes of Connecticut numbered one thirty-fourth of the population but con-

tributed one-third of the convicts.[14] George Park Fisher, later to be on
the Divinity School faculty, remarked that to demand of the South
immediate emancipation was like telling an eagle in midair with a lamb
in its talons to let go at once.[15]

To persuade the South one must recognize the problem of the South,
so argued Benjamin Silliman in an address in Center Church on the
Fourth of July, 1832. He would freely concede that difference in circumstance rather than in moral sensitivity accounted for the banishment
of slavery from one region and its perpetuation in the other. None could
deny that the North had supplied the slaves for the South and that the
South was not insensitive. Virginians themselves had recently said
that "slavery is an intolerable evil; bitter to the slave; costly to the
proprietor; dangerous to the morals of youth . . . a blot on our national
honor . . . an insult to the purity of our religion and an outrage on the
Majesty of Heaven!"[16]

Leonard Bacon was even more insistent that the approach to the
South be conciliatory and discriminating. The first principle of Christianity is that the slave is a brother of the human race and a brother in
Christ. But this does not exclude the dilemma of the Southern slave
owner who would welcome emancipation but retains his slaves because
he does not see how to set them free. "You say he makes money out of
them; much less than if he invested in the stock of the proposed New
York and New Haven Railroad. Does he commune with them? you
inquire. No, because he is a Presbyterian, and they are Baptists, and
they won't have him. Would I permit a slaveholding Presbyterian in
the South to occupy my pulpit? I would not accept him simply because
he was a Presbyterian, nor exclude him simply because he was a slave-
holder. I would ask him why."[17]

But if this were the state of affairs, what then could be done? The
answer given was colonization, the return of the Negroes to Africa. The
plan met with a hearty response in the South. Jefferson had suggested it.
One hundred and forty-three emancipation societies sprang up in the
United States, and of these one hundred and three were in the South.[18]
This very fact commended the plan to the Northern moderates because
here was a move toward the abolition of slavery on which the North and
the South would collaborate. A national society was founded, and a

colony secured in Liberia. The migration began, but at the end of ten years only fifteen hundred Negroes had been transported, whereas the natural increase in the population in the United States had been five hundred thousand. Liberia, moreover, was proving unhealthy. Of the immigrants and agents two hundred and thirty had died.[19] Furthermore, groups of free American Negroes declared themselves against the plan. "We are content," said they, "to abide where we are. We do not believe that things will always continue the same. . . . This is our home, and this is our country. Beneath its sod lie the bones of our fathers; for it, some of them fought, and bled, and died. Here we were born, and here we will die."[20]

The reformers reconsidered. Some who had at first supported colonization, such as William Lloyd Garrison and the philanthropist Arthur Tappan, came to the conclusion that the Negro problem would have to be solved in this country. The colonization scheme was a diversion from the preparation of Negroes for emancipation without repatriation. Colonization was lulling the conscience of the South and consuming the resources of the North. Tappan became more extreme in his charges and claimed that the colonization society was "a device of Satan and owes its existence to the single motive to perpetuate slavery."[21]

To Garrison the society was suspect because it did have support from the South and from slaveholders. He was resolved to have no part with any society which did not renounce slavery. This brought into question the very theory of societies. They constituted, as we have observed, a new technique for dealing with particular ills. A society directed itself toward a specific objective and one only, seeking to enlist those in favor of the single end, however much they might diverge at other points. Leonard Bacon held to this view with regard to the American Colonization Society. It does not prevent anyone, said he, from being an abolitionist. William Lloyd Garrison can agitate all he pleases for abolition through some other society, but this society is neutral as to slavery because its only objective is colonization. It is equally neutral with respect to Sabbath breaking and intemperance.[22]

Garrison would tolerate no neutrality; not even a temperance society could avoid the issue. The American Tract Society was torn and for long held to the principle that the Society is not "to be used as an instrument of attack on slavery *as such,* or for . . . its abolition in the South." Such was the judgment of Jeremiah Day and Eleazar Fitch, Chauncey A. Goodrich and Leonard Bacon.[23] Missionary boards were rent. The American Home Missionary Society under Bacon's impact declined to disown slaveholding members. The American Board of Commissioners for Foreign Missions ruled that its function was to evangelize not to correct all the ills of society. Responsibility, however, could not be so readily disclaimed in the case of slaves owned by the missions to the Cherokees and Choctaws. The connection with these missions was severed in 1860.[24]

In the meantime Garrison and the Abolitionists excoriated alike the slaveholders of the South and the temporizers of the North. *The American Antislavery Almanac* for 1838 illustrated the months of the year with woodcuts showing the torturing of slaves in chains, slaves whipped, fugitives shot, families separated, and an Abolitionist lynched.[25] The *Liberator* carried at its masthead a cut of a slave block with the words "Slaves, horses and other cattle for sale."[26] From the *Oberlin Evangelist* these lines were reproduced:

> There's a stain on the "flag of the free,"
> There's a wail in "the home of the brave,"
> There is blood on the skirts of thy Ruler and thee,
> My country, the home of the slave.[27]

Whittier, the Quaker poet, contemplated with equanimity the dissolution of the Union:

> Make our union-bond a chain,—
> We will snap its links in twain.[28]

But that, replied Bacon and the moderates, will not free the slaves. Instead, indiscriminate denunciation is welding their chains. "The antislavery societies, by their doctrine of immediate and unqualified abolition . . . have divided the north and united the south. The southern agitators, by their doctrine of superlative excellence and inviolable sacredness of slavery . . . are rapidly making the north unanimous, and will ere long produce a division in the south."[29]

Bacon's analysis at this point may be questioned. A modern historian has declared that "the full Southern defense of slavery was formulated before, rather than after, the attacks of the Abolitionists . . . and the threat that war would be the result of the infringement of 'Southern Rights' had been made before the birth of the American Anti-Slavery Society."[30] Yet no one can question Bacon's judgment that *if* the South were to be won, exaggeration and malediction must be eschewed. For himself he would combine colonization and emancipation. His program was couched in the formula of the *"immediate duty* of emancipation"

Leonard Bacon

but not the duty of *"immediate emancipation."*[31] The distinction was rather too subtle for the common man, but there was one reader who grasped it. When in 1864 someone told Abraham Lincoln that Dr. Bacon was supporting his re-election, Lincoln mused, "Bacon? Let me see, what do I know of him? Didn't he once write a book on slavery? . . . I read that book . . . and at first did not know exactly what to make of it; but afterwards I read it over more carefully, and got hold of Dr. Bacon's distinctions, and it had much to do in shaping my own thinking on the subject of slavery."[32]

What Bacon meant was that here and now he was ready to support all efforts at Negro improvement in this country looking toward eventual emancipation. In July, 1826, five young men met in the pastor's study of Center Church and formed two societies, one an antislavery society and the other an African Improvement Society. Among the founders were Theodore Dwight Woolsey and Leonard Bacon. The latter society was to be composed of Negroes and whites, and the board of managers was to include both races in expedient proportions. The caste line was thus broken. A church for Negroes was founded in New Haven with

Simeon S. Jocelyn as the pastor.[33] A Bible class of twenty adult Negroes received instruction from two Yale tutors, and the members of this class in turn taught the eighty scholars in the Sunday School.[34]

When in 1829 the African Education Society was founded Leonard Bacon was again active. The most feasible way of implementing the program appeared to be the establishment of a school for Negroes in New Haven. Jocelyn was elated, but inauspiciously William Lloyd Garrison also sponsored the plan, and unhappily just after a Negro insurrection in Virginia. An editorial in the *Connecticut Journal* for September 9, 1831, reads in part: "We had the pleasure of hearing Mr. Jocelyn's statement. . . . No man has done more than he to elevate the colored, yet we cannot get away from the fact that at present the black population is, as a mass, degraded. Their general viciousness has created antipathy. The general feeling, prejudice if you like, is that a college for blacks will be totally ruinous to the city. Our citizens will shrink away from it as contamination. It will lower the tone of public morals, drive away from our city its female schools—its throngs of summer visitors and will stop the vital stream of the city, the influx of young men to Yale College. We are not opposed to such a college, but its location for its own prosperity must be elsewhere."[35] A mass meeting of citizens rejected the school by a vote of 700 to 4. Jocelyn wrote to the *Connecticut Journal*, "Our beautiful city is clothed in sackcloth. Our proud elms hang their heads."[36] Not long afterward even the Negro church had to be given up.

In the meantime Lyman Beecher, like Bacon, was manfully struggling to combine the two approaches, colonization and emancipation, by a process of gradualism. At Lane Seminary in Cincinnati, where he was president, the students led by Theodore Weld conducted a prayer meeting of several days' duration. Northerners and Southerners participated. With all the fervor of a Finney revival the group emerged with the resolve that so drastic an evil as slavery admitted no temporizing. When old Beecher held firm, the students migrated to Oberlin. Beecher called them "He-goat men, who think they do God a service by butting everything in the line of their march." Of the Beecher children only Catherine upheld her father. Harriet and Henry Ward bolted to the "He-goats." When in after years Harriet needed documentation for

Uncle Tom's Cabin, she appealed to the researches of Theodore Weld.[37]

Then in 1839 New Haven was shocked into a more acute sensitivity by a strange visitation. A Spanish vessel, the *Amistad* manned by Negroes

AFRICAN SABBATH SCHOOL.

Come thou with us, and we will do thee good.—Num. x. 29.

merits and receives this certificate as a token of approbation for the kindness shown to   by introducing   into the African Sabbath School.

Superintendent.

New Haven,   183

was apprehended in Long Island Sound, and the blacks were lodged in the New Haven jail, charged with mutiny and murder. The owners of the vessel were two Spaniards, Ruiz and Montez, who claimed that they were transporting legally acquired slaves from Cuba for sale on the island of Principe. The slaves had mutinied and killed the captain.

Others of the crew escaped in a small boat. Ruiz and Montez and the cabin boy, who spoke both the language of the blacks and Spanish, were spared in order to steer the *Amistad* back to Africa; but they had tricked the blacks and had sailed east only by day but northwest by night. The Negroes discovered the deception in the harbor of New York and took over the vessel until they were apprehended by the Coast Guard. The owners demanded the return of the vessel. The Coast Guard demanded indemnification for bringing in the prize. The Spanish government demanded the extradition of the mutinous Negroes. But the case was already in the hands of an American court. An international incident was rapidly developing. President Van Buren desired to conciliate Spain but did not feel that he could override American justice. He placed a vessel, therefore, in the New Haven harbor with instructions if the case went against the blacks to turn them immediately over to Spain, but if in their favor to lodge an appeal at once before the Supreme Court.

By treaty England and Spain had agreed that any slaves taken after 1820 should, if discovered, automatically be freed. Nevertheless the trade still flourished. Blacks were captured in raids on the African coast, transported to Cuba and there fitted out with Spanish names and false papers back dated to make it appear that they had been taken prior to 1820. This had been going on for nineteen years. Were these Negroes on the *Amistad* old slaves or new slaves? Ruiz and Montez produced papers to show that they were old slaves, but were the papers falsified? And were these Spaniards the violators of an international agreement?

Thus far only the story of Ruiz and Montez had been heard. How could the Negroes' version be obtained since they did not speak English? This was the hour of destiny for Josiah Willard Gibbs. For forty years he had uneventfully been teaching Hebrew, Greek, Arabic, and Sanskrit. He was a famous philologist. Could he find the key? A phrenologist had had his turn, had felt all the bumps of the captives but without illumination. A deaf and dumb expert had had a try, but the sign language scarcely settled the crucial question, which was when these Negroes had been made captive.

Professor Gibbs went down to the jail. He indicated to the captives that he wished them to count. As he pointed, perhaps to his fingers, they began: "Eta, fele, sawa, nani," and so on up to "pu" for ten. Gibbs recorded the sounds. Then he went to New York and visited the vessels in the harbor until he found a Negro who both understood the numbers and spoke English. Here was the interpreter.

Now the true story was disclosed. These Africans had been captured not many moons since, and transported to Cuba. Fifty-four of them, including several women and three little girls, had been equipped with Spanish cognomens. Their leader, Singbe, for example was called Cinque. He was a magnificent figure; witness his portrait in the New Haven Historical Association by Jocelyn, the brother of the former pastor of the Negro church in New Haven. They had been transferred to the *Amistad*, the story continued, and chained in the hold. Then Singbe had succeeded with his toe in prying loose a nail from the floor. With this he had picked the one lock which secured the chains running through the iron collars of all the captives. The Negroes armed with sugarcane knives appeared on deck. The rest of the story as told by Ruiz and Montez was correct, save at the point of the papers. The essential point had now come to light. These were but recent captives in violation of international treaty. The case was pleaded in Hartford by Roger Baldwin for the defense. The judge was in an awkward position because to accept the version of the Negroes was to impugn the good faith of the Spanish officials in Cuba who supplied the false papers. The judge, though no Abolitionist, was not devoid of integrity and declared the Negroes free. The case was at once appealed to the Supreme Court. John Quincy Adams, who by reason of the infirmities of age had retired from the bar some five years earlier, was persuaded to take the case. A letter came to him in English from Ka-le, one of the captive boys:

"Mr. Adams: Dear Friend, I write because you talk to high court. The Spaniards say we bought in Havana. They lie. We bought in Mendi. We speak no Spanish. We speak little English. We read Matthew, Mark, Luke, John. Mr. Adams, you have children. You sorry Mendi people take them to Africa. Mr. Adams, we want to go free."

Friends averred that the lad had composed this letter entirely by himself. He was able to do so because during the year of incarceration the captives had been receiving instruction in English from Professor

George E. Day and the students of the Divinity School. All those concerned for the slavery question in New Haven were vastly interested and when one of the captives died, Leonard Bacon preached the funeral sermon.

Before the Supreme Court John Quincy Adams reviewed all the legal aspects of the case and declared that according to the covenant between England and Spain these men, being recently enslaved, were subject to liberation. Then, rising above all legal technicalities, he declared that in any case nations could not by their laws abridge the fundamental law of the liberty of the individual. "Gentlemen," said he, pointing to the Declaration of Independence hanging on the wall, "are these the principles by which our country shall be known?" The slaves were declared free. They were returned to Africa accompanied by missionaries.[38]

One might have supposed that this repatriation would revive the plan of colonization. Rather it served to point up the failure. To send back Negroes lately come from Africa was one thing, but quite another to repatriate those long since uprooted, without memory of their land and language and sapped of vitality by generations of slavery. One could not expect them to display the mettle of those English exiles for religion who tamed the American wilderness. Colonization manifestly had failed. The year in which Leonard Bacon gave it up was the very year of the *Amistad*. Curiously the American Missionary Society, founded to repatriate the captives, had as its main objective abolition—how different from the other missionary societies—and the preparation of the Negro for freedom in the American society. Benjamin Silliman now contemplated the day when the highest offices of state, the bench and the bar would be open to the Negro.[39]

One would have supposed that since the colonization issue was no longer divisive the antislavery forces could now pull together. Perhaps they might had not the problem at this juncture assumed a political cast. The Missouri Compromise of 1820 had established that slavery should not be introduced above the line of 36° 30'.[40] Some argued that the compromise was a tacit acceptance of slavery south of that line. The Northern Abolitionists would not have it so and encouraged the Southern slaves to seek asylum in the North. In 1844 a Yale graduate, the

Reverend Charles T. Torrey, resigned a New England pastorate and from his residence in Baltimore assisted in the escape of nearly four hundred slaves. Detected, he was condemned to six years of hard labor. He died in prison in 1846 of pulmonary tuberculosis at the age of thirty-three. A friend wrote:

> My countrymen weep not for him;
>   He has passed to the home of the just;
> But gird you with sackcloth and mourn for the land:
>   O, weep lest beneath the AVENGER'S strong hand,
> All your hopes sink in shame to the dust.[41]

But was it right to assist runaway slaves? Would not this infuriate the South, and would not the saving of a few slaves forge chains on those remaining? So long as a slave was property in the South, were not even those Northerners who favored emancipation obligated to return the slaves in the hope of an eventual universal release? Should the Abolitionists by the clandestine methods of the underground railroad goad the South into secession in which case the slaves would not be freed?

In the 1840's and '50's the Rhetorical Society of the Divinity School under the presidency of Nathaniel William Taylor was agitating the following questions: Should fugitive slaves be returned? In 1845, the president of the Society answered in the negative. In 1849 the question was whether slaves should be induced to run away from their masters. This time Hadley was in the chair and the vote of the president and the Society was affirmative. In 1850 the question was: Was the fugitive slave law Constitutional? The president and the Society said yes. In 1852 the query was posed whether there is a law higher than the Constitution. The president and the Society answered no.[42] Hadley recorded in his diary: "Spoke of fugitive-slave law, which Mac says is constitutional and ought to be obeyed, Bush says is unconstitutional and ought not to be obeyed, and I say is constitutional and ought not to be obeyed."[43]

Moses Stuart was among those who supported Daniel Webster in the conviction that for the very sake of emancipation the Union must be maintained, and to that end fugitives should be returned. This does not mean, said he, that we condone slavery. The point is simply that we have no jurisdiction. We are told that there is a higher law than the Constitution, that we are bound to disobey the Constitution. Yes, but can my conscience tell Virginia what is right? Slavery among us has indeed taken its worst form. Social relations are destroyed. Slaves live in concubinage. Ignorance is profound. The morals of the owners are corrupted. But injudicious attacks simply rivet slavery upon the South. Let us follow the things that make for peace. What will the United States be after nearly one-half is a smoking ruin?[44]

John Greenleaf Whittier was appalled by the compromises employed to preserve the land from becoming a smoking ruin. In a dream he saw a fugitive Negro woman take refuge in a church only to be shackled by the minister himself.

> I woke! and lo! the fitting cause
> Of all my dream's vagaries—
> Two bulky pamphlets, Webster's text,
> And Stuart's Commentaries![45]

Then came the Kansas Nebraska Bill whereby, as some held, a Northern route for a Western railway was secured by conceding to the South the possibility of slavery above the line established in the Missouri Compromise. The Nebraska Territory was to be divided. The present Nebraska should be free, but in Kansas the question should be settled by a referendum.[46] This was too much for the American Tract Society. Jeremiah Day, Eleazar Fitch, and Chauncey A. Goodrich declared that the members could not shut out from their minds and hearts certain events of recent occurrence—the repeal of the Missouri Compromise, the invasion of Kansas by armed men avowedly for the purpose of controlling elections in the interest of slavery.[47]

In 1854 a meeting was held in New Haven at which the aged Nathaniel W. Taylor spoke. The Nebraska Bill, said he, "is a mean attempt to violate a fair bargain. . . . Now, Sir, I will give you my honest opinion of the grand ulterior design of this movement. It is to nationalize slavery. . . . We have conceded enough and long enough. . . . Sir, I am a Union man. . . . I went for the Compromise of 1850 [the reference is to the admission of California as a free state with the proviso that in Utah and Nevada the question be settled later by plebiscite]. On this spot I made a speech for compromise, and in the same circumstances would make it again. . . . I am glad I made it. . . . Again the tempest is on us, and we can trust compromises and plighted faith no longer.

Enough of concession. . . . Let the North unite . . . lay aside past differences of Whig and democrat, abolition and free soil . . . and gird themselves to the struggle for the rights and liberty which our Constitution gives us. . . . Sir, if worst comes to the worst, I could lay off the garments of my profession and put on a soldier's coat in the cause of freedom. (Tremendous and long cheering and shouts of applause.)"

Dr. Bacon arose. "Slavery," said he, "ought to be *prohibited in these territories*. Because [it] is . . . the plainest and grossest violation of natural justice. Clergymen, they tell us, have no right to meddle in politics. My venerable friend here (Dr. Taylor) will be assailed with obloquy tomorrow for having spoken on this question."

Dr. Taylor: "And so will you."

Dr. Bacon: "Yes, so will I. And I am willing to be."

Professor Silliman spoke: "Never before . . . have I addressed a public assembly upon a political question. . . . But, gentlemen, a real crisis has now come over us, and now for the first time, I tremble for my country. . . . I would not be devoid of charity. I have many friends in the South whom I respect. I love my country—my whole country! But I love more that *principle*, dearer to our fathers than their country, dearer to them than their lives—*Liberty*."[48]

Since the slavery issue in Kansas was to be settled by a referendum both the slave and the free states sought to control the elections by pouring in immigrants, some of them not averse to violence. In March, 1856, a company of some forty men of Connecticut, mostly aged under thirty-five, were ready with their families to set out for the contested area. A great farewell meeting assembled in the United Church to raise money for the expedition and particularly to supply the emigrants with rifles. Henry Ward Beecher was invited to give the main address. A full account was given in the *Independent*, the journal edited by Leonard Bacon. "The church was filled with an audience of the most prominent citizens of New Haven. Many clergymen were present, together with a goodly representation from the Faculty of Yale College." The leader of the expedition explained that the rifles would be used only for defense, and if not needed against the Border Ruffians would still be useful against wolves and game. "We mean," he said, "to vote for freedom, *peacably and courteously*, . . . but if an attempt is made to prevent us, we will go to the ballot-box with a ticket in one hand and with a *rifle in the other!*"

Mr. Beecher spoke for an hour and a half, painting a vivid picture of two types of civilization developing in this land. The question as to which should prevail, said he, will be settled in Kansas. Complaint is made that the Northern emigrants have gone armed. They have gone with their Bibles. Nevertheless, until the causes of war are eliminated, wars cannot be done away. The best method to prevent war in Kansas is to be ready for it. It were a shame that the company setting out from New Haven should lack the requisite means of defense. (Great applause.)

The audience sang Whittier's "Song of the Kansas Emigrant" to the tune of "Auld Lang Syne."

Professor Silliman spoke. He expressed the hope that the Sharp's rifles would not be put to their fullest use, but he believed in "meeting manfully the present exigencies." Wherefore, he desired that the list of subscriptions should be headed: "B. Silliman, one Sharp's Rifle." (The price of a rifle was twenty-five dollars.) The Reverend Mr. Dutton gave one; so did his sister and thereby wrecked the girl's school of which she was mistress, since most of the scholars came from the South.[49] The account continues: "Stephen D. Pardee—I will give one for myself, and also one for my wife!"

"Mr. Beecher—'I like to see that; it is a shot right and left!' (Great laughter.). . . .

"Mr. Moses Tyler—'I will pledge one Sharp's rifle from the *Junior Class in Yale College!*' (Great applause.)

"Professor Silliman (rising from his seat and sweeping the galleries with his eyes)—'There are FOUR classes in Yale College!' (Laughter.) . . .

"Messrs. Dunlap and Rider, of the Senior Class of Yale College, contributed one."

The number subscribed in all was twenty-seven. The total receipts "made the collection for Kansas in the North Church *one thousand dollars.*

"The meeting then adjourned."[50]

The next half decade nullified the verdict of Henry Ward Beecher that the issue of freedom and slavery would be settled in Kansas. Leonard Bacon ruefully shook his mane as there emerged, so far as he could see, but three possibilities: war, compromise, or separation. Of the three he had come to prefer separation.[51] Two weeks after this statement came the attack on Fort Sumter. Bacon bowed. There was nothing now but to see it through. The North was singing that the Lord had "loosed the fateful lightning of His terrible swift sword," and "His truth is marching on."

CHAPTER XII

A Permanent Habitation

In the period immediately following the Civil War Yale Divinity School was on the verge of closing. Even before the war attendance had declined from an average of eighty-seven during the years 1838 to 1843 to only twenty-two in 1858. The main reason for decline was obviously not the war but that the old faculty was dead, dying, or decrepit. Taylor, died in '58, Goodrich in '60, Gibbs in '61, and though Fitch lived until '71, he was in practical retirement. Let this be a warning against constituting a faculty of men of the same age. The school would have been closed save for the second Timothy Dwight, grandson of the first. His task was at once to secure endowments and buildings recruit a new faculty and enlarge the curriculum.[1]

To retrieve the school's material basis was Dwight's first task. The finances of the Divinity School had long been in a precarious state. The salaries of Gibbs and Goodrich were frequently in arrears, even though Goodrich was a most liberal benefactor. Timothy Dwight regularly contributed his own salary. The new faculty whom he recruited were active in the raising of funds, none more so than Leonard Bacon whose great prestige and acquaintance in the churches aided no little. In 1869 he wrote from New York to his wife, "Monday evening, on our arrival at Brooklyn we took rooms at the Mission House and after tea went to see Mr. [Lyman] Beecher. We found him very seriously ill." The letter goes on to report calls on various prospective donors and concludes, "This is pretty hard work, but so far I am well except that my feet are a little stiff and lame—partly because of new stiff-soled boots. In great haste, your loving husband."

Lame legs built stout girders for the Divinity School. In 1867 Dwight reported assets totaling two hundred and fifty thousand dollars including a recent gift of thirty thousand dollars from Augustus Street establishing a chair in Ecclesiastical History to be named for his father Titus Street. In 1871 ex-governor Buckingham, who had already given generously,

Timothy Dwight the Younger

established the Buckingham Professorship of Sacred Literature. Samuel Holmes of New York endowed the Professorship of Hebrew Language and Literature. In 1884 to '85 Henry Winkley of Philadelphia, a complete stranger to the school, gave fifty thousand dollars to establish a Professor-ship in Biblical Theology. These sums were adequate at a time when the maximum salary was around twenty-five hundred dollars.

All of these new chairs were in need of "a permanent habitation," as Leonard Bacon phrased it. The school had never been adequately housed. Taylor and Gibbs had at first lectured in rooms above the old chapel. Divinity Hall constructed in 1835 to '36 had no classrooms and in any case was conceded to the theological department only under the express stipulation that it might at any time be reclaimed by the academic.[2] In 1866 the claim was pressed with the intent either to use the building for the undergraduates or to raze it to provide for Durfee Hall.[3] The Divinity School began casting about for new funds and a new site. The most favored location was the corner of College and Elm across from the Methodist Church, directly in line with a diagonal crossing the Green. But Professor Dana had requested this location for a museum; hence "with reluctance" the Prudential Committee recommended that the ground be allocated to the Divinity School. From various sources funds were secured.

On a gray July day in 1869 Leonard Bacon radiantly knocked on the door of George Leon Walker, pastor of Center Church, and invited him to attend the breaking of ground. The laying of the cornerstone on September 22 of that year was observed with impressive exercises,

The Daily Graphic, June 15, 1875
The Divinity School Buildings in 1875

commencing in Center Church at half past two. Leonard Bacon presiding, rejoiced that they were about to lay "the cornerstone of an edifice to stand for ages"—it was demolished in 1931.[4]

The building when completed was pronounced by the undergraduate *College Courant* to be "a fine specimen of the renaissance style," giving the effect "not so much of splendor as of massiveness and chaste elegance. The more sophisticated *Yale Courant* expressed concern lest religion languish amid such elegance:

"Judged from outside appearances, theology at Yale must be in a thriving state. A glorious day seemed to have dawned upon it; a day in which the millennium is dimly shadowed forth. A career of greatness,

hitherto unknown, now lies before it. Its ranks are being recruited from
the noblest youth of the land. It glories in a new and gorgeous edifice,
furnished in luxurious style. It has swept away all traces of its former
lowliness. . . . But, alas, we fear for the results. Amid such mighty and
radical changes will orthodoxy stand unshaken? Are black bricks and
stones of divers colors consistent with sound doctrines? Surrounded by
such magnificence, will theologues preserve their piety and keep alive
their zeal? On graduation, will they be ready to preach the gospel to
the poor on small salaries or to live in humble dwellings? Will many
of them be missionaries? It is with sad forebodings that we think upon
the probable answers to these solemn questions.

It was not thus that the fathers who planted the Church in the
land, were fitted for their work. They fasted, they lived in huts, they
endured hardships. But, O, shades of the Puritans; to what have these
degenerate days brought your descendants!"[5]

The annual catalogue for the year 1870-71 proudly announced that
the rooms were all furnished. The building was heated with steam,
lighted by gas and equipped with fireplaces and bathrooms. Among
the undergraduates the Sons of Belial circulated the report that the
Divinity students on occupying the new premises for some two weeks
did not discover the bathrooms. This on the authority of Professor
Benjamin W. Bacon. The fireplaces were used until 1891 and then
banned because of the great fire in the roof. Of this disaster there is a
lively account from the pen of Delia Lyman Porter:

"One of the incidents of our first year together was the famous
Seminary fire. We had started one evening to pay some calls, (dressed
in our gladdest rags) when the fire alarm rang, and as we walked up
Wall street, we found our Seminary on fire, flames issuing from the roof
of Edwards Hall." Professor Porter went up to recover his already copious
lecture notes, until those below, seeing smoke belch from his windows
on the third floor, sent up a rescuer to conduct the professor in his
evening clothes through a Mississippi flood of waters from the fire hose.[6]

The building program plus the new professorships so quickly re-
plenished the student body that the building when completed was
already inadequate. A chapel followed, facing on Elm Street, made
possible by the munificence of Frederick Marquand of Southport, Con-

necticut. His name has been carried over to the chapel in the present buildings on Prospect Street. At the semicentennial exercises of the school in 1872 the catalogue printed a ground plan showing the portion of the quadrangle completed and the portion contemplated. Mr. Marquand then contributed half of the expense for another dormitory, eighty thousand dollars on condition that within a stipulated time the remainder should be subscribed. It was, and the companion building erected. The two dormitories were called East and West Divinity. In 1908 the names were changed respectively to Edwards and Taylor Halls.[7]

Library facilities were still inadequate. The books named for their donor "The Trowbridge Library" constituted only a small reference collection. For their housing Mr. Marquand, in 1881, again generously contributed funds. The building was named in honor of Leonard Bacon.

Throughout this period the student body continued to be predominantly Yankee and Congregational, though with a steady rise from other sections and sects. Although some data are lacking, it is possible that in 1860 all of the students may have been born in New England. In 1901 the percentage was down to 12 per cent. The great gains were in the numbers from the Middle West. The South always contributed a few; in 1865 directly after the Civil War there were 9 per cent, but in 1900 only 7 per cent. The Far West sent very few, throughout this period only about 2 per cent. Foreigners were well represented. In 1900, for example, a class of 56 had twelve from abroad; three from Canada, three from Japan, two from Turkey, two from Germany, one from Ireland, and one from Scotland.

Increasingly the number of graduates who settled in New England exceeded the number of those born in the area. In 1858, 59 per cent were born in New England and 50 per cent settled. In 1902, 16 per cent were born in this region and 43 per cent settled. This shift may have been because the students from the more conservative sections of the country had difficulty in returning to their own constituencies and were driven to transfer to New England.

The Established Disciplines: Theology

In the years between the Civil War and the new century the courses of study in the Divinity School were divided into pairs of threes. The

inherited three were theology, Bible, and practical theology. The
innovated three were church history, social ethics, and missions. In the
ancient three theology had been regnant—too regnant, thought President
Woolsey, who hoped the new curriculum would be better balanced. At
the same time he recognized the new imbalance in that theology, the
queen of the sciences, was represented only by a *locum tenens*. The
work of Nathaniel W. Taylor had been taken over by his son-in-law,
Noah Porter, but only out of filial piety.[8] He was teaching in the
College and believed that philosophy and religion should there be taught
by one man and that that man should not teach anywhere else. He stated
his point bluntly when in 1854 George Park Fisher was made College
Pastor and Professor of Divinity with assignments in instruction. Porter
remonstrated to President Woolsey that the man who took the students
through "the sour labor" of abstract metaphysics should be allowed to
sweeten the diet by teaching also morals and Christian evidences and
that one not grounded in the philosophical disciplines should not be
teaching theology at all. Nothing personal against Professor Fisher was
intended, to whom Woolsey forwarded the letter. Fisher replied that if
he were restricted to preaching he would not hold the place for a day.
He could be effective as College Pastor only if he shared in instruction,
and if he were not competent for this, neither was he competent to be
pastor. Fisher won. On Porter's death Fisher wrote a very warm
encomium. Porter's position was derived from his distaste for mass education. He was instrumental in introducing training through intimate
encounter. It was said that a student would no more think of striking up
a familiar conversation with President Woolsey than with East Rock
but that Professor Porter was "every student's friend." His classes became conferences in which his fancy was kindled and words of "felicitous
glowing statement fell from his lips." In discipline he was understanding
and some suggested that in his theology he modeled the government of
the universe on his own administration of the College. He kept eternal
damnation on the books and then let everyone off.[9]

Yet for all his desire to concentrate on the College, he did teach
theology in the Divinity School for nearly two decades. In his teaching
and in his published works he brought to the fore the problem of
knowledge through the Scottish philosophy, with which student notes

reveal his father-in-law, Nathaniel Taylor, to have been concerned. The problem of knowledge preoccupied the age of Enlightenment from Locke through Kant. Edwards had wrestled with it and for long in New England his solution had held sway until the Scottish Realism appeared to be a more effective reply to Hume. Taylor had availed himself of the new view but in no systematic way and with no greater precision than his sources. Porter was teaching philosophy and came directly to grips with the epistemological problem. He took a middle ground between the pure empiricists and the intuitionists. There must be an impact from without upon the knowing subject. Only in the case of its own body does that subject have an immediate experience of material reality. In other instances there is immediacy only of *matter as being* and not of secondary characteristics which may be erroneously apprehended. Reason can, however, detect and correct the error. The process of knowing was described by Porter as "rational intuition." The mind must receive and does receive but in receiving is active in applying to sensation judgment, analysis, and revision.[10]

But when it came to religious knowledge he appeared to shift from immediacy of experience to inference. In a sermon *Agnosticism, a Doctrine of Despair*[11] Porter treats God as the postulate necessary for all thinking and doing. Science must assume God, for what science can there be if the universe is devoid of rationality? History requires God if it be anything more than a mere sequence of events. Morality is nothing without God. Personality on the outside is necessary to sustain personality on the inside. Freedom calls for God. Without a personal, willing, acting God the universe in but mechanism. Progress is but an ideal hope without God to insure it. The future life is insubstantial apart from God. Nature exhibits "remorseless insensibility." "An earthquake swallows up tens of thousands of living men. The jaws of the gulf that opened to receive them swing back to their place, and forthwith flowers adorn the ghastly seam, as if in mockery of the dead who are buried beneath. . . . Of another life there are no tidings and few suggestions, a possibility, or perhaps a probability, but no hope. . . . Now let God be seen to break forth from His hiding-place, and to manifest Himself in the Christ who conquers death and brings immortal life to light through his arising and ascension, and the hope that had been reached as a conclusion of assured conviction is shouted forth in the song of triumph, 'Blessed be the God and Father of our Lord Jesus Christ, who . . . has begotten us again into a lively hope by the resurrection of Jesus Christ from the dead, to an inheritance incorruptible and undefiled and that fadeth not away.' "[12]

The argument appears to be inferential. God is necessary to make sense out of life. One wonders whether the validity of the inference is not based on the experiential. A friend tells of a hiking trip with Porter in the Adirondacks. In 1874 when he was sixty-four Porter took with him some companions and guides on a climb through the wildest route of the region. Toward the end of the day, as they were on a high eminence, "long slanting shafts of radiance burst between the peaks and streamed miles and miles across the bosom of the forest basin beneath." The guides picked up the knapsacks. Porter gazed immovably and said only "Let's stay." That meant chancing the weather under the sky, but the guides dropped the knapsacks and prepared supper. Porter watched until the light was gone, then rolled up in his blanket. At dawn he was again at the point of lookout and watched the pageant of the sunrise. As the journey was resumed, his elation marked him as one who like Moses had talked with God and wist not that the skin of his face shone.

Yet the vision of the ineffable is not a communication of detailed information, and Porter's pupils were taught "to tolerate the vast, unexplored spaces of darkness with which things eternal are begirt. They learned a certain reticence of speech and thought regarding the inner nature of the Godhead, the atonement, and the mysteries of the divine life embodied in human life." That was why Porter could be at once the stalwart critic and the stanch friend of heretics such as Theodore Parker, the Unitarian, and Tyndall, the Darwinian. It was Porter who stoutly defended Bushnell and made Congregationalism large enough to contain Theodore Thornton Munger. When warned that his patronage of heretics might damage Yale, Porter answered, "If it be a question between the welfare of the College and the performance of duty, let the duty be done, and let the College suffer."[13]

After eighteen years he was excused from serving for Leah and returned to his Rachael. Leonard Bacon took over theology and relieved him. It was George Park Fisher's turn to have misgivings about a newcomer.

There was apprehension, he testified, among the younger men "that there might be some want of freedom in the presence of his [Bacon's] positive character and emphatically outspoken opinions. All apprehensions of this sort were soon dissipated. We found him uniformly gentle and considerate, not in the least disposed to press unduly his own ideas upon our acceptance, and helpful and obliging in the highest degree. Fertile in new plans, he was fortunately at the furthest remove from obstinacy in insisting upon measures which were not acceptable to his colleagues. . . . In our conferences he brought out of his full mind treasures new and old. . . . As to the students he was lenient in his judgments, kindly and yet searching, and eminently wise and stimulating in his criticisms. He never manifested to either professors or pupils any of the faults which have commonly been thought to have been characteristic of old men."[14]

But Bacon was not primarily a theologian. His contribution was rather in the field of American Church History, a consideration of which will be deferred until the next chapter.

At the laying of the cornerstone of Marquand Chapel in 1871, President Woolsey announced the coming to the chair of theology of Samuel Harris. He was fifty-seven when he came and had never written a book. He was sixty-nine before he did any writing, and after that produced four ponderous volumes. They savor more of the classroom than do the previous theological works of New England, produced primarily by ministers. Harris had long been teaching. Systematic arrangement of points was not, however, what struck his students; the novel element in his presentation was the frequent quotations from current literature and notably the poets: Wordsworth, Whittier, Browning and even Goethe, esteemed like Virgil as a pagan saint. Harris had not quite the temerity to introduce into the text of a sober work on theology a citation from *Alice's Adventures in Wonderland*, but he accorded her the distinction of a footnote.[15]

One of his students wrote, "I can see him now, sitting in his chair in the class-room, his pale face turned toward the window, and irradiated with the inner light of the Son of Righteousness, his deep set eyes reflecting the heavenly vision which was his, his voice finely modulated and in perfect harmony with the thought, as he repeated those lines from

Wordsworth's 'Ode to Immortality from Recollections of Early Childhood,' beginning,

> So in season of fair weather,
> Though inland far we be,
> Our souls catch sight of the immortal sea
> Which brought us hither;
> Can in a moment travel thither,
> And see the children sport upon the shore,
> And hear the mighty waters rolling evermore.[16]

In theology Harris was not a path breaker. His task was to teach the
fundamentals, not to be startling. From Taylor he derived his faith in
the moral government of the universe. From Bushnell he appropriated
the blending of the natural and the supernatural. With Wordsworth he
saw God immanent in nature. Like his great predecessors he combined
the diverse strands in modern Christianity. He believed, said he, (though
not quite so succinctly) in a religion of the heart without sentimentality
or pantheism, a religion grounded in history without aridity, a religion
of reason without dogmatism and speculative coldness. What does this
add up to if not Pietism, the Reformation, and the Enlightenment?[17]

His greatest distinction lies in the extension of Noah Porter's treatment of the problem of knowledge to the sphere of religion. One has
the feeling that with Harris moralism was a deep ingredient in his conviction as to the possibility of knowledge. If there is no possibility of
knowing, there can be no morality because morality depends on choice,
and choice requires the knowledge of alternatives. But to be unable to
do anything was just too much for this son of the Puritans. To be in-
active because forever undecided was for Harris a supreme example of
moral dereliction. A student in Yale College of the class of '73 recalls a
sermon which he preached to the undergraduates. The day was hot and
the hearers on the hard benches more than usually uncomfortable. Harris
spoke of the need of positive belief in religion and gave the agnostics
a hard drubbing. "His fervor increased as he went on, and the most
hardened Sophomore was interested. Finally he paused a moment and
then raising his long arm, with dilating eye and ringing voice, he exclaimed, 'Some men are nothing but interrogation points all their lives.'
As he hurled out this sentence and pointed with quivering finger to some
of these wretches up among the rafters overhead, a wave of horror

thrilled the crowd. Even the tutors looked aghast. Never before had it seemed such a horrible thing to be an interrogation point as it did at that moment."[18]

In wrestling with the problem of religious knowledge Harris did not proceed to argue from Biblical revelation, let alone from miracles. Following Locke the problem of the credibility of the witnesses to the miracles had been so far pursued that by the end of the eighteenth cen-

Samuel Harris

tury there was more of a disposition to believe in the miracles because of the Gospel than in the Gospel because of the miracles. After Bushnell, miracles were defended as possible because the supernatural is only the direct operation of will in temporary suspension of the natural, but no evidential value was discovered here. Harris took this ground but did not reject the miracles. Continental criticism left his assurance unscathed. Had not Baur devoured Strauss and Renan consumed Baur? With composure one might watch as fish swallowed fish.[19]

Harris took over from Noah Porter the doctrine of rational intuition but made explicit the claim to immediate religious experience. God, said he, is not merely a postulate required to explain all other postulates. God is among the data of experience. "The knowledge of God, like the knowledge of man and nature, begins in experience, and is ascertained, defended and systematized in thought." "The reality of our knowledge of God is a primitive datum of consciousness." "Man being rational is so constituted that in the presence of God . . . he will know him; and he will know that he knows God in the act of knowing him." "Physical science and religious knowledge are, as knowledge, the same in kind, differing only in their objects." The knowledge of God is primary for "if man cannot know God, he cannot know anything."[20]

This immediacy of divine experience might seem to reduce the need for a self-revelation of God in Christ. One does have the feeling that Harris is not stupefied like Edwards and Bushnell by confrontation with Christ. There is indeed a fine passage on the combination of opposites in the character of Christ, reminiscent of Edwards' sermon *On the Excellency of Christ*, but there is hardly the same sense of awe and wonder. The reason, however, is not so much that the immediacy of religious experience rendered unnecessary a historical revelation as that the revelation in history was not concentrated at a given point in time. The incarnation of God was discerned in the geologic and the evolutionary ages. Harris, in accord with his time, had gone beyond Bushnell's rhapsodies over the geologic eons to include the progressive stages of the emergence of sentient life culminating in man, God's colleague in a continuing creation. The incarnation was anticipated by the theophanies of the Old Testament and continued in the supernatural community, the Christian Church, and the panorama of creation and the drama of redemption were seen moving forward to a stupendous consummation. The inconspicuous no less than the spectacular is suffused with the energizing of God's majesty.

"It is not only in storms that the ocean reveals its strength; but in the calmest day its gentlest swell moves in upon the beach with a majesty which could only have been acquired by traversing the ocean's breadth, and concentrating in itself the ocean's power. So every act of God is majestic with the love and power of the Godhead; whether creating a world or redeeming it, raising or prostrating kingdoms, or bringing in mighty reformations, or giving gracious consolation to the afflicted, or drawing a child to himself, or listening to the sighs of the penitent, it is all the acting of godlike majesty and love, which has swept across the ocean of God's eternal counsels, and gathered into its gentlest movement, the eternal power and love of God."[21]

Harris also found that God had a plan for the ages. Bushnell had envisaged the consummation in terms of solar galaxies. Harris like the millenarians and the apostles of progress came back to earth. With Edwards and Beecher he found the locus for the realization of the future

The Faculty in 1881

| Harris | Fisher | Bacon | Barbour | Day | Dwight |

The Faculty in 1922
Standing: Professors Archer, Weigle, Bailey, Dahl, Tweedy, Wright, and
Macintosh
Seated: Professors Porter, Bacon, Beach, Dean Brown, Walker, Sneath, and
Dinsmore

holy commonwealth in these United States. "God has always acted," said he, "by chosen peoples. To the English speaking people more than to any other the world is now indebted for the propagation of Christian ideas and Christian civilization. It is a remarkable fact in this day that the thinking of the world is done by the Christian nations; that the enterprise and energy of the world are mainly theirs. They alone are colonizing, and by their commerce and enterprise pushing their influence throughout the world. So also the political condition of the Protestant nations is that of constitutional government, popular education, and a growing regard for the rights and welfare of the people."[22]

Well may such optimism now appear to have been incredibly naïve. Yet conceivably Harris was right that no moment in history was ever more propitious than 1874. The world was at peace. The Civil War was over. The Union had been saved. Slavery abolished. The temperance cause was making strides. Educational reform was astir. The state was responsive to the popular will and ready to assist moral reform. A people nurtured by Calvinism and endowed with a new and rapidly expanding land had received an unparalleled opportunity. But the glorious end could not be achieved without toil and many frustrations. "Broken hopes, thwarted plans, bitter discoveries of human wickedness, toil without visible results will sober and sadden you. Death will overtake you while you feel that you have accomplished nothing, and you will be able only to look to Jesus to pardon an unprofitable servant; yet, in the assurance of victory, labor; and, in the distant future, looking down on the renovated earth, you will hear and join the voice of the great multitude, as the voice of many waters and the voice of mighty thunderings, saying: 'Alleluia, for the Lord God Omnipotent reigneth!' "[23] From the encounter with philosophical and religious skepticism Harris emerged to reaffirm the American apocalyptic dream.

After Harris systematic theology at Yale was not systematic until the coming of Douglas Macintosh. The immediate successor of Harris, George B. Stevens, had been transferred from the field of New Testament, and although he wrote some books on theology proper, he never ceased to deal with what was essentially Biblical theology, despite the institution of a new chair devoted to that particular field and manned by Frank C. Porter.

CHAPTER XIII

The Established Disciplines:
Bible and Homiletics

While toward the turn of the century theology decreased, Biblical study increased. There were sometimes three men in this field occupying themselves with language, exegesis, and Biblical theology. During the last forty years of the nineteenth century, there were in all as many as nine men giving instruction in these areas. This little company was large enough to develop schools of thought. The younger split from the older, notably Bacon and Porter from Dwight and Day with Stevens in between. The younger philologians, Harper, Curtis, Sanders, and Moulton, were ranged also with the rising generation.

Benjamin W. Bacon in reviewing his life gave a candid picture of Biblical instruction as conducted during his students days by Dwight and Day. Johannine authorship of the Fourth Gospel was considered to have been established for all time. Objections to the Mosaic authorship of the Pentateuch were regarded as "an assault of hostile critics." Classroom instruction was philological and exegetical. Critical questions were adroitly parried. Dwight did not undertake to give an introduction even to the whole of the New Testament but would go through a single book examining the meaning of every word. In so doing, said Bacon, he fought "no battles save rear-guard actions," and Day was a "pacifist of the pussy-foot type."[1]

Oddly enough all of these men had studied in Germany. There they had learned something: all things excellent are not Anglo-Saxon, professors may drink beer and still be Christian, to celebrate Christmas and light candles on the altar is not necessarily popish. Although they did learn German *Gründlichkeit*, in the realm of ideas they brought back mainly a reinforcement of what they took. The composite origin of Genesis had long since been accepted by Gibbs and Stuart. In the Old Testament the more drastic reconstructions of Wellhausen and Gunkel had not registered and for the New Testament the views of Paulus, Strauss, and Baur were considered negligible aberrations.[2]

German higher criticism invaded Yale by way of Scotland. George E. Day warned his class against the work published in Edinburgh of W. Robertson Smith, *The Old Testament in the Jewish Church* (1881). Because of it, Smith had been dismissed from his chair at Aberdeen. In this book he maintains that the method of revelation is the method of education. God's word is delivered in the language of men and is not exempt from the necessary laws and limitations of human receptivity and expression. Scripture exhibits various levels and many passages are properly excluded from devotional use. The Bible as history must be studied according to the same rules as other ancient books. The revelation of God which it contains will not be borne in upon us by external testimony but will become a spiritual certainty only through the testimony of the Holy Spirit.

This book Day described as "bad." Benjamin Bacon rebelled, not simply because he was young, but also because he was a Bacon. His grandfather Leonard, when W. Robertson Smith was deposed at Aberdeen, had proposed that he be invited to lecture at the Divinity School, and Benjamin's own father had sent him a copy of the book.[3]

To leave Dwight and Day with only this account of their teaching and significance would, however, be quite unfair. None would have been quicker to say so than Benjamin Bacon. When Dwight died, Bacon in a memorial address paid him a just and glowing tribute. As "Tutor Tim" in Yale College he contributed, like Noah Porter, to breaking down the state "of armed neutrality" between the faculty and the students. When in accord with the traditional concept of his tutorial function he sprinted after some miscreants and found himself gaining, he called, "Gentlemen, if you do not run a little faster, I shall be obliged to overtake you." His youth was marked by a rollicking gaiety and his age by a genial drollerie, which beguiled alike his pupils and colleagues. He it was who saved the

Divinity School from extinction, and he, who on succeeding Noah Porter as President, made of Yale a university not merely in name through an act of Legislature but in fact by developing the schools and departments into something more than fringes to the College. In the Biblical field the contribution of Timothy Dwight lay in the translation of foreign works and in his share in the labors of the committee which produced the American Revised Version of the Scriptures.[4] Bacon described Dwight as "humorous and humane; as sound in judgment, as indefatigable in labor."[5] Until his death in 1916 he was a symbol of the continuity of the gerenations beneath the elms. Robert Dudley French of the class of 1910 thus wrote of Dwight's latter days:

"Among the alumni who were in college during the years that followed his retirement, his figure is remembered like some mid-winter sunset in New Haven,—a vision of the elder hours withdrawing amid a glory of color, wherein the towers of the college and the venerable elms upon the Campus seemed to have a share. In some such sunset hour, perhaps, we had caught a glimpse of the ex-president, stoop-shouldered, wrapped in thought, shuffling slowly across the Campus or up Hillhouse Avenue; and we saw him as a visitant out of the well-nigh forgotten past. At all other times and seasons, the college world and all that was in it belonged to us, who were the youngest of the family of Yale; but at such a time, as we saw this old man moving in slow dignity before us, apparently oblivious of us and all our noisy ways, it came suddenly upon us that Yale had known many years before ever she knew us and that her strength ran far into the past.

"In those years, he appeared but seldom in the public life of Yale; but on one occasion, every year, he stepped out of his retirement to stand for a moment before us, sign and symbol of the past. On Commencement morning, when all the degrees had been given, and the last hymn had been sung, there fell a hush on the crowd in Woolsey Hall, as Timothy Dwight stepped forward, from his place beside President Hadley, to pronounce the Benediction. In that silence his voice, though it was a little faint and husky, reached every corner of the hall, and to each of us it seemed the voice of the old Yale calling down the peace of Heaven upon us who were of the new."[6]

Much the same can be said for Professor Day with this addition that when Benjamin Bacon came to the Divinity School in 1881, Day was within two years of the age when now retirement is obligatory. This was the man, let it be remembered, who had taught English to the *Amistad* captives in 1839. He was basically a teacher of Greek and of Hebrew. His greatest scholarly contribution, like that of Dwight, was in translating foreign works and in serving as Secretary for the Old Testament

George E. Day

Section of the American Committee of Revisers from 1871 until the work was completed.[7]

A new translation had been needed partly in the interest of contemporary English and partly to take account of an improved text. The first need had long been recognized in Yale circles. In 1769 Ezra Stiles had said that he desired no departure from the King James Version until "the English dialect of the last two ages shall have become obsolete and unintelligible to posterity."[8] This would be, he thought, when the westward migration had reached the Mississippi. The river was attained much sooner than he ever divined, and the new translation came out coincidentally in 1833, the work of Noah Webster. Inasmuch as the Bible influences the national language, said he, it must be correct, grammatical, and appropriate. Obsolete expressions should be replaced by current terms. For example: *who* for *which, know* for *wist, bring* for *fetch, sixty* for *three score, perhaps* for *peradventure, cows* for *kine, interest* for *usury, hinder* for the Elizabethan *let, shun* for *eschew, killed* for *slew, by no means* for *God forbid, insane* for *mad, toil* for *travail, plunder* for *spoil, Holy Spirit* for *Holy Ghost.* Euphemisms should be substituted for all expressions "offensive to delicacy" or inappropriate "before a promiscuous audience." For *to stink* he would substitute *to be odious.*[9] Josiah Willard Gibbs reviewing the work of Webster regretted that it had never been accorded its due. He added a further list of emendations such as *brothers* for *brethren, intimate* for *familiar.*[10]

The American Revision Committee enjoyed the services of several Yale men in addition to Day. The chairman of the New Testament Company was Woolsey. Dwight and Hadley were members. The principles of Webster and Gibbs are less in evidence than might have been expected because the concern of the translators of the 1880's was not so much to modernize the English of the King James Version as to bring the translation into line with the enormous advances in the recovery of the true text, especially of the New Testament. Since the King James three great manuscripts of the New Testament had become available: the *Codex Alexandrinus,* the *Sinaiticus,* and the *Vaticanus.* Westcott and Hort had incorporated the new findings into an improved text. The American Revised Version utilizing these materials was meticulous, exact, and literal. For precision it was superb, and this work is the most enduring monument of Dwight and of Day in the field of scholarship.

In 1886 when Day at the age of seventy relinquished his teaching, he devoted himself to building up the remarkable library on foreign missions which now goes by his name.

Day was replaced in the teaching of Hebrew by William Rainey Harper, who kindled such enthusiasm for the subject that George Park Fisher had to plead with the students to devote some time to the other disciplines. Benjamin Bacon remarked that Harper could never have evoked such interest had he not combined the study of language with historical criticism as the incentive.[11]

When in 1891 Harper left to become the president of the University of Chicago his post was taken by his friend Edward L. Curtis from McCormick Theological Seminary, whose only regret in leaving Chicago for Yale was that now he would be as remote from Harper as before. In other respects Curtis welcomed relief from the school where for ten years he had been battered by the ultraconservatives who were outraged by his claim that God loves all of His children alike. What then, they said, of the elect? Even more disconcerting was his statement that the Bible is an oriental book and he who would understand it must "wear the garb of the orient, dwell beneath Syrian skies; must be semitic in his intellect, receiving truth by intuition, passionate and intense in feeling and utterance, and skilled in symbol." Creeds are tentative, said he, and the Westminster Confession not immutable.[12]

After coming to Yale Curtis put to flight armies of aliens in the battle for higher criticism. The methods used in testing Livy, said he, must be applied also to the Pentateuch and to the Gospels.[13] The enduring scholarly work of Curtis is the volume on *Chronicles* in the *International Critical Commentary*.[14] In the preface he declared that as history, the books of Chronicles were worthless yet historically valuable because they idealized the past in order to provide a norm for the present and a program for the future. One may well doubt, said he, whether Judaism could have survived in that era of pressures from Persia, Greece, and Rome had not the religion been centralized about Jerusalem, the Temple, and the priesthood, all so exalted by the Chronicler. In teaching the Bible to children Curtis advised no premature injection of criticism. But, when questions are raised, said he, the young should be given candid answers.[15]

In 1900 Curtis was reinforced through the coming of his friend Charles C. Torrey as professor of Semitic Languages. He taught only in the Graduate School but many of the Divinity students took his work, sometimes in Hebrew and more particularly in Aramaic and Syriac. Throughout the years until his recent death he has kept his colleagues in ferment through revolutionary hypotheses. Even before coming to Yale he had set forth his views: the books of Ezra and Nehemiah were by the same author as the books of Chronicles and of no more historical value; there was no return from exile;[16] Cyrus, the leader of the supposed return, is interpolated in the Second Isaiah, and thus there is no need to assume a Third Isaiah consisting of the chapters in which Cyrus is not mentioned.[17]

In 1886 George Barker Stevens came to Yale in the field of New Testament. Both chronologically and theologically he lay between the older luminaries and the new. He had studied in Germany and had learned one thing which other Yale teachers had missed—that the Bible contains more than one theology.[18] Stevens made that fact plain in the title of his first publication, *The Pauline Theology*, in 1892 and again in the second, *The Johannine Theology*, in 1894. The first book accepted the traditional Pauline canon but denied that the theology was a unit. In a later work in 1905, *The Christian Doctrine of Salvation*, Stevens plainly said that we must distinguish "between the contingent thought-forms of the first Christian thinkers and the essential religious life and fundamental Christian certainties concerning God and the experience of salvation, which they were seeking to expound."[19]

Stevens' first work on Johannine theology did not seek to settle the question of authorship but recognized that the picture of Jesus there given differed from that in the first three gospels. In 1899 a comparison was more fully developed in *The Theology of the New Testament*. Here Stevens frankly said that "the Gospel of John is a distillation of the life and teaching of Jesus from the alembic of the apostle's own mind. It is the interpretation of the meaning of Christ's words, deeds and person, derived from intimate personal relations with him and colored and shaped by a long life of Christian thought and experience."[20] This does not mean that it is inferior to the Synoptics because these accounts also were fashioned by men subject to error. For example, in the Synoptics there are predictions that the Son of Man should come with power before the generation then living should have passed away. Since this had not come to pass, either Jesus was mistaken or the disciples misunderstood what he had said. Stevens could not tolerate the first alternative and had none left but the second.[21] If then the writers of the first three Gospels were in error on this point, the way was open to regard the interpretation of John's Gospel as equally valid and perhaps even more satisfactory. Stevens certainly found it more congenial because of the doctrine of eternal life rather than of the advent of the Great Day.

In his final book Stevens was still the Biblical theologian, though one has the feeling that he was not so much deriving his theology from the Bible as discovering it in those selected strands which met his need. Any atonement, he declared, in a sense of expiation, propitiation, or substitution was to be rejected as the result of the contingent thought forms of the Apostle Paul. The true atonement is "the eternal passion of the heart of God on account of sin," and this Stevens declared to be the Biblical position.[22]

In all of his thinking one wonders how far he may have been influenced by his younger colleagues. In his first work he acknowledged indebtedness to Frank Chamberlin Porter, who as a young man succeeded John E. Russell in the chair of Biblical theology. Porter had completed his doctoral dissertation on *The Yeçer Hara; a Study in the Jewish Doctrine of Sin.*[23] The purpose was to discover how far Paul was original in his doctrine of sin. The approach was genetic, because one cannot properly speak of Paul's "contingent thought forms" unless one considers where they had come from, how far they had been developed up to Paul, and in what respects he introduced modifications. Porter's influence on the thinking of the Divinity School was so deep that it calls for a more extensive treatment, but since his impact came mainly after the turn of the century, the description will be deferred.

Bacon will receive like treatment. His comments on his teachers have already been noted. His coming to the school belongs here. Already he had been in the parish for twelve years. During that period he had pursued the questions raised by W. Robertson Smith and all the more readily because a master of the linguistic tools. As a lad Bacon had been on the continent while his father was a pastor at Geneva and thus had mastered French and German, and at Yale the pedestrian drill with Day in Hebrew and Dwight in Greek had not been in vain. Bacon's first book, published in 1892, was entitled *The Genesis of Genesis*. The subtitle was really more arresting, *Bibles within the Bible*. The introduction was a magnificent plea for the higher criticism. The details of the analysis in the body of the work need not detain us. In such an area later studies render the earlier obsolete, yet the specialists assert that Bacon's book is still worthy of study for its pregnant suggestions.

When in 1895 Stevens was transferred to theology as successor to Harris, Bacon presented his candidacy for the chair of New Testament. George Park Fisher, who had preached Bacon's ordination sermon at Lyme, was dubious. Delia Lyman Porter (Mrs. Frank C. Porter) is our witness. "When the New Testament chair became vacant and the successful Oswego pastor [Bacon] was being considered, our famous Professor George P. Fisher, (then the uncrowned King of the School) was so exceedingly afraid that in spite of all his brilliant ability, this outspoken young scholar would wreck the stable and sure foundations of the school by his radical views, that it seemed impossible to engineer the permanent invitation. . . . Things were practically at a deadlock . . . when in the cushioned seat at the South end of our living room nook, I said, 'Ben, if you will take the chance, declare your willingness to come *for one year only on trial* I believe you will surely in the end win over Professor Fisher and get the permanent appointment!' "[24] Bacon made the venture, came for a year and stayed for a life.

Another of the ancient disciplines to be expanded was pastoral theology. After Goodrich the chair was first held by James M. Hoppin who must have been an interesting person. At any rate he had many interests. Trained first in the law, he devoted himself to the ministry and ended by teaching art. He wrote several books on Greek and Renaissance art. As an adjunct to his work in the Divinity School, he produced a hefty tome entitled *The Office and Work of the Christian Ministry* (1870). Frankly he said he had written it so he would not have to say it. The students could read all this, and the class period could be devoted to practice preaching. One of the merits of his book is a lack of dogmatism. He recognized cordially that there is more than one way of delivering a sermon. Some men handle a manuscript without constriction; others are hampered save in extempore preaching. Aware of styles and periods of preaching, Hoppin described the American variety as "doctrinal and experimental; it aims to reach the conscience and will through the understanding, and to bring men to an *immediate* decision in matters of the soul. It deals with these doctrines as if they were the greatest of truths, and the only truths worthy of an immortal soul's attention. It is therefore characterized by the most intense and often terrible earnestness."[25]

Lewis O. Brastow, who succeeded Hoppin, also brought out a manual on preaching entitled *The Work of a Preacher* (1914), valuable partly because of its rich store of examples from ancient and contemporary preachers. The same quality appears in another work entitled *The Modern Pulpit* (1906), which surveys types of preaching in various periods and lands. Of the American preacher Brastow said, "His product is less sentimental, less affectionate, than that of the German, less fervid and rhetorically brilliant than that of the Frenchman, less dignified and churchly than that of the Anglican, less Biblical, less sympathetic, and less evangelical than that of the English nonconformist. But in general it will hardly be questioned that it is more thoughtful and after its kind instructive." Even more significant was the differentiation of styles of preaching in the sections of the United States. The preaching of the North appeared to him to be intellectually deliberate, independent, and virile; that of the South emotional, oratorical, effusive, and conservative; that of the West intensely practical, tenacious of encrusted theology, and wholly averse to historical criticism.[26]

Brastow's greatest contribution to his students was "the merciless love" with which he dissected their sermons without wounding the authors. One of them describes him, the onslaught over and the oil poured: "He stands in that front pew nervously cutting the railing with the thin edge of his hand. He throws down the paper on which he has made his analysis, makes a movement suggestive of gathering himself together. Every fiber is tense, in the grip of the one idea, which in a marvelous way makes him insensible to everything else. With that delving gesture in which he seems to reach down beneath the surface for the truth which an instant later he holds up before us, he enforces the message that we must go deep into the secrets of God, and the mysteries of the human heart, down far beneath the easy surface, if we are to hold up before men the truth that shall win them."[27]

A new development in the department of pastoral care was elocution. Samuel Silas Curry was entrusted with this charge. He wrote a good many books on the subject in which he decried all tricks. One must give attention, said he, to enunciation, accent, change in pitch, and depth of tone, but expression is the fruit of reliving that which is read. He deprecated the Barn Yard Symphony style, which necessitated reading a poem on God revealed in torrents, meadow streams, pine groves, and avalanches of snow with strivings to reproduce the appropriate noises. Better to suggest the awe and reverence which the entire passage is designed to evoke.[28]

The greatest adjunct to the department of pastoral theology was the establishment of the Lyman Beecher Lectureship in 1871. The donor was Henry Sage of Brooklyn, who desired to found a lecture series on preaching in honor of his revered pastor, Henry Ward Beecher. The latter is said to have remarked, "No, name it for my father. At his best he was greater than all his children put together." No lectureship on preaching is more distinguished than this. A history of the series from

the founding to 1950 has been admirably furnished by Edgard DeWitt
Jones in his book *The Royalty of the Pulpit* (1951). In its Foreword
Halford Luccock notes how these lectures illustrate the changes which
have taken place in the sermon itself. "In the 1870's there were still
sailing the seas, as approved models, many of the old three-decker sermons, formidable frigates and imposing, if difficult to manage. As the
series goes on, we can trace the changes from more formal, traditional
oratorical forms to direct, conversational speech."[29]

During the thirty years to the turn of the century there were many
distinguished men in the series. Henry Ward Beecher led off. Among
those who followed were Phillips Brooks, R. W. Dale, Washington
Gladden, Andrew Fairbairn, Henry Van Dyke, John Watson, better
known by his pen name Ian MacClaren, and George Adam Smith. Notes
on the whole series would scarcely be in order here, but a word on the
opening lectures by Henry Ward Beecher may not be amiss. Edgar
DeWitt Jones has culled some of his nuggets. "Great sermons, young
gentlemen, ninety-nine times in a hundred, are nuisances. They are like
steeples without any bells in them; things stuck up high in the air,
serving for ornament, attracting observation, but sheltering nobody,
warming nobody, helping nobody.

"A sermon is not like a Chinese firecracker to be fired off for the noise
which it makes. It is the hunter's gun, and at every discharge he should
look to see his game fall."[30]

In discussing the call to the ministry Beecher confessed that he had
nothing to say from personal experience. "I never had any choice about it.
My father had eight sons. Only two of them ever tried to get away from
preaching; and they did not succeed. The other six went right into the
ministry just as naturally as they went into manhood." But there are
some who have to make a decision. Among the signs of a call are fruit-
fulness in moral ideas, power in moving men, a living faith and good
health.

"There's one thing more. I do not think that any man has a right to
become a Christian minister, who is not willing and thankful to be the
least of all God's servants and to labor in the humblest sphere. If you
would come into the ministry, hoping to preach such a sermon as Robert
Hall would have preached, you are not fit to come in at all. If you have

a deep sense of the sweetness of the service of Christ; if the blood of redemption is really in your heart and in your blood; if you have tasted what gratitude means, and what love means, and if heaven is such a reality to you that all that lies between youth and manhood is but a step toward heaven; if you think that the saving of a single soul would be worth the work of your whole life, you have a call, and a very loud call. A call to the ministry is along the line of humility, and love, and sympathy, and good sense, and natural aspirations toward God."[31]

CHAPTER XIV

The New Disciplines

Among the new subjects introduced into the curriculum of the Divinity School during the last four decades of the nineteenth century Church History was not so much new as renewed. In the years following the Revolution the subject had been taught by Ezra Stiles. The intent had been that he be succeeded by Professor Kingsley, but he proved always to be otherwise occupied, with the result that this discipline lapsed until the appointment of George Park Fisher to the chair in the Divinity School in 1861. In the meantime, the subject had not been wholly neglected for the book most frequently withdrawn from the Library, after the works of Edwards, was Mosheim's *Institutes of Ecclesiastical History* and later Neander's *General History of the Christian Religion and Church.* Yet Yale as a seminary was behind others in caring for this field. Andover made provision for Church History in 1824, Union in 1850, Lancaster in 1853. Still, in all of these seminaries Church History was a relatively late addition to the curriculum. An acute observer accounted for the comparative neglect both on the ground of scanty sources and provincialism of time and place. The New England pastor had left Europe behind and New England's past was utilized to shame the decadent rather than analyzed for light upon the present. The growing cultivation of Church History was a faint admission of need for light and betokened a waning confidence in the American dream.[1]

The method of presentation followed the several German schools. In the period of the Reformation the main interest in Church History had been polemical. The great work was *The Magdeburg Centuries,* designed to expose the corruptions of Rome. This treatment was by chronological segments without progression or laws. The late seventeenth and eighteenth centuries brought forth two great movements, Pietism and the Enlightenment, both of which affected the teaching of history. Pietism disparaged institutionalism as dampening to piety, and dogma as tending to aridity. Hence, attention was focused on the interior life of individuals, and Church History was thereby reduced to spiritual biographies in which the heretics at times outrated the orthodox. The exponent of this view in the early eighteenth century was Gottfried Arnold; the same interest is apparent also in Neander.

The Enlightenment was interested in objectivity. Fanaticism, superstition, and bigotry were condemned in favor of the sound, the sober, and the reasonable. The ideal for the historian was a complete detachment. This was the slogan of Mosheim, author of the famous *Ecclesiastical History*.

The emotional aloofness sometimes took the form of presenting everything with equal coldness, or again with equal warmth. In the latter case the historian like an actor projected himself equally into each successive situation of the past. The extreme of this method was illustrated by a Protestant historian who expounded Roman Catholicism with such sympathy as to make a convert and prided himself at this supreme instance of his objectivity.

Neither Pietism nor the Enlightenment made a whole out of Church History. The Hegelians then sought to discover certain laws in the historical process. The familiar assumption that thesis and antithesis resolve themselves into synthesis was applied to the history of the Church and with such confidence that by this rule documents could be dated, assuming that those which reveal a clash must antedate those which exhibit the resolution. The method when applied to the literature of the New Testament by Ferdinand Christian Baur led to quite untenable results, but his attempt to surmount the fragmentation of history was significant.

George Park Fisher, the first professor of Church History in the Divinity School, was a mellowed Puritan. A student described him in his mature years as handsome, with an expansive dome, bald, circled by white hair falling over his collar, sideburns white, cheeks fresh and rosy, eyes twinkling. He was an inimitable raconteur and his stories quickly made the University rounds as when he told of a mother who took her young son to see the famous picture of the Christians in the arena about to be devoured by the lions. The lad, pointing to a young lion on the outskirts of the picture, exclaimed, "Mother, that little lion over there ain't getting any!" The Fisher home on Hillhouse Avenue was the scene of sparkling parties to which distinguished visitors were invited, and always several delightful young women. However, Fisher did not approve of women speaking in public until he heard Mrs. Ballington Booth in

George Park Fisher

United Church. He immediately proposed to invite her to preach in Battell Chapel. He did not disparage his own powers of persuasion and delighted to tell of German scholars who had modified their opinions as a result of talking with him. He liked to tell also of his interview with the Pope, presumably not with the same result.[2]

Such gaiety was not at all out of accord with the Puritan tradition in which laughter and tears were often wed. Fisher knew both. The diary of his student years in Germany[3] tells of walks with the daughter of his landlady. After a trip during the summer vacation he makes this entry: "August 18, 1852. Today I returned [to Halle] from Dresden. Was saddened to learn of the death of Fraulein. She was somewhat unwell when I left, but able to come out of her room and bid me adieu; but, alas, how little did I think it was the *last* adieu in this world. . . . God only knows when I shall be called. . . . I also received . . . the cheering intelligence that my mother and sister are well. May God keep them and love them! And may he keep me, not only in life, but in purity of heart and holiness of walk and conversation. May I be like Jesus, and through his Grace, be humble, prayerful, sober-minded, industrious, reverent and anxious to do good, and finally may I be prepared for the rest which remains for those who love our Lord!"

Humor and pathos both were native to this Yankee Puritan, but neither appears in his writing. For this there was also a tradition. Bellamy and Emmons had not spiced their theological works with the brilliant quips with which they regaled their students. And more influential in all likelihood was the German fashion in writing Church History, where objectivity, to the severe exclusion of the author's predilections, was the goal. Fisher's *History of the Christian Church* (1888), *The Reformation* (1873), and *History of Christian Doctrine* (1896) were all marked by impartiality, absence of bias and utter fairness alike in exposition and in the allotment of space. The scope was magisterial. His *History of Christian Doctrine* is still unsurpassed for coverage, and the documentation is impressive. But the books do not enable one to understand why Williston Walker should have called his predecessor "keen, vivacious and witty,"[4] nor why Benjamin Bacon should have referred to Fisher's "gracious and genial address" with "a flow of anecdotes."[5] Such qualities ill comported with the severe detachment demanded of the historian.

One pitfall of this detachment is a possible secularization of Church History, which, if there be no sense of commitment, makes it like any other history. The religious factor may even be neglected. The tendency is marked in Fisher's *The Colonial Era* (1892). True, the avowed intent was to describe the colonial era, not the colonial church; yet in a culture in which the church played so conspicuous a role, one might have expected the church historian to make religion the dominant factor, but Fisher would not inject his prejudices, nor even his convictions.

Fisher was wrestling with the dilemma which acutely confronts any university teacher: how to combine objectivity and commitment. The answer may lie in distinguishing occasions. Fisher's sermons in the college pulpit make abundantly plain that he was never that monster execrated by Samuel Harris, the interrogation point. Nor was there any doubt in Fisher's theological works. Here he accommodated old approaches to new data. The argument from design was made to incorporate the theory of evolution, and advancing physiological knowledge was impressed into the service of apologetics. He used Tyndall's description of the ear, "this lute of three thousand strings"[6] to illustrate God's design. Fisher's other works dealt with the grounds of theistic belief, the supernatural origin of Christianity, and the refutation of radical Germans. Fisher distinctly belonged to the New England way, and his early misgivings about Benjamin W. Bacon show that his studied detachment, though not a mere pose, was certainly far from being the whole man.

Leonard Bacon in teaching American Church History was inhibited by no Continental patterns. His pragmatic purpose was avowed. "Why may not," said he, "the 'annals of a parish' be as lively with illustrations of human nature, and as rich important practical lessons, as the annals of an empire? If in speaking of the fathers of New England and particularly of New Haven, I have insisted more on their virtues than on their faults and errors, it is partly because while their faults have been often and sufficiently blazoned, their virtues have been, to the popular mind, but imperfectly illustrated. . . . If I have spoken freely of the secular constitution of the Church of England, and of the evils resulting from it which made our fathers exiles, it is no more than becomes a man and an American; and the candid reader will observe, that in so doing, I have not spoken at all of the Episcopal Church as it is organized in this country. I am far from imputing to American bishops, chosen by the people of their charge, and responsible to those who choose them, the sins of English prelates under the Stuarts."

Bacon did not feel constrained to suppress enthusiasm for "the first settlers of New England [who] generally came hither, not for the improvement of their outward condition and the increase of their estates, not for the sake of putting in practice any abstract theory of human rights or of civil government, not even for mere liberty of conscience, but for the one great purpose of extending the kingdom of God, and promoting their welfare and the welfare of their posterity, and the welfare of the world, by planting Christian institutions, in the purest and amplest form, upon this virgin soil. It was this purpose, which gave to their enterprise its character of heroic dignity."[7]

In the year 1891-92 the Divinity School first introduced a course in social ethics. The time was propitious. The blithe confidence of Samuel Harris with his near equation of the kingdom of God and American culture was receding. Men were coming to realize how much was amiss in the American social scene even though some of the big disclosures were to come only after the turn of the century. Lincoln Steffen's *The Shame of the Cities* and Ida Tarbell's *The History of the Standard Oil Company* did not come out until 1904. These books pointed up what was already evident to the discerning, that the abolition of dueling and slavery and the mounting crusade against intemperance had not cauterized all the sores of society. Two, perhaps three, great problems confronted the land: One, corruption in government, notably in the cities; two, growth of monopoly and the exploitation of labor; and three, discrimination against minorities, the immigrant, the Negro, and others. And, of course, there was the perennial problem of the destitute, the deficient, and the criminal.

In the year 1891-92 Professor Arthur Fairbanks was called to lecture on the relation of the classes in society; socialism, communism, and the labor question; pauperism and charity; crime, its prevention and the reclamation of criminals. He was succeeded by W. Blackman, who continued until 1902. He introduced what has ever since been an annual event, a sociological trip to New York to visit "such institutions as the hospitals on the East River islands, a Bowery lodging house, the Relief Bureau of the *New York Journal*, the University Settlement in Delancey Street, the Tombs, the Criminal Court Building, the People's Bath House in Center Market Place, Mulberry Bend, the Young Men's Institute in the Bowery, Mills Hotel for Men, the workrooms of the International Christian Alliance, and the Grace Church Settlement on Fourteenth Street."[8] The men of that generation evidently were not equal to a visit to the morgue.

The social philosophy underlying these courses is nowhere disclosed. One learns more from the first treatment of social questions in the Lyman Beecher Lectures by Washington Gladden in 1887 entitled *Tools and the Man* (1893). *Laissez faire*, he claimed, was based on an entirely unwarranted optimism that if everything were left alone all would work out for the good. That certainly, said he, is not true in the case of the public domain, which has been shamefully alienated in the United States. Moreover, what is now private property is not to be regarded as sacrosanct and may be reclaimed by the state in case of public need. Nevertheless, the role of the state is not to be unduly magnified, for the state cannot as yet be regarded as a Christian institution. The state may protect and educate the citizens, curb monopolies, endeavor to provide for all an equal chance, suppress parasites, such as gamblers, saloonkeepers, and lazy paupers, limit the hours of labor, require sanitation in factories, offer arbitration anywhere and require it in the case of semipublic utilities. This program was certainly very moderate and hardly introduced the welfare state.

An actual example of social action on the part of the Church was afforded the students of the Divinity School by the example of Newman Smyth, pastor of Center Church, member of the Yale Corporation, citizen of New Haven. As president of the New Haven Law and Order League he was active in promoting the enforcement of the liquor laws against the serving of drinks on Sundays. Significantly the stress was not on Sabbatarianism nor on temperance as such but on curbing the economic loss incurred through drinking away the week's wages. Another point was municipal corruption in law enforcement. The New Haven *Evening Leader* for September 27, 1894, carried the headline "Police Again Critisized, Rev. Dr. Smyth Fires Another Volley at Corruption, Patrolmen Who Wink With the Other Eye and Take Free Drinks." Smyth charged that in ninety-seven places in New Haven liquor was illegally sold and the police were instructed by their superiors "not to be too damned officious."[9] In court he produced the evidence.

The rights of labor equally engaged his activity both in championing the workers and in averting conflict. In the case of a threatened strike on the New Haven Railroad Smyth was the mediator. And when a strike was imminent on the streetcar system in New Haven, his behind-stage efforts were again successful. In celebration of the settlement the New Haven Road put on all its cars that night and offered the whole town free rides. The people thronged the streets and kindled bonfires. "There is a lot of good nature," remarked Smyth, "lying round loose among people generally if it can be touched off right."[10]

A third major subject introduced into the curriculum was that of Christian missions, though as yet there was no full-time appointment. In 1897 Brastow and Blackman were asked to give a course to those preparing for the mission field. The next year the Reverend D. E. M. Bliss of New York was engaged to lecture an hour a week on the subject. The course was required of Juniors.[11]

The delay in providing specific training for missionaries does not indicate a lack of interest in missions or a failure to supply recruits. On the occasion of the semicentennial in 1872 an account was given of all the missionaries who had gone out from Yale, both the dead and the living. The report says that of eight hundred and fifty Divinity graduates, thirty-one had been foreign missionaries.

The death rate among the earliest was appalling. One reads: Aitchison, China, five years, died aged thirty-three; Griswold, West Africa, died after two years; Lockwood, among the Cherokees, one year, died aged thirty-one; Marsh, among the Zulus, six years, died aged thirty-six; Mitchell and wife, never reached Persia, died of ague on the way at Aleppo; Parry and wife in Ceylon, two and a half years, died of cholera; Shipman in the Sandwich Islands, six years; Smith in Turkey, five years, died of cholera aged thirty-four; Righter in the Levant, two years, died aged thirty-two; Stevens on the way to China died at Singapore, aged thirty-six; Whittelsey in Ceylon, five years, died aged thirty-nine; Stoddard in Persia lost his wife from cholera after eight years of service. He served twelve years.

Interesting details of many of these men are reported. Stoddard, for instance, took with him a telescope by which the Persians were much impressed. Finding them oblivious to time, on which Western society is pivoted, he constructed sundials and then sent to Connecticut for clocks and afterward for instructions on how to repair them. He constructed a microscope, a camera, and a balloon. The comment is "that not one of his . . . attainments was thrown away."

Among the retired missionaries the best known was Peter Parker, pioneer of the medical missions in China. He went there in 1834 intending to devote himself only to the diseases of the eye but soon discovered the impossibility of specialization. The applicants were so numerous that periods for reception had to be restricted to one day in two weeks. Applicants camped on the ground the night before clinic days. Two thousand cases were handled during the first year. In twenty years his hospital treated fifty-three thousand patients. Because of hostilities be-

tween England and China, the mission was for a time closed, and Parker
returned to this country. He tells us that "after arriving in New Haven,
I expressed to President Day, Prof. Silliman, Prof. Kingsley and the
Faculty of Yale generally, and to other friends in New Haven, my views
of the peculiar state of affairs in China, and of the favorable opportunity
for the American Government to proffer friendly offices to the contending powers, and to establish treaty relations with China. With one voice
these gentlemen said, emphatically, 'You must go to Washington, and
there express the sentiments and views you state to us.' In company with
Rev. Dr. Bacon, early in January, 1841, I proceeded to Washington. The
administration of President Van Buren was near its close. On calling on
the President and the Hon. Mr. Forsyth, Secretary of State, I was referred
to the cabinet officers of the incoming administration. As Dr. Bacon will
remember, we called on Mr. Webster, Secretary of State elect. He listened
attentively. . . . On taking leave, Mr. Webster rose up and with a grave
voice said, 'What you have now stated to me *orally*, will you be so good,
Sir, as to give me in *writing*.' " The upshot was that Parker himself was
sent to China as the United States Commissioner to negotiate a treaty
and that he incorporated in it permission for the building of Christian
churches.

At the conclusion of the biographies the semicentennial report gives
this summary. "This completes the list of thirty-one missionaries. . . .
Let it be noticed also that eighteen of these missionaries were born in
New England, where most good things are expected to originate. . . .
All but five were married men. . . . Nine were missionaries to China;
seven in Turkey; four in Africa; three in India; two in Persia; one in
Syria; one to the American Indians and the Sandwich Islands; a second
one to the Sandwich Islands; one to Siam, and to Micronesia. They have
touched the four quarters of the globe. They have wrought in a dozen
different languages. They have reduced some of these to writing, preparing books and translations of the Scriptures. . . . It may have been
noticed also that many of these missionaries died young. Possibly some
may think their lives were almost thrown away. But we doubt if any
other thirty-one students of this Seminary, taken at random, have done
as much to spread the truth and bless the world as they. Men have died
young in this land also. . . . But the missionaries do not all die young."

Spaulding and his wife had been forty-three years in Ceylon, Goddell was fifty-three in Turkey, Walker and Bushnell thirty years in Gaboon. Our Savior's life was short. The apostles died young, and the Gospel must be preached.

"We only wish that the proportion of foreign laborers from this Seminary had been larger. It does not compare favorably with other Seminaries. Here it is only one to twenty-eight; in Princeton one to eighteen; in Andover and Union one to sixteen. With nearly sixty thousand evangelical clergy to forty millions of people in this country, and less than two hundred missionaries to four hundred millions of people in China, it would seem as though a just compassion would spare a few more men to that dark land."[12]

Forty years later in 1902 George Park Fisher was able to report that the total number of foreign missionaries from Yale was certainly not under one hundred and twenty. Presumably he was speaking of the entire university, and some of these may have gone out directly from the college or the medical school without having studied in the Divinity School. Among the more recent missionaries mention was made of Robert Hume in India and of his services in distributing a million dollars worth of relief during the famine. A tribute was paid also to Horace Tracy Pitkin, the martyr of the Boxer Rebellion![13]

In the meantime the Divinity School was laying the foundations for a chair of missions by providing the literary tools. Professor George E. Day, as already noted, devoted his retirement to the building up of a collection. "Old Yom" the students had come to call him (the word for day in Hebrew is "Yom"!). Venerable as the ancient of days and as indefatigable, he scoured the secondhand bookstores of Europe. When "Old Yom" began his work, the greatest collection in the world on missions was in Denmark and numbered 5,200 volumes. By 1900 Day's collection had reached 7,159. The work was continued after his death, and in 1921 the report was 20,742 volumes. Harlan P. Beach, assessing the library in that year, said that the Missionary Research Library in New York had a wider scope because it was not contiguous to a university, but that in his judgment the Day Missions Library was the foremost in the world.[14]

A word should be said about interest at Yale in sacred music. We have already noted the revision of Psalmody by the first Timothy Dwight. The second Dwight and Leonard Bacon were the authors of hymns. The latter prepared a collection for missionary meetings and innovated in Center Church a monthly Sunday evening missionary rally devoted so largely to songs as to be called the Monthly Concert.[15] By 1850 the abhorrence of Ezra Stiles for an organ in a church or university would scarcely have been intelligible. Two years later Horace Bushnell gave his address on religious music before the Beethoven Society at Yale. No man did more to achieve a revolution in religious music in this country than Lowell Mason and none did more for musical education of the children in the churches and public schools than he. Mason was resolved to correct the Psalm singing of the earlier days, which according to George Bacon was performed in "a style so whimsical, so full of odd conceits and affectations, so uselessly involved and intricate, as to be little better than absurd." As for hymn singing, words and tunes were so disjunctured that the various parts would sing in turn. "Stir up this stu, Stir up this stu, Stir up this stu," before combining on "this stupid soul to pray."[16] Mason was opposed not only to such infelicities, but to the "use of current love songs, the vulgar melodies of the street, of the midnight revelers, of the circus and the ballroom—in special seasons of revival."[17] Lowell Mason became the choir master of the Bowdoin Street Church in Boston during the pastorate of Lyman Beecher. His labors gave to the choir of that church a national reputation, and thereby he became the educator of the land.[18] Today his best-known compositions include the tunes for the hymns: "When I Survey the Wondrous Cross," "Nearer My God to Thee," "My Faith Looks Up to Thee," "Blest Be the Tie that Binds" (Boylston), and "Work for the Night is Coming." In 1875 Lowell Mason's collection of sacred music was given to the Divinity School and housed in a room designated by his name.[19] In the very same year a musical society was founded in the Divinity School which should provide for lectures in church music and develop musical talents. The society sponsored a glee club. In 1897 the name of the society was changed to that of the "Society of Sacred Music and Liturgics of the Yale Divinity School."

Records of student activities during this period are scant. In 1895 the Leonard Bacon Debating Club was founded, a revival of the society which had flourished in the days of Nathaniel W. Taylor. The topics had a wide range from the ecclesiastical and the homiletical to the social, political, and literary. Something approximating modern field work began in 1898 when the students became associated with a settlement known as Welcome Hall on Oak Street. Until that time apparently the only outlet for religious expression available to the Divinity students was work in the Sunday schools.[20]

In this period undergraduate opinion on the Divinity students was not precisely flattering. An observer cited by John Addison Porter in his *Sketches of Yale Life* (1886) considered a room in West Divinity Hall desirable because of the opportunity afforded to study that psychological rarity, the theologue. One of the Divinity students wore a fez given him by a cousin in Bulgaria. Another had a parlor organ. This "Theologue sits and pumps the chronic spasms of jagged melody from its ancient chest with Christian fortitude, happy in the thought that physical exercise is not incompatible with devotion in the shape of variations on the *Missionary Hymn*." Another may be seen through his window practicing the benediction. Some day, said the observer, we shall be listening to these ministers. "Today we see but the ungainly, loquacious, green, sportive Theologue. . . . [The type that] ropes in the little girl that peddles toothpicks and supports two fathers and eleven brothers, gives her a twenty minutes' lecture on annihilation, predestination and homiletics."[21]

What a pity the editor did not live to see the John Addison Porter prize awarded to five students of Divinity: James Hayden Tufts (1888), Philip Whitehead (1914), George Stewart, Jr. (1921), Dumas Malone (1923), and Liston Pope (1940).

CHAPTER XV

The Age of the Deans

EDWARD L. CURTIS

Shortly after the turn of the twentieth century the Yale Divinity School was again at the ebb. Once more the reason was a failure to practice retirement control. All of the venerables dropped out in close succession. Samuel Harris had retired in 1895. His successor G. B. Stevens died suddenly at the age of fifty-two in 1906. George Park Fisher continued until 1901. He was then seventy-two and had served forty-six years. It was too long. The students of his latter days say that he merely repeated his textbook, and one member of the class impudently sat with the work in view of the professor, and in case of an addition made an annotation to Fisher's evident irritation. Yet he was jocular about his eventual leave-taking and compared himself to the man who so often spoke of his approaching demise that someone testily told him "to stop talking and get on with the dying." George E. Day had for some time been active only as the Librarian of the Missions collection. He died in 1905. Brastow, despite the newly enacted rule setting the age of obligatory retirement at sixty-eight, was permitted to stay until seventy-two in order that he might qualify for an allowance. He finished in 1907. If one strike an arbitrary line at 1905, apart from Brastow, the staff was reduced to Edward L. Curtis, age fifty-two, Frank C. Porter, age forty-six, Benjamin W. Bacon, age forty-five, and Williston Walker of the same age. These four men in the middle bracket were already scholars of distinction, but they were too few to maintain the school.

Attendance declined. In the academic year 1906-7 there were indeed ninety-eight students, but of these only forty-eight were candidates for the B.D. degree. The previous year the number had been fifty-four. The entering class sank to only thirteen. The reason was not the dearth of theological candidates, for Yale College in that year had thirty, of whom not one elected Yale's own seminary.[1] The *Yale Alumni Weekly* pronounced the Yale Divinity School to be numerically in a state of "stagnation not to say recession."[2]

Edward L. Curtis

Plainly there was need for new faculty appointments. This required money. Moreover, the buildings called for renovation, and the curriculum for revamping. Everything needed to be done first. No men without money and no money without men! President Arthur Twining Hadley intervened. He was the son of that Professor James Hadley whose diary has frequently been cited. Arthur Hadley was the first lay President of Yale. Some in Divinity sensed a certain chilliness to their school on the part of this president who had been preoccupied not with revelation but with railroads. One wonders whether the suspicion was altogether justified. Hadley certainly was not indifferent to religion. Witness his baccalaureate addresses and his readiness every Sunday to walk out to Dean Brown's house on Edwards Street to greet the minister of the morning and to walk back with him to Battell Chapel. A college president who today would walk two miles for anything would be considered devoted. But Hadley did want a university each of whose constituents should maintain the high standards of the College. He proposed now that the

Divinity School institute an administrative dean. Hitherto the dean had been little more than a presiding officer at faculty meetings. Frank K. Sanders was chosen for the post. He came from the field of Semitics in the College and consented to be dean in the hope of promoting his discipline. However, what the School needed at that juncture was not a shot of Semitics. Sanders' primary commission was to raise money. When after four years he ended with a deficit, Hadley saw no way out but to impose tuition on the Divinity students. Theodore Thornton Munger, a member of the Corporation, was heartily in favor. "Why should divinity students be coddled? Are they poor? Then let them go and earn," said he. When the matter came to a vote in the Divinity School faculty, Bacon and Walker were in favor; Stevens, Curtis, Brastow, and Porter were opposed. The motion was lost. Sanders resigned.[3]

Then it was that Edward L. Curtis was appointed Acting Dean. In 1905 the outlook alike for funds and students was most bleak. Curtis was a scholar and did not relish administration and money raising, but someone had to step in. If it be said that Timothy Dwight the Younger saved the Divinity School from closing during its first crisis, on the occasion of the second none so fully merits acclaim as Edward L. Curtis, devotedly served by Porter, Bacon, and Walker. In June, 1905, the Corporation agreed to meet one-half of the Divinity School's deficit of thirty thousand dollars if the School itself would raise the remainder. That summer Curtis, Walker, Porter, and Bacon in apostolic fashion, two by two, canvassed the area and by August had secured one hundred and forty subscriptions covering the required sum. Among the donors were Chauncey Depew, Charles Scribner, and Timothy Dwight. New faculty appointments were made forthwith. William B. Bailey, who since 1901 had been conducting field trips to New York for the students, was invited in 1906 to offer a course in "Welfare, Work and Practical Philanthropy." In that same year the first appointment was made to the chair of the Theory and Practice of Missions in the person of Harlan P. Beach. Systematic Theology was taught for the year 1907-8 by Marion Leroy Burton, who then left to become successively pastor of the Church of the Pilgrims in Brooklyn, president of Smith College and president of the University of Minnesota.[4] An invitation was then extended to George

Wobbermin of Breslau in Germany. He declined. The faculty looked next to Canada and approached Douglas Clyde Macintosh, who accepted. When he entered the country, an immigration official accosted him on the train with an inquiry as to whether he was employed in the United States. He answered affirmatively and was informed that he must then return at once to Canada. "That is strange," said he, "since an ex-President of the United States [William Howard Taft] is a member of the Corporation which engaged me." "Why, what are you going to do?" asked the official. "To teach at Yale University." "Oh," said the official, "I thought you were going to work." Macintosh was appointed to the Yale faculty on February 15, 1909. On that very same day a colleague, Henry Hallam Tweedy, received appointment to the chair of Homiletics, and an invitation was extended to E. Hershey Sneath to transfer from the College to the Divinity School as Lecturer on Ethics and Philosophy of Religion. He was appointed in 1910.

The renovation of the buildings was undertaken. Anson Phelps Stokes, Secretary of the University, said that his first speech before the Corporation was on the subject of bad bathroom facilities at the Divinity School. He had been lodged there on his first night as an officer of the University and had discovered that the tin bathtub suffered from a serious depression. During the next four years more than twenty thousand dollars was expended on repairs and improvements including the linking of the Divinity School buildings with the University's heating plant.[5] In the general rejuvenation of the School details were not overlooked. Professor Porter informed the School that the organist needed more practice but could not play without a blower. Therefore a member of the senior class was engaged to blow at twenty cents an hour.

The libraries in 1900 included the Day Missions Collection, which aimed at comprehensiveness; the Lowell Mason Library of Church Music subsequently transferred to the Music School; and the Trowbridge Reference Library, which, as already noted, was a small working collection of four thousand books. There was no thought of enlargement because only a short sprint away was the University Library, housing major theological sets, not to mention such superb gatherings as the Dexter Collection on Congregational History. The Trowbridge Library needed primarily duplicates, which were authorized on the request of the Librarian, Frank Chamberlin Porter.[6]

The most drastic need of the School was the revision of the curriculum. Around 1900 strident criticism was being leveled against theological education. In 1899 this was the liveliest topic of debate at the meeting of the International Congregational Council. The attack stemmed mainly from those imbued with the resurgent Renaissance ideal of the universal man proficient in all disciplines. The difficulty was that since the Renaissance the disciplines had increased beyond the capacity of an individual. President Elliot of Harvard, who addressed the Council, had sought by an elective system to provide that an entire university if not an individual should embrace everything. President Hyde of Bowdoin, applying this principle to theological education, demanded expansion of the curriculum in the direction of philosophy, ethics, sociology, and literature,[7] and another speaker proposed to achieve this range by consolidating the four theological seminaries of New England.[8] *The Congregationalist* polled recent seminary graduates, who on the whole appeared fairly satisfied with their training, though one praised his teacher in Hebrew for enabling him to acquire the language with a speed equalled only by the velocity with which he had forgotten it.[9] *The Congregationalist* editorially warned against trying to cram everything into a theological course and thought that if the minister were expected to deal with domestic sorrow, labor disputes, political policy, and social custom, he would have to be left to learn something after leaving the seminary.[10] The most discriminating remarks at the Council came from the lips of Frank Chamberlin Porter. Recognizing that thoroughness demanded concentration and one man could not encompass all, he abandoned the concept of a core to be mastered by all. The ancient tongues are valuable but not imperative for a grounding in Biblical studies and these afford a discipline not incapable of being matched in philosophy and ethics. He cut deeper than any other by voicing the fear that Christianity like the Judaism of the time of Christ might be separated "from the world in form with conformity to the world in spirit."[11]

The upshot of the discussion at Yale was the introduction in 1907 of a curriculum with a wide range of election. The student might enter one of three fields: A, historical, mainly Biblical with Hebrew; B, philosophical with work in philosophy and science without Hebrew; C, practical with courses in sociology and law and without Hebrew. Greek was still required in all. The result was a meager election of group A with the great majority promptly gravitating to group B.[12]

Such variety was justifiable only if the students were actually aiming at diverse types of Christian ministry. In 1910 the faculty, aware of this point, shifted the alignment from subjects to professions and differentiated four varieties of the Christian ministry. The first was pastoral service; the second missions; the third religious education, which included teaching in colleges and directing religious education in churches; the fourth was social service with an eye to work in social settlements and in the YMCA. All four ministries required a core training in the fundamental disciplines with attention in each one toward special requirements. For example, in missions the student would study comparative religion and the history and customs of the country to which he was destined. The fourth field required sociology and constitutional law. In order to provide such a wide range of training the school proposed to draw freely on the entire resources of Yale, and here was the justification for the close association of a theological seminary with a great university center. For some years to come the faculty continued to experiment with the arrangement of courses.

There were other significant changes. The School definitely announced that it was unsectarian and enforced the point by declining to exercise its prerogative to send a delegate to the Congregational National Council in 1907.[13] Subsequently, after the interdenominational character of the School had come to be well recognized, this prerogative was resumed. The stipulation of adherence to a prescribed creed was abandoned, and Douglas C. Macintosh, a Baptist, when invited to the faculty, was asked only one question of a remotely theological nature, namely, whether he favored "open" or "closed" communion.[14]

The faculty were not unaware that a curriculum so diversified would distribute the students' activities all over the campus and might mean a less intimate association within the school. A corrective was sought in social functions for the entire Divinity community. The *Quarterly*

reported in the spring of 1911: "The social life of the School has been at
flood tide since our last issue. St. Patrick's Day was celebrated with the
assistance of Puzzling Pierson, prestidigitator, who entertained the faculty
and students and their friends in the Lowell Mason Room during the
evening. The interest of the occasion was heightened by the fact that
Mr. Pierson is an old acquaintance of us all, having been the assistant
to the superintendent of the Divinity buildings for the last ten years."[15]
Mr. Pierson is to this day the Superintendent of Buildings in the year
of our Lord 1957.

News of these doings reached the world without, and an observer
reported in *The Congregationalist* that there were rumors of "wild revels
and most undignified procedures in connection with 'stunt nights,'
when both students and professors play horse to an almost inconceivable
extent. One hears of Professor Bacon being tried by his colleagues for
orthodoxy, with Professor Walker doing to perfection the part of the
judge; as well as of the sleight-of-hand performance by the professor of
systematic theology, to say nothing of minstrel shows."[16]

The School was now definitely on the mend. Attendance was steadily
mounting, and between the fall of 1906 and the spring of 1909 the
number of candidates enrolled for the B.D. degree increased from 46
to 60. The great problem now was to secure a dean who would be not
only an administrative head but who would relate the School to the wider
Church constituency, interdenominational and national in scope. The
day was gone when Yale could or should serve only the Congregationalism of the Connecticut valley. The University was much concerned for
the outreach of the Divinity School, and William Howard Taft, now
President of the United States, made a trip from Washington especially
for a meeting of the Corporation to discuss the affairs of the School.
Overtures as to the deanship were made to a number of distinguished
men who declined the assignment.[17]

Dean Charles R. Brown

Charles R. Brown, who had the courage to undertake the deanship,
was at the moment recovering from the strain of an exacting and notable
pastorate in California. Born in Virginia, reared in Iowa, trained for

the ministry in Boston and exercised in the pastorate in Boston and in California, he represented the whole country. Denominationally he was what today would be called "an ecumenic." His mother was a Presbyterian, his father a Methodist, and he a Congregationalist. At one time, to discover what Christian Science was all about he had taken a course under Mary Baker Eddy and received a diploma as a practitioner. Like Smyth he had been a mediator in labor disputes.

Charles R. Brown

Brown had already given the Lyman Beecher Lectures at Yale in 1906 on the topic *The Social Message of the Modern Pulpit,* in which Brown announced that the need of the hour was not the reconciliation of science and religion, not a restatement of theology, not a readjustment of polity, not an outburst of philanthropy, not even a rekindled passion for souls, but a "thorough application of the principles of the Gospel of Jesus Christ to the conditions of every-day life." Brown took as his text the word of the Lord to Moses, "I have surely seen the affliction of my people which are in Egypt, and have heard their cry by reason of their taskmasters. . . . And I am come down to deliver them. . . . Come now therefore, and I will send thee unto Pharaoh, that thou mayest bring forth my people the children of Israel out of Egypt." The parallel between modern labor and ancient Israel, said Brown, is great, but there is a big difference. Now there is no Canaan to which to go. The free land of the West has all been pre-empted by private ownership. We must "have it out with Pharaoh right here."[18]

The great problem, he continued, was not production but distribution, and particularly a distribution of profits to those whose toil created the wealth. With passionate indignation he leveled the indictment: "Are there not hundreds of weary working-men, taxed steadily beyond their strength, wearing out before their time, receiving far less than an equitable share of the prosperity they help to create, and forced by necessity to serve with rigor? Are there not hundreds of tired clerks and book-keepers, insufficiently paid, working often far into the night, in close, dark quarters, with abundance of bad air, sometimes in those hideous little 'upper berths' of offices put in against the ceiling like swallows' nests to save floor space and rent? And all the while many of those who reap the profit from this exacting labor are rejoicing in a useless and debilitating luxury which is made possible for them by the lack of equity in the sharing of the profits of the business."[19]

The solution which Brown had to offer was not socialism. He had too little confidence in human nature to suppose that men would put forth their best without the incentive of private reward, and again he had too little faith in men to suppose that government bureaucrats would be able to solve the ills of society. At the same time he had a deep confidence in the residual decency of mankind and believed that even the robber barons could be touched by an imaginative picture of what was actually going on. In any case a quickened public conscience could bring pressures to bear for the correction of abuses. Precisely because this improvement was possible, the laborer should not bow down to the golden calf of violence. The minister's role was mediatory. Let him smite the conscience of the exploiter, sensitize the feeling of the consumer, and moderate the intemperance of the laborer.

Today this platform sounds very moderate. Brown was in the middle of the road. The Socialist club in California shredded him as a stand-patter, while for the same statements the ministerial association considered him a firebrand. The Yale Corporation was to the right of middle and looked dubiously on his appointment. In the meantime, in a suburb of New Haven Brown delivered his great address on Abraham Lincoln. Brown was persuasive on any theme, but on Abraham Lincoln he could bring an audience to its feet or to its knees. The Yale Corporation invited him to become the dean of the Divinity School.

He was not to assume his duties until the opening of the academic year the following September. In the meantime, Curtis carried on despite a failing heart and eyesight half gone. He was eagerly awaiting his release from academic duties. The ultimate release came on August 26, just a week before Dean Brown took over.

The new head of the School set out at once to recruit students from across the land. Professor Luccock once remarked that Dean Brown had preached in every preparatory school and college in the United States except Notre Dame. Born in the South he set out to reclaim the South. The task was delicate because Yale was looked upon askance on account of the higher criticism. At one Southern Presbyterian college the dean sought an entrée through an alumnus. The president of the school dubiously inquired whether Brown was orthodox. "In essentials," was the answer. The president questioned the expediency of exposing the students to such attenuated Christianity, but as a Southern gentleman agreed that the dean might call. The president began, "Where were you born?" "In Virginia," answered Brown. "Then how do you happen to be a Congregationalist?" "My father was a Methodist, my mother a Presbyterian who taught her children the 'Shorter Catechism.' I compromised on Congregationalism." Brown knew how to pull the stops. Virginia and the Shorter Catechism did it. He was invited to speak in chapel and later to give the commencement address.[20]

As an ambassador Brown was fortunate to have been more conservative than some of his colleagues, and when Bacon and Porter made him doubtful of the Virgin Birth he handled the question with superb finesse. He would say, "What do I believe about the Virgin Birth? Exactly what the Apostle Paul believed. And what did he believe? He never mentioned it."

During Brown's administration from 1910 to 1928 the advances were marked. The enrollment went up from 114 to 162, the faculty from 9 to 15, the funds from close to nine hundred thousand to something over a million and a half. The number of states represented increased from 28 to 36, and the denominations from 10 to 16. The Methodists held first place in numbers, the Disciples second, the Congregationalists third, with Baptists and Presbyterians following. The school was no longer recruited predominantly from New England. The South Atlantic and Midwestern states each sent more. The Far West and foreign countries had a few.[21]

The new curriculum which had been fully elaborated during Curtis' administration was first implemented under Brown. Indeed one of the conditions for its actual inauguration was the securing of an administrative head. Throughout his deanship the scheme was retained with modifications and enlargements. The requirement of constitutional law in the third area lasted but for a year. The curriculum was continually enriched by the addition of entirely new subjects and by the endowment of fields hitherto but partial and tentative.

The two areas most heavily stressed and most characteristic of the period were social service and religious education. The former had received some attention before the turn of the century, but funds were not available for a full appointment. Dean Brown solicited one hundred thousand dollars, the gift from Gilbert L. Stark—the gift made possible the chair named after him in Practical Philanthropy. William B. Bailey, who had been giving some instruction during the previous decade, was appointed to the chair in 1916.[22] Later Jerome Davis was appointed on this foundation.

The great popularity of religious education was due to the concepts of Horace Bushnell's *Christian Nurture* and the intense need occasioned by the secularization of education in the United States. In 1912 E. Hershey Sneath was appointed Professor of Ethics and Religious Education. He and Mrs. Sneath endowed the library in religious education named for their son.[23] The daughter of Horace Bushnell, Mrs. Hillyer, established the Horace Bushnell Chair of Christian Nurture in which the first incumbent was Luther Allan Weigle appointed in 1915. In the same year Benjamin Winchester was made an assistant.

The Chair of Missions had had but tenuous support, and when Harlan P. Beach came in 1906, his salary could be promised for only three years. The gift of D. Willis James made possible Beach's permanent appointment in 1914 as head of a department of missions in which two years later he was assisted by John Clark Archer.[24] Beach was succeeded in 1921 by Kenneth Scott Latourette.

One chair was carved to fit the occupant. Henry B. Wright had long taught classics in Yale College. He was distinguished as a personal evangelist on the campus and was much interested in the developing laymen's movement, the YMCA. In 1914 the Stephen Merrell Clement Foundation provided for a Professorship of Christian Methods, a phrase broad enough to cover his varied interests.[25]

A special grant, the Mattatuck Fund, brought Charles Allen Dinsmore, after his retirement from the Congregational Church at Waterbury, to give courses in the Bible as literature and on religion in literature. He began in the fall of 1920.

The old subjects were of course maintained. Edward L. Curtis was replaced by George Dahl. Young men were given trial instructorships with an eye to future appointments. The *Yale Divinity Quarterly* in 1920 reports that Dumas Malone was being tested in Church History, Roland Bainton in New Testament, and Robert Calhoun in the History of Religious Education—curious that no one of the three is now working in the area of his apprenticeship.

The breadth of the new curriculum was signalized to the constituency by a change in the name of the institution.[26] No longer should it be called the Yale Divinity School but the Yale School of Religion. Two reasons were assigned: first, that the scope of instruction went beyond Christianity to include comparative religion; second, that the new name would parallel those of the School of Law and the School of Medicine and would accentuate the position of the Divinity School in a university cluster.[27] The new name was but short lived. To avoid confusion with the Department of Religion the old title was restored in 1920.

With the inauguration of President Angell in 1921 the relations with the University became ever more cordial. Divinity students were encouraged to avail themselves of Yale's full resources. One course was widely taken, that by Richard Swanson Lull in Organic Evolution. Dean Brown was quite right that at Yale Moses and Darwin were adjusted. No one had done more to mediate in this area, as in labor disputes, than Newman Smyth of Center Church. Coming to grips with evolution and immortality he pointed out that biological evolution has reached its ultimate in man. Advance henceforth lies in the improvement of sentient beings. For this advance death is not requisite as it was in lower forms to make room for better bodies. Death may be discharged, and that development of spirit which arleady takes place while in the body can be continued beyond the body.[28] One who so conceived of evolution scarcely needed to take a course for confirmation but many students came from areas where the theory of evolution was still vehemently denied. For that reason Dean Brown himself urged the Divinity students to enroll in Lull's course.

Field work, hitherto on an informal basis, began to be elevated into a recognized discipline with faculty supervision. The move was intimately related to the agitated question of charging tuition. Under Dean Curtis' administration in 1908 the *Yale Alumni Weekly*[29] had pointed out that throughout the University apart from the Divinity School, the average yearly cost per student was $284.83 to which the student contributed on the average $132.84, but the average cost for the Divinity student was $829.99 with no contribution. The *Yale Divinity Quarterly*[30] had already explained that the high cost was due to the small number of students and was higher for the same reason in Forestry and Art. An increase in enrollment appeared then to be the solution. In any case the Divinity student could not pay tuition because the highest average salary paid by any Protestant body in the United States was only $800 a year, and if the student graduated with a debt, he would never be able to come into the clear.

At the same time the feeling was strong that the Divinity student should not be coddled and should give a return for scholarship aid by high academic achievement and church work. Some scholarships were instituted as prizes for distinguished scholastic records. Others were called work scholarships in return for which a stipulated number of hours a week should be devoted to one of the churches, settlements, or boys' clubs. At first a graduate student was in charge of making assignments. From 1913 to 1928 Professor Dahl took over the arduous load with student help. Insofar as possible the type of work selected was designed to provide a practical apprenticeship, but very little supervision could be afforded.

Work in the Graduate School for the doctor's degree fell either to the

Department of Semitics or to the Department of Philosophy. In 1920 a Department of Religion was organized under the direction of Douglas C. Macintosh, and graduate work in Religious Education was organized as a subdivision of the Department of Education.

CHAPTER XVI

The Biblical Phalanx

The Biblical field continued to hold the center of interest. The New Testament had come to be the battleground for theology and the Old Testament was by this time as placid as the field of Gettysburg a century after the fray. Harper, Curtis, Torrey, and the young Bacon had fought the good fight and won the day for higher criticism—at any rate, in most of the centers of theological learning, though the general public in many regions was still behind. The task of teaching the Old Testament and Hebrew fell to Curtis' successor and son-in-law, George Dahl. His assignment was to mediate the new position to students who came from conservative backgrounds.

Every generation has its own problem. In the second and third decades of our century attention shifted from Genesis to Jesus. America was just coming to grips with the radical New Testament criticism of Germany to which previous Yale scholars had been oblivious. Significantly, Torrey moved into the New Testament field with his assertion that the Gospels and the first fifteen chapters of Acts had been translated directly from Aramaic documents. The evidence consisted partly in the prevalence of Semitic idioms in the Greek and partly in mistranslations due to incorrect vocalization of the Aramaic manuscripts written without vowels. Torrey, rendering the Gospels back into Aramaic, discovered the possibility of some surprising mistakes. Luke 11:48 in the Greek reads, "Your fathers killed the prophets and you build them." The English has supplied, "build their tombs." Change but one vowel in the Aramaic and the phrase becomes, "And you are their sons." Again in Luke 24:32 the disciples on the walk to Emaus say one to another, "Was not our heart burning within us?" Alter one vowel and its reads, "Were not our minds obtuse?"[1] Such contentions were accepted by Torrey's Yale colleagues, notably Dahl and Bacon, but stoutly contested by the Chicago school who felt that Palestinian Jews writing Greek would ordinarily introduce Semitisms.

Torrey used conclusions in the philological area to support far-reaching deductions in the historical. He assumed that the Aramaic originals were unitary documents, so that if one verse were early the whole must be early. The "abomination of desolation" in Mark 13:14 he took to be a contemporary reference to the attempt of Caligula to erect his statue in the Temple at Jerusalem in A.D. 42. The entire Gospel was to be assigned the same date.[2] The first half of the contention Bacon conceded, but the second he warmly contested. The two men frequently debated in the Semitic and Biblical Club. As tension mounted Bacon waxed warmer and Torrey cooler. Students wondered whether they would be implacable enemies for life, but the next day heard them greet each other, "Good morning, Charles." "Good morning, Ben."

Bacon occupied the chair of New Testament introduction. His colleague, Frank Porter, was the Winkley Professor of Biblical Theology. Everyone thought of Bacon as the more radical of the two. He was a warrior from his youth and scented the battle from afar. Porter was one of the meek who inherit the earth without casting fire. The Divinity School saw high humor in a mock trial not of Frank Porter but of Benjamin Bacon for orthodoxy, but the joke struck closer to the truth than was supposed.

New Testament Introduction: Benjamin Wisner Bacon

Not for naught did Bacon come from a great Puritan family. His scorn for the timidity of Dwight and Day was in tune with the bolder spirit of his grandfather Leonard Bacon. The grandson was a knightly champion of a tradition in which an inalienable core was conserved along with continual adaptations and restatement in terms of enlarging thought and altered conditions. He was more receptive of critical studies from abroad than most of his American contemporaries and was highly impatient of the "wait and see" attitude with reference to German scholarship. Already he had made the plunge with his two works on Old

Testament criticism. Now he was to apply the same methods to the New Testament.

His methodology was eclectic, and in his treatment of miracles one observes the influence of three German schools. The first was the rationalist method of Paulus who explained miracles as the misunderstanding of natural events, the second the mythological method of Strauss who considered miracles dramatizations of ideas in the form of myth, and the

Benjamin W. Bacon

third was the "aetiological," as Bacon called it, of Baur who believed the New Testament materials to have been selected and reworked in accord with the interests of the Christian community.

These three approaches were combined by Bacon in his interpretation of the single miracle of the feeding of the five thousand. In accord with the rationalist approach he held that no miracle occurred at all though he ascribed the misunderstanding not to the eyewitnesses but to the later legend makers. What actually happened was that only some in the throng had forgotten to bring food. By an example of generosity Jesus induced those who had remembered their lunches to share with the others and thus all were fed.

To the legendary elements Bacon applied the mythological methodology of Strauss. The details appended to the narrative by the redactor were designed to exalt Jesus as outdoing Elisha, who fed one hundred men with twenty barley loaves (II Kings 4:42-44), whereas Jesus fed five thousand with five loaves and two fishes. Note that in the Fourth Gospel the loaves are distinctly said to have been barley.

For Bacon, vastly more significant for the understanding of the Gospel account was the practice of the early Church. In this approach one discerns the hand of Ferdinand Christian Baur to whom Bacon paid a high tribute as the first to insist that the New Testament is to be understood in terms of the life, the controversies, and the interests of the early Christian community.[3] From this point of view the miracle of the loaves was interpreted as an anticipation of the Christian love feast. Just as in the primitive assemblies the throng was seated on the greensward in companies, and the presiding officer blessed, broke, and distributed the bread, so here, after the seating, the Lord took bread and having given thanks broke it and gave to the disciples for distribution. At the end, the unconsumed portion was gathered in baskets. The Gospel does not say what was done with these fragments, but in the early Church they were taken to those unable to be present.[4]

Thus in interpretation of the single incident we find the rational, the mythical, and the aetiological method.

Bacon's primary concern was not, however, to explain miracles nor even to trace the rise of an early Christian literature, though this endeavor occupied most of his attention. The goal was to recover a picture of the advent of Christianity, of those events, experiences, ideas, and interpretations which constitute the basis for and the essential meaning of New Testament religion. The only way to find out is through a rigorous, critical examination of the literary sources. But we are never to forget that books did not come first. The life of the early Church centered not around gospels but around sacraments. Baptism and the Lord's Supper were the two foci of the Gospels themselves. Jesus' Galilean ministry starts with his baptism by John and the Judean ministry centers upon the Last Supper.[5]

Paul, the earliest witness, states that the Lord in the night in which he was betrayed took bread, and broke it. Paul stressed baptism also as a dying and rising with the Lord.[6] Both sacraments signified that Christ died *for our sins*, that his sacrifice was an atonement effecting reconciliation with the Father.

Is this an interpretation forged by Paul or did Jesus so conceive of his own mission? One may legitimately wonder because the Gospels have little about the atoning quality of his death.[7] Bacon saw a development in Jesus himself as to his role in God's plan. He commenced as the successor of John, the son of David, to awaken Israel to repentance. Rejected in Galilee he made an excursion into the region of Tyre and Sidon where the Canaanite woman persuaded him that he had a mission beyond Israel. Yet his obligation was first of all to his own people and for that reason he set his face to go up to Jerusalem.[8]

The authority by which he did so then became a problem for himself as well as for his critics. He began to assume the role of Messiah who should cast out the false shepherds of Israel, purify the Temple and rally the people. There was indeed a very real possibility of success. As a matter of fact, he did dominate the Temple for a few days after the cleansing, and he would never have been crucified if his challenge to the hierocracy had not been so menacing as to constitute a political danger in the eyes of the Roman authorities.

The attempt failed, and before the end of the week Jesus perceived that he had been no more successful in Jerusalem than in Galilee. He profoundly believed that God would intervene and that there were those of his generation who would not taste of death until they should see the Danielic Son of Man coming on the clouds of heaven. Those modern interpreters, said Bacon, who refuse to take this literally are mistaken. We are no more to be offended that Jesus thought in the imagery of his time than that he spoke Aramaic.[9] He was not particularly concerned about the hour of the coming, deprecated specific predictions, and even at the moment saw already the hand of God at work in the casting out of demons. At the same time he did expect a divine intervention in the near future.[10]

First, however, must come his own death. He was now to assume the role of the martyred Maccabees, who gave themselves as a propitiation on behalf of Israel. Jesus likewise prepared to lay down his life with the assurance that his disciples would sup with him in the banquet of the kingdom. The shepherd was smitten. The flock was scattered. Peter first rallied the brethren. To him first came the experience of the risen Lord.

Of necessity now some change had to be made in the interpretation of the meaning of Jesus. He had not redeemed Israel. The religion which centered about him had therefore to become individual and could then be universal. The titles Son of David and even Son of Man lost their appropriateness in favor of the New Man, the New Adam who should make of his disciples new creatures. By his cross he had won reconciliation with the Father, and men need no longer torture themselves in the impossible endeavor to placate God through works of the Law. This was the gospel Paul elaborated. It grew directly out of the gospel of Jesus.

The first three Gospels, all later than Paul, fall short of his profound insights. Mark makes of Jesus the wonder-worker whom God highly exalted.[11] Both Mark and Luke are interested in softening the Petrine-Pauline controversy over the keeping of the Jewish Law. Mark, stemming from Peter, outdoes Paul in ridiculing dietary regulations[12] and the Lucan writings by a companion of Paul represent the Apostle as willing to accept certain food laws.[13] Matthew then lapses into the very legalism Paul decried and portrays Jesus as the new Moses promulgating the higher righteousness from the Mount.[14] John's gospel, though later than the three, returns to the gospel Paul received in that Jesus is the Lamb of God that "taketh away the sins of the world." At the same time primitive Christian eschatology is spiritualized as eternal. In the Fourth Gospel we have our charter of liberty.[15] Like John we may discard thought forms provided we penetrate to essential meanings.

Bacon was as free as his colleagues to discard mythology but more insistent that Christianity is rooted in an act of God in history. "To the historian of religion the historical Jesus that really counts is not the Rabbi, however sublime his heavenly wisdom. . . . Neither is it the second Moses who gave the new law. . . . It is the Martyr of the kingdom of God, who dedicated his blood as an atonement for the sin of his people. . . . The vital fact which lies at the foundation of the faith is the fact that Jesus made this self-dedication in the night in which he was betrayed. . . . Faithful unto death to the cause of God's kingdom, he poured out his blood as a libation for the sin which stood between the 'many' in all lands who were waiting for that kingdom and the divine fulfillment of their hope. If any think it an obsolete idea to imagine that the wrath of a justly offended God can be propitiated by such prayers and offerings of self-dedication, that is nothing to the point for the impartial historian, who can only record the fact that Jesus did make this self-dedication, assuring those in whose presence he made it that it should not be in vain, but that he would confess those in the presence of the Father who joined him in like self-surrender here on earth, and making tryst with them at the heavenly feast of Redemption. It is the business of the theologian, not the historian, to say whether this religious idea that forms the very basis of Christianity is capable of expression in terms acceptable to modern thought."[16]

Yet Bacon did not disdain to be both the historian and the theologian. "I am not so foolish," he wrote, "as to imagine that Paul thought he could offer the world a 'gospel of peace' by anything which does not bring men into contact with the living God by showing Him at work. Telling men the beautiful system of ethics Jesus taught in Galilee does not give them a gospel. Telling the marvels of healing that took place while he went about preaching repentance is not a gospel. Telling how he was martyred for the kingdom's sake is not a gospel, unless somehow, somewhere, you can show that the hand of the living eternal God was at work in the matter."[17]

As a teacher Bacon passed sentence on himself as "the worst possible."[18] In a sense he was right. No teacher "made fewer concessions to human finitude." Robert Calhoun recalls: "I seem to remember from the first day onward a marvelous intricacy of internal and external evidences, patristic parallels, Aramaic originals, single, double, and triple traditions, *logia* and redactions, unrolling imperturbably as the Amazon, for us to sink in or swim as we might. Most of us sank . . . yet somehow we did not wholly drown. . . . The inexhaustible patience and gracious restlessness of a teacher whose full mind engulfed ours and carried them along by massed learning and fluent thought . . . gave us confidence. . . . By dismay we were moved to emulation, and by emulation we nonspecialists achieved, little by little, not mastery but some measure of appreciative insight. For us New Testament study took on once for all the stature in which he had brought it visibly before our eyes."[19]

Students who were bewildered by his erudition and disturbed by his conclusions were reassured by his prayers. "The deep reverence with which he read the Bible, the awe which crept into his voice as he talked, with utter humility and yet as a friend may, with God, the chaste beauty of his diction with never an awkward phrase or a jarring word to mar the worship, the transparent sincerity which made it impossible ever to suspect that he had forgotten the Deity and was addressing his remarks to the congregation in the form of prayer—shall we ever forget those hours?"[20]

In public address he was quite able to cast aside professional terminology and to speak simply and profoundly of the things of the spirit. After his alumni address in 1922[21] the entire audience rose spontaneously to its feet and Oscar Maurer, pastor of Center Church, ejaculated, "Now I know how the Greeks felt about their orators."

BIBLICAL THEOLOGY: FRANK CHAMBERLIN PORTER

The bridge which linked the Old Testament and the New was Frank Chamberlin Porter. His field was Biblical Theology and included of

Frank C. Porter

necessity both Testaments. He was besides a specialist in the intertestamental period. Of all the men on the faculty during the first quarter of the century none was so influential in forming the minds of the students as was he. This was partly because he dealt with ultimate questions. Not for him to settle the problem of the Aramaic originals. Not for him to determine the dates of the sources of the Gospels. The question for him was what the New Testament as we have it means for Christian faith and experience. He was influential also because he was perhaps more than any other the very epitome of the prevailing Liberalism.

He was actually more radical from the point of view of the historic Christian tradition than his colleague Benjamin Bacon, though few realized it because Porter was so demure and diffident. His teaching technique was also disarming. He would review the opinions of critics more radical than he and having refuted them would appear by comparison to be on the side of the pillars. His power rested not primarily upon his writings although he produced two books: *The Messages of the Apocalyptical Writers*[22] and *The Mind of Christ in Paul*.[23] He was urged to write more by colleagues, students, and not the least by Mrs. Porter, herself so dynamic that there was never a hiatus between the resolve and the result. Against all pressures Frank Porter held his own. Once at a picnic at the close of the school year each was asked to tell of summer plans. Mrs. Porter said, "We are going to Paris on Saturday *if* Frank has finished his book." Mr. Porter said, "I am going to Paris on Saturday. I do not know what Mrs. Porter will do." Neither was his impact due to skill in lecturing. His multifarious notes on sundry scraps of paper deployed on the desk in no discernible order made the hearer fidget, and his suspended sentences reminded one of a crow circling to find a fence post on which to alight. His power lay in the richness of his thought, the transparency of his spirit, the gentle self-effacement of his character. John Moore (B.D. 1918) aptly spoke of Professor Porter as "trailing the Beatitudes."

He gathered up many of the strands in the New England tradition. Jonathan Edwards had deeply affected him, and he was fond of commending to his classes the sermon "On the Excellency of Christ." The Neoplatonic strain in Edwards reappeared in Porter. The whole Edwardian stream meant more to him than students suspected. When his successor in the library undertook to make room for newer books by carting the New England theologians to the basement, Porter looked on ruefully and remarked, "We were nurtured on those men." He had studied also in Germany and was fully acquainted with the new schools. In 1893 he published an article in the *Andover Review* on "The Liberal and the Ritschlian Theology of Germany."[24] His comment was that Liberalism substituted for Christ the Christ idea, whereas Ritschlianism was tied to the Christ of actual history. He questioned whether Liberalism was Christian and whether Ritschlianism was reasonable. Here was the problem of faith and history with which Porter was to wrestle all his life. What is now called demythologizing was his constant preoccupation.

Porter was likewise affected by Coleridge, Wordsworth, Bushnell, and Munger, pastor of United Church in Porter's student days.[25] From Coleridge he has learned that to enter into religion one must submit oneself as a many-stringed instrument to the fire-tipped fingers of the royal Harper.[26] Wordsworth formulated in a sentence Porter's whole principle of Biblical interpretation: the object of poetry is "truth, not individual and local but general and operative, not standing upon external testimony but carried alive into the heart by passion—truth which is its own testimony."[27]

In order to answer the question what is true, valid, and vital in the religion of the New Testament, Porter formulated four canons. The first was that the valid is the universal rather than the particular, that which can be repeated in our experience and not some unique event which by its very nature is incapable of repetition and therefore of verification. There was an implicit danger here that Christianity would be denuded of its essential character as a religion based upon a unique event in history, the incarnation of God in Christ. That was why Porter himself inquired whether Liberalism was Christian. The second principle was that the universal truths can be conveyed best through symbolic mythologies. Said he: "May not help toward an understanding come from the recognition that the question of the place even of the gospels in actual Christian experience is not only, and perhaps not primarily, a question of past historical fact, or of permanent historical forces and processes, but also of the power of the mind to clothe its deepest feelings and highest apprehensions of truth, its most living sense of God and the unseen world, in concrete narratives or pictures, and that, whatever their precise relation to fact, these pictures, in any case, have their real significance as the language of faith and emotion, in their transformation of things seen into symbols of things unseen and eternal?"[28]

Even the Christology of Paul was mythical. He had no single Christology, but "took his Christological language from the Old Testament, the Apocrypha, the Wisdom Literature, from the Greek Mysteries and from the Logos of the Stoics." Every one of Paul's varied Christologies was an analogy, a figure of speech, a mythology by which to express the exceeding wonder of all that he had known in Christ.

The next two canons have to do with what old New England would have called "preparation for salvation," the approach needful on the part of man if he is to apprehend the universal truths which the mythologies enshrine. The first response—this is the third canon—is wonder, emotion, passion, transport. The Epistles of Paul were themselves the fruit not of ratiocination but of ecstasy. Consequently, "after the work of scholarship, Paul will still, as before, be best read and most truly appreciated by those who most nearly share his experience, those to whom the power to call God, Father, and Jesus, Lord, and the experience of divine love as an indwelling Spirit make the soul glow with gratitude and lift it up to an exultant consciousness of freedom and of essential immortality."[29]

The fourth canon is that there must be an ethical response. "The wonder of the Gospel picture of him [Jesus] is that no one can behold it without feelings and decisions that involve character; that no one sees in it more or other than he wills to see. One cannot even see a fact which condemns him or commands him, unless there is in him a spirit of humility and obedience. . . . No critic's Life of Christ can in the name of history free men from the requirement of obedience and faith toward him. Still in the Gospels stands a holy and loving One who says, Come unto me, believe in me, and no one who sees and hears can escape decision, no one can come and believe who does not become as a little child."[30]

The application of these four canons is well illustrated in Porter's exegesis of two passages in the Pauline Epistles. The first is Romans 8:38-39: "For I am persuaded, that neither death, nor life, nor angels, nor principalities, nor powers, nor things present, nor things to come, nor height, nor depth, nor any other creature, shall be able to separate us from the love of God, which is in Christ Jesus our Lord." "There are here," writes Porter, "a number of conceptions of current Judaism such as the principalities and the powers. But when we have placed these expressions in their time have we finished? No, this is far more the language of lofty emotion than the language of the time. It belongs to Paul, not to his contemporaries, for it is Paul's vision and passion that it contains; and because it is the language of emotion it is the language of all times. It glows with an inner fire, and we have not really read it unless by it our souls are set on fire. The feeling so far masters the form that it is no less impressive in English than in Greek, to us to whom principalities and powers and height and depth do not stand for realities of the unseen world, than to those in whose view of the world such conceptions had an established place. It is of value to trace these ideas to their origins and understand them in their connection, but it is of far greater value to follow the march of Paul's thought through the chapter, to feel the pulsation of his heightening emotion and to respond with inner exultation to this final triumphant challenge of Christian certainty against all the powers of the universe. This then is poetry; it is inspired religious literature; and what the historical critic can do with poetry concerns its body, not its soul, passing events or current opinions, the storehouse out of which the words are drawn, but not the life with which they are endowed. For the right reading of a poet, one in whom thought is touched and vitalized by passion, the question is almost irrelevant whether he supposed the concrete objects in which he clothed his thought and his emotion to be actual or not. He may have supposed some things actual which we know to be fancy, some events historical which we find to be legendary, some occurrences extraordinary of which we understand the causes and connections; but if he used his materials poetically and if the poetry is good, if the thought is of the universal quality, the feeling human and intense, and the language fit and beautiful, then we can still use it with a delight quite unimpaired by our differing knowledge."

The other example is Philippians 2:5-8: "Let this mind be in you, which was also in Christ Jesus: who, being in the form of God, thought it not robbery to be equal with God: but made himself of no reputation, and took upon him the form of a servant, and was made in the likeness of men: and being found in fashion as a man, he humbled himself, and became obedient unto death, even the death of the cross." "The use of traditional ideas in this passage is unmistakable. Jewish mythology knew of heavenly beings who had attempted to seize upon the throne of God and had been cast down in disgrace. To them Paul contrasts the figure of a heavenly being who renounced all such impious ambitions and who because of his utter self-humiliation and obedience was lifted to a place of unparalleled glory by the side of God. Greek mythology was not without its figure of a divine being, a god, who descends into human life, enduring the hardships for the sake of bringing help to men in their weakness and suffering. What then is peculiar in this account by Paul of the drama of the incarnation of the divine Christ? What is there to praise in such a substitution for the human Jesus of the gospels of this mighty figure traced in the outlines of myth? Is not such a divine drama just the sort of thing that marks Paul's departure from Jesus and that impels us to return to Jesus from Paul? If it were either as speculation or as mythology that Paul introduced and valued this dramatic picture we should have to assent to the criticisms implied in such questions. But this is to Paul neither myth nor theology; it is a hymn to Jesus Christ, and in his image a hymn to self-sacrificing love, a glowing picture of its divine beauty and greatness and its assured blessedness; a picture of the truth that the way to be first is to be last of all and servant of all. Of the two great sins of Biblical interpretation, that which makes poetry or allegory of what is simply matter of fact, has been far less harmful in its effect than that which makes either history or doctrine of what is in truth poetry."

The preceding passages are from Porter's printed works in which he voiced his confident conclusions. In the classroom and in manuscript he was often tentative, yet precisely in the areas where he could not make up his mind he was often of the greatest stimulus. Constantly he was grappling with the problem of faith in relation to history. He desired to emancipate faith from the incertitude of historical fact never absolutely recoverable. At the same time he well knew that Christianity stems from a deed of God in history. Porter addressed to himself the question, "Do the truths [of Christianity] depend in any sense on facts, and do they in any measure give evidence as facts? . . . Every affirmation about the life and teaching of Jesus, even the assertion that he really lived, however we come to it, remains an historical affirmation and cannot become anything else. If we are to be really free from dependence upon historical criticism in matters of Christian faith we must be prepared to listen without fear to any assertion whatever from the side of history as to matters of fact. It is only an adverse judgment of value, the assertion that the ideals present in the gospels are not true, that Christian faith may deny. Let us suppose that Jesus never lived or that the picture of him in the gospels is so far an idealization that the historical Jesus is hidden from us, would it follow that the ideal is untrue?

.... To me it seems that our Christian experience justifies us only in saying that it comes to us as truth and works in us as a saving and renewing power, through the gospel picture of Jesus Christ; not that the truth of the picture depends upon its historical actuality. . . . We assent to the truth, and would assent to it no less if the picture were proved fiction and not fact. . . . Poetic truth in any case is the best and the highest that they contain and impart, truth that is to say not past but eternal, not local and particular but universal, not human but divine."

He sums up his position by saying: "We ought then to apply both to Paul and to the gospels, and within the gospels both to the words of the evangelists and to the words of Jesus, the principles that condition the right reading of great books; we ought freely to respond to them, with transport and with wonder; and we ought to apply their vision of truth to our own present world and to our daily life. But this means that our religion is to be not only that of Jesus but also that of the apostles, that of the New Testament. We are not only with Jesus to see God the Father in Nature and in man, but also with Peter and Paul and John to see God the Father in Jesus the Son. . . . If we read the New Testament as the literature of Christian faith and feeling this means that we shall undertake to share that faith and love and reverence with which the gospel picture of Jesus is drawn and his place in religious experience described."[31]

The universal in Christianity is ethical in content and ethical in demand: Not a marvelous and magical effect of the death of Christ upon the mind of God or upon his conduct toward us, not the dogma that Christ dies for our sin, his death being for the benefit of those who assent to the dogma, but the inward ethical appropriation of the death of Christ, the will to make it our own in character and conduct, is the greater thing.[32]

In reviewing Bacon's book, *Jesus and Paul*, Porter inquired whether the atonement is to be interpreted in any other way than that "Christ is altogether, even in his death and resurrection, that which the Christian is and should strive to be." In other words Porter endeavored so to universalize Christianity that Jesus becomes the prototype in all respects of the Christian who can aspire to enter into every experience of His Lord; whereas Bacon looked upon Christ as a unique figure standing at the very apex of history.[33]

Yet Porter was not prepared to divorce faith from history. "At certain points," said he, "it is not clear that history can pursue its own way without offense to religion, or that religion can dispense with positive convictions as to matters of fact. This is especially the case in regard to the life of Christ. Here the effort to maintain a relationship of independence and indifference between history and religion fails."[34] Nor is it necessary to be skeptical with regard to the whole life and teaching of Jesus. As to the details we cannot be sure, but we can recover the total impression of his life and character.[35] When we have done so, our attention will be directed away from the dogmas about Christ. There is something perverse about inquiring into the self-consciousness of Jesus when he was so unconscious of self.[36] The meaning of the Jesus of history is that he lifted man beyond history. "The greatness of Jesus, his secret and his divinity . . . is most nearly disclosed in the power that he had to produce in men a living faith that was not bound to his earthly presence, that was not contained in the words he uttered and the life he lived, though it had its first expression there, that did not depend on accurate recollections of all that he had said.[37]

"It must be confessed that the relation of the historical Jesus to present religious faith is a peculiar and difficult example of the relation in literature between historic fact and poetic truth, between the particular and the universal; but I would urge that it is an example of that relation, and that only by treating it so can religious faith in the end free itself from an anxious and burdening dependence upon historical criticism."[38]

In the thought of Professor Porter one observes again the three main emphases which have been persistent in the New England tradition: First, the Reformation with its emphasis upon faith in that which God did in history; second, the Enlightenment with its insistence that the valid is the simple and the universal; and third, Pietism with its warm emotionalism.

CHAPTER XVII

Theology and Church History

SYSTEMATIC THEOLOGY: DOUGLAS C. MACINTOSH

Douglas Macintosh was one of the most thought-provoking members of the faculty in the 1920's. *The Festschrift*[1] written by his students in his honor is an exciting discussion of the issues of which he had made them cognizant. Calhoun and the two Niebuhrs, Northrop, Bixler, Krusé, Bewkes, George Thomas, and others paid him homage though frequently challenging his conclusions. Reinhold Niebuhr, at a dinner in honor of Macintosh's sixtieth birthday, referring to the title of a recent article by him, said that the next book might be entitled "My Former Students and Other Battlelines." In response to the toast Macintosh recalled a professor of philosophy who when congratulated on the number of his students in distinguished posts replied, "Yes, and no one of them is teaching the truth." Macintosh believed that there is a truth and that he had it, and that this truth is of paramount importance. He could suffer a disagreement with regard to the Christian ethic of war with more equanimity than with regard to the method of being certain about the Christian God. His debates with his students were not devoid of emotional strains because he was no liberal relativist but a scion of the Puritans who believed and cared.

He was actually of Puritan descent going back to John Cotton through Seaborne Cotton, so named because he was born at sea. Back in England this Seaborne begot descendants who later came to Canada and turned into Macintoshes. One would have expected their religion to be Presbyterian, but the family history was so crossed with searchings of the deep things of the spirit that a more congenial home was found among the Baptists. Here was another combination of the Reformation and Pietism.[2] Like his ancestors, Douglas Clyde Macintosh was an evangelical never happier than when engaged in deputation revivalism. He was a Bible Christian who, when the faculty subjected themselves to an examination in the content of the English Bible, scored above all his colleagues.

At the same time like Jonathan Edwards and the whole New England

Douglas C. Macintosh

tradition he was concerned that religion should be consonant with and supported by philosophy and natural science. And he was fully abreast of that radical Biblical criticism in which the humanist science of historiography had issued. But research implies uncertainty. If all were known there would be no research. Religion, however, can brook no uncertainty —not on the points which vitally matter. Therefore, religion must be independent of historical research. Even more unequivocally than Porter, Macintosh maintained that Biblical scholars must be absolutely unimpeded, even should they come out with a demonstration that Jesus had never lived at all. The Christian, however, cannot hold his faith in abeyance while the historians are settling such questions. Faith, therefore, must be emancipated from history.

In a work entitled *The Reasonableness of Christianity*, a title reminiscent of the Enlightenment, Macintosh covered one hundred and thirty-five pages before arriving at Jesus at all, and then justified his procedure: "It has been through no oversight that nothing has been said of Christology or of the historic Jesus. There is an important tactical advantage in showing how extensive and vital is that content or essence of Christianity which can be defended successfully without any assumption as to particular facts of history. We escape the danger of infecting the entire content of essential Christian belief with the necessary incertitude of historical opinion. All that has been said of the reasonableness and truth of Christianity is demonstrably valid, whether we have any Christology or not, and whatever we may or may not believe about the historic Jesus. It would still be valid if it should turn out that Jesus was essentially different from what has been commonly believed, or even that he was not truly historical at all. . . . it is the systematic thinker's task to lead faith to a sure foundation, independent of the uncertainties of historical investigation. . . .[3]

His whole approach was largely tactical. Macintosh emphatically did not reject the Jesus of history and later in his book gives what he takes to be the assured results of New Testament study thus far. What he retained of the historical Jesus was very considerable, but the point was that *if* this had to be relinquished, nevertheless, the Christian view of God and of goodness and of the life to come would still be true and right.

The argument proceeds along Kantian lines to justify the interpretation of life in terms of "moral optimism" as reasonable and plausible. Moral optimism recognizes the reality of evil. God had to allow the possibility of evil in order to provide for the actuality of good (the position of the old Edwardeans) but evil can be overcome and if men strive to do their best the good will triumph. This view induces a heroic attitude toward life. It is not unmistakably nullified by ascertained facts. It entails a number of implications which turn out to be essentially Christian. Thus the Christian picture of life is validated as that view which, better than any other, invests life with meaning and significance.[4]

Still, what had thus far been said does not go far beyond a plausible conjecture. How does one know that values are values? How does one know that God will validate them? Or that there is a God and that He is good? If one cannot assume a revelation of God in Jesus Christ in the Scriptures how then is one to know? The problem of religious knowledge is at once posed. Macintosh realized that a prior question must be raised as to the possibility of knowledge at all. One might have surmised that a man with the three names Douglas and Clyde and Macintosh would have been in the succession of the Scottish Common Sense Realists and one might have expected a Yale man to be in the line of Noah Porter and Samuel Harris. But these connections are fortuitous. Macintosh was not trained at Yale. Unwittingly he did stand in the Scottish and Yale succession of Epistemological Realism.

Some of the characteristic terminology of the Common Sense philosophy appears in Macintosh's whimsical parody of the Parable of the Prodigal Son: "A certain father named Common Sense had two sons. The elder was science and the younger philosophy. This son having received his portion of the inheritance went into a far country and squandered his substance in riotous imagination until he began to be in want of any positive truth and fain would fill his belly with the husks of skepticism. Having gained nothing from his wanderings save sophistication, he resolved to return to his father, whose forgiveness was more readily won than was the respect of the suspicious and censorious brother to whom the father had rightly said, 'Son, thou art ever with me and all that I have is thine.' "[5]

We have already seen that Reid of the Scottish school asserted immediacy in the experience of external reality though conceding a measure of possible error. Noah Porter introduced the more precise view that experience is of matter as being and not of secondary characteristics. Macintosh combined this view with the Kantian that the mind in knowing is active in casting experience into categories. All admitted error which by critical reason could be detected and corrected.[6] The position of Macintosh was the middle ground between the pure empiricism which yields nothing but incoherent particulars and the subjective rationalism which can never get beyond the knower to the known. Macintosh defined truth not as the relationship of absolute identity between idea and reality—this is unattainable—but a sufficient identity for practical purposes. He said that his definition of truth was intellectual but his criteria pragmatic. Again a middle ground between the view that there is no truth or if there is, one cannot know it and the view that truth exists and this truth is fully attainable.[7]

His pragmatic criteria of sufficient truth for practical purposes requires then a definition of the practical purposes. What he meant was enough truth to make sense out of the universe and to give point to the life heroic. He needed a belief in a good and personal God; a belief in immortality for the rectification of wrong and a continuance of the valuable. He needed a belief in the Christian law of love and self-sacrifice. How then, particularly apart from Christ, could certainty as to these values be achieved?

Here like Harris and others before him he carried over his empiricist epistemology into the area of religion. Divine reality can be immediately experienced. At this point he was admittedly indebted to Schleiermacher whom earlier New Englanders had rather paralleled than borrowed. But if religious reality can be experienced, there is more than an analogy between science and religion. Science is a way of learning by experience through examination, hypothesis, experimentation, and the formulation of laws.[8]

In precisely the same fashion, said Macintosh, the affirmations of Christian faith are capable of verification. Religious experience is a laboratory in which to conduct the experiments. The experience may be past or present and the whole of Church History discloses a rich roster of personal cases. In religious experience there is immediacy, and there is also error. Here too there is need for a critical monism or a critical realism. That is to say the religious object is real, but our apprehension is partial, inaccurate, and in need of correction.

If, then, we seek to test our religious assumptions we must, so to speak, set up experiments. We are not simply to sit and wait. Macintosh, on the one hand, hailed the "theologians of crisis" because they insisted on a real transcendent religious object, but criticized them because of their passivity. With the early Edwardeans he believed that there can be a preparation for salvation. On the part of man it involves "the right religious adjustment," an openness of the spirit, especially a readiness to conform to God's will. "He who does the will shall know the doctrine" of the righteousness and love of God. Thus, moral optimism will be confirmed by religious experience.

To quote Macintosh: "As a result of acting intelligently on the hypothesis of the existence of a God great enough and good enough to justify our absolute self-surrender and confident, appropriating faith, there comes a religious experience of spiritual uplift and emancipation in which, as a complex of many psychological elements, there can be intuited empirically, or perceived, the operation of a Factor which we evaluate and interpret as divine, because of its absolute religious and spiritual value. It is here then, and not in traditional creeds or sacred books as such, that we find revelation."[9]

As one reviews Macintosh's books today some sense returns of the initial thrill of emancipation which excitedly emerged as his course unfolded. One could now let the New Testament critics go their way. One could reply to any reproaches from the natural scientists that in religion one was but using their methods and that the grounds of religious certainty were quite as assured as their own. Right religious adjustment might indeed make exacting demands but the Christian experience of the ages demonstrated its possibility. And if one's own experience were inadequate one could turn to history and there find, as it were, a treasury of the accumulated merits of the saints, who had made the right religious adjustment and experienced the assurance.

But then all the questions returned. The students began to inquire. George Thomas asked whence came the moral values which were to be tested by the right religious adjustment. Seelye Bixler wondered whether religion can be empirical. "Religion can not allow its interest to be centered exclusively in the factual world, nor can it forget that the bridge between the world of fact and that of meaning must take its form from the ideal as well as the real." Again he pointed out that religious experience is not like that with which the scientist deals. "The mystics themselves claim that the experience of God is neither describable nor communicable, and further, that it is not dependable, since the 'right religious adjustment' is often made without positive results." Richard Niebuhr held that theological science cannot be made subject to human values and Reinhold Niebuhr found Macintosh's system altogether too neat. "Neither the vital thrust of life, nor its organic unities nor its disharmonies nor its highest possibilities can be expressed in terms of logic and rational consistency. The dynamic and creative energy of life can be described but not comprehended by reason." Finally Northrop maintained that science offers no help on the problem of certainty unless science adopts a new monistic metaphysics. For if reality be held to consist of an infinite number of separate entities no knowledge of ultimates is at all possible.[10]

One of the most interesting points in this whole discussion in 1937 is that no one made a plea for return to the historic revelation of God in Jesus Christ as the ground for religious and for Christian knowledge. Many of these authors, writing twenty-five years later, would speak differently.

In Macintosh, more perhaps than in his colleagues, one felt the persistent conflict between the Enlightenment and Pietism, a conflict which did not end with his generation. He should not have expected his uneasy synthesis to satisfy another generation. There was, however, a deeper synthesis than the theoretical which grappled his students to him. Seelye Bixler records that a reading of *Theology as an Empirical Science* prompted a visit to New Haven at the time of great vocational hesitancy on the ground of personal inadequacy. All of this doubt Macintosh dispelled. Soren Vetsigian, who for years now has been carrying on behind the iron curtain, once gave a paper before a seminar conducted by four professors. None appeared impressed and the author was dejected until Macintosh told him that his paper might make an article. That was the day which made of Vetsigian the author of several books in Armenian. When Macintosh was paralyzed and almost deprived of speech, Mrs. Macintosh told him that she had written to one of his former students telling him that he was her husband's favorite son. The stricken man rallied and speech returned to enable him to say clearly, "No, three thousand." That was the number of his favorite sons.

Overpowering was the witness of his own faith when he lost his first wife. The week following happened to be his assignment for chapel. He did not flinch, but on the first day read as his Scripture the verse from the prophet Habakkuk: "Although the fig tree shall not blossom, neither shall fruit be in the vines; the labour of the olive shall fail, and the fields shall yield no meat; the flock shall be cut off from the fold, and there shall be no herd in the stalls: yet I will rejoice in the Lord, I will joy in the God of my salvation."

CHURCH HISTORY: WILLISTON WALKER

Williston Walker, who succeeded George Park Fisher as Professor of Church History, was another scion of Puritan stock. His father, George Leon Walker, had been pastor of the First Congregational Church in

Hartford and then of Center Church in New Haven. He was himself an accomplished historian, and his book *Some Aspects of the Religious Life of New England*[11] is a gem. Mrs. Williston Walker was a Mather, and never did her husband write so much *con amore* as in his account of the role of the Mathers in New England.[12] Alice Mather Walker was evidence of the continual vitality of the dynasty, a vibrant raconteur of Yankee yarns and in the Women's Missionary Society as powerful as a grist mill in a freshet. Her husband was no whit behind her in flair. His lectures ranged from the dramatic to the amusing, and perhaps he was more convincing in the latter because laughter is the mark of detachment. As a doctor of philosophy of Leipzig he was committed, like George Park Fisher before him, to the cult of historical objectivity. In teaching there are two techniques by which objectivity can be achieved. One is to treat all men and movements with equal involvement. The danger of this method is that the historian is merely an actor who is today Othello and tomorrow Lear, one who can as readily impersonate Ignatius Loyola as John Calvin. The second approach to historical objectivity is to portray all men and movements with equal detachment, and this Walker did. This method divorces the historian from what he relates and as an exponent of this approach Walker stood aloof, unrolling a fascinating panorama, provocative frequently of merriment, but never of tears.

Yet it was not because he was a stranger to tears. When in Geneva Walker attended a performance of a dramatization of the sacrifice of Isaac, a poignant portrayal of the agony of Abraham resolved in obedience to slay the only begotten son of his age, yet wishing rather to stab himself, Walker came out in tears.

He had a decidedly serious aim and when called upon to formulate his objectives in the teaching of Church History declared that the first was to make "the minister feel that the difficulties with which he was surrounded were no greater and no more formidable than those which his brethren in Christian service had encountered in the past." As to the meaning of Church History he "pointed out the bond of unity which runs through all the variety of forms, of organization, or types of worship, and of theological statement in the Christian Church, which is to be found in Christian experience." Here was a Pietist interpretation of Church History which illustrates again what one observes in nearly all the men of that period, the continual and uneasy attempt to hold the Enlightenment and Pietism in balance. Walker's third point was that "the story of the church is essentially that of a divinely guided process, and one moving forward to a larger realization of the kingdom of God."[13] This is Calvinist. So here again, the three ingredients of the New England tradition were brought together: Reformation, Enlightenment, and Pietism.

Williston Walker

His commitment to the Congregational denomination was marked. He served as one of the committee of nineteen to draft a new constitution; he was the American official delegate to Geneva for the celebration of the four hundredth anniversary of the birth of John Calvin;[14] and he served as one of the committee of three on church unity between the Congregationalists and the Episcopalians. He was an ardent proponent of the incipient ecumenical movement, though never at the expense of basic Congregational principles. These, however, were never narrowly construed. His historical catholicity and objectivity enabled him to demolish many of the absolute pretensions of the sects, including his own. In December, 1919, he became the first provost at Yale and in that office did signal service in the organization of departments. In 1920 he was made dean of the Graduate School. His scholarship in the field of Church History is nowhere finer than in the New England field in which he was rooted. His *Creeds and Platforms of Congregationalism* is a superior piece of editing.[15] Along with it goes his *History of the Congregational Churches in the United States* in the American Church History Series. Unsurpassed are some of his minor articles like the one already mentioned on the Mathers, and another on the Sandemanians[16] and one on "Why Did Not Massachusetts Have a Saybrook Platform?"[17] despite the desire for it not only on the part of the Mathers but also of their opponents.

One would expect that a historian with this Puritan heritage, if he should turn to the Reformation, would fasten upon John Calvin. Walker loved him, but did not suffer enthusiasm to lapse into adulation. The life entitled *John Calvin* is sober, sound, and scrupulously candid.[18] The treament of the Servetus episode glosses nothing damaging to Calvin. This was and probably still is the best single volume on John Calvin and well merited a translation into French.

Walker's histories of the Reformation[19] and of the Christian Church[20] were on the order of textbooks, clear in arrangement, balanced in selection, straightforward in style, objective in presentation, fashioned altogether after the Lepizig model in the tradition of Mosheim's *Institutes of Ecclesiastical History*, entirely lacking in the sparkle which graced the author's classroom style. Particularly the one volume on the history of the Church has been the prevailing staple in theological seminaries and ministerial libraries for the last quarter of a century.

CHAPTER XVIII

The Making of a Minister

HOMILETICS: CHARLES R. BROWN

The caption of this chapter was the title of a book
by Charles Reynolds Brown, who, in addition to being Dean of the
School, gave courses in homiletics and pastoral care. In his judgment
the first requisite in the training of a minister is to teach him to preach.
Social activity is important; pastoral care is extremely important. The
Dean himself, when in the pastorate, made at least one thousand calls a
year. He did not forget that the Apostle Paul "was not so enamoured of
the drag-net as to forget the value of the hook and line."[1] Yet the sermon
is the acme of the minister's endeavor. The most fundamental training is
of the heart. There must be a message to declare and a deep sense of
urgency. "The man who can stand before a waiting congregation of
expectant people and not feel . . . the tug and pull of their need upon
his own moral reserves, . . . is altogether too wooden to be in the
ministry for a single hour. . . . You may be thoroughly sure that in any
congregation you face there are men and women fighting more devils
than were ever cast out of Mary Magdalene. . . . You may be sure that
. . . there are men and women sitting quietly in their pews who can
scarcely keep the tears back as they reflect upon the bitter experiences
through which they have been passing. They need to have some man
preach to them until the heavens open and the angels of comfort are
seen ascending and descending for the help of the sons of men." The
preacher must remember that he is not in the pulpit "to lecture on
botany but to raise flowers."[2]

Assuming all this, there are certain skills which will make the sermon more effective. The Dean possessed them in supreme measure, and one may well surmise that he was more influential as a teacher of preachers by example than in the tutorial role. To be sure, his critique of student sermons was helpful but to witness the man at work was not only a lift but also a pull.

He held strongly that preaching should be basically Biblical and expository. He knew by heart all the great passages of the Bible, and his reading of Scripture was actually recitation. The sermon in his judgment should be exposition, not merely of a passage but of a book, chapter by chapter. The primary reason is that the Bible is the source book of the Christian religion; another, that if the minister proceeds in this way he will always be sure of his topic for the next Sunday; and furthermore, if he treats the Bible in course, when he comes to a ticklish theme such as divorce, he will not be suspected of having selected the topic in order to strike at individuals.

The sermon should be delivered without a manuscript. Those who heard the Dean in his prime never suspected that he had paid a price to acquire that flow of easy, felicitous speech which was the marvel of those who heard him whether in the pulpit or the committee room. Yet he records that when in his early ministry he weaned himself from the manuscript, truly he became apostolic in that he was beaten with rods of mortification. "By day and by night," said he, "I have been in the deep, right there in my own pulpit."[3]

The Dean always enjoined careful preparation of a sermon. It should have structure but not protruding bones. He told with glee of a minister in the college chapel who announced his points as Roman I, Roman II, Arabic 1, Arabic 2, one in brackets, two in brackets. When he came again, at every new point the junior class would cross their legs. The leader of the prank was suspended but Dean Brown said that had he been in power at the moment he would have recommended the young man for an assistant professorship in the department of homiletics.[4]

The sentences in a sermon should be simple, not resembling an archipelago with outlying islands.[5] There should not be a "Sabbath day's journey" between the noun and the leading verb. The vocabulary should be Anglo-Saxon, leaning heavily to the monosyllabic. Take the following paragraph from his *Yale Talks*. He had been telling about the apostles as fishermen on the lake of Galilee and continued, "They had wintered and summered with that old lake. They had fished it by day and by night and in all weathers. They knew every cove along its shores and every deep hole where the fish might lie. They knew all the best places to fish, for they had tried them out a hundred times. They knew what sort of sky was best for fishing, and from what quarter it was best to have the wind blow. You could not tell them anything about fishing in the Sea of Galilee."[6] Of the ninety words in this paragraph only one is of Latin derivation, the word "quarter." Eighty of the words have but one syllable, and the remaining ten only two.

Such a renunciation of the full resources of our language makes for clarity at the expense of a certain impoverishment. The Dean compensated by rhythm. Read out loud the above paragraph and observe the poetic cadence of the lines. Variety was further introduced by the modulations of a voice which measured up to his own specifications as "strong, resonant, flexible and pleasant."[7]

Another device of good sermonizing was the use of piquant expression. He would never employ a hackneyed metaphor. Instead of saying "sticks out like a sore thumb," he would say "stands out like a bonfire against a dark sky."[8] He had a genius for summoning a deceased metaphor back to life. Preaching at Yale he would not say "solid as a rock," but "solid as East Rock."

He remarked that a minister responsible for two sermons a week may find himself encumbered with two white elephants. That is trite enough! But see what he does with them. The minister, said he, will have to carry water for them all week, as boys do when the circus comes to town. He will have to curry the beasts, forage to fill such huge stomachs, and scurry around to secure new blankets for their backs in the Sunday parade. The preacher becomes so desperate that he decides to go out of the show business.[9] Then there is some hope for him.

After displaying to the students all the arrows in his quiver, the Dean ended with this comment: "When the day of judgment comes, the Son of Man sitting upon the throne of His glory and separating ministers

on his right hand or on the left as a shepherd divideth his sheep from
the goats, will not look at our barrels. Our barrels will not be there. The
contents of those barrels will all have been rolled up like a scroll and
consumed with fervent heat. But the people to whom we have preached
will be there. Some of them on the right hand and, alas for us! some of
them on the left! And that will be the terrible and searching test applied
to our work as preachers. The type of character we have produced, or
have failed to produce, as we have done our work with fidelity and
efficiency or as we have scamped it with slovenly or chilly indifference—
that will be the test applied to determine whether we ourselves shall be
found upon His right hand or upon the left. The final significance of
every sermon is to be manifested at last not in the profundity of its
thought or in the grace of its literary finish but in the spiritual results
which it achieves."[10]

HOMILETICS: HENRY HALLAM TWEEDY

Brown's colleague in the field of homiletics, Henry Hallam Tweedy,
was an admirable complement. Brown was a son of the soil, Tweedy a
scion of the gentility, with the face of an archangel and the fingers of a
virtuoso. Brown would describe an uncut diamond student as a "bucket
of pure dirt." Tweedy would be more apt to call him an unfinished
symphony. He was himself an accomplished pianist, and it was a joy
to hear him and Grace Tweedy at two pianos.

In the pulpit Tweedy was less virile than Brown, yet in his own way
equally telling. No more gripping sermon was ever preached to Yale
undergraduates than Tweedy's on the responsible use of wealth. He had
less of the genius for the inevitable metaphor, but a greater facility in
apt and brief quotation. The sermon on "Unrighteous Forgetfulness"
well illustrates his message and style. It dealt both with what to forget
and what not to forget. We would do well to forget past faults and
failures. "Why lash our minds with whips of scorpions to no purpose?"
We must forget prejudices and grudges. Those who harbor resentment
"are about as happy as a company of morose toads imprisoned at the
bottom of a dank well." We are not to forget, said he, to return books.
We are not to forget letters to friends and calls on invalids. To forget

the legacy of our forebears and the privations endured for our sakes by our parents is a crime. We have no right to forget those by whose toil we live. We shall be impoverished if we suffer ourselves to forget higher moments when we have been vouchsafed visions of God: "It may have been a day when from the summit of some snow-capped crag we watched the sunlight pour in a luminous flood over Alpine valleys, or a night when we saw the moon rise over 'the billowing vast of the un-

Henry Hallam Tweedy

plumbed sea.' Or it may have been those other moments—moments when we faced the miracle and the mystery of life, as we bent over a cradle and pondered on the unsolved problem of life's beginning, or stood by the bedside of a friend, as he drifted out of our lives into the unknown. Somehow at such times we became conscious of a great invisible Companion. . . . Our heads were in the sunlight, the spiritual atmosphere was fragrant, our minds were thinking the thoughts of the Infinite Spirit after him, and our hearts were living temples of that mysterious Presence which we call holy, not only because it is hallowed but because it makes us whole." Such moments we dare not forget.[11]

Tweedy, not being dean, had more time as a teacher than Brown and could not only read and mark but could also talk over student sermons. Both men had a larger assignment than simply teaching and preaching. Brown gave a course on the Care of the Parish. Tweedy likewise. And there is every reason why two men should be covering the same ground when students are numerous. In parish work, said Tweedy, "Nothing will take the place of sympathetic companionship. . . . A certain amount of advice, comfort, warning and rebuke can be administered to a crowd;

but for delicate readjustments and difficult needs, nothing will atone for the lack of those quiet hours when two friends talk face to face alone."[12] With regard to church administration he had a pungent word when he said that churches seeking ministers behave as if they had taken for their motto the text "Give me a kid that I may make merry with my friends."

To the training for preaching and pastoral work Tweedy added two other assignments: religious education and public worship. He gave no direct instruction in the former but was gladly enlisted in an enterprise to provide guidance to parents and graded materials for children in the field of religion. With E. Hershey Sneath he was a collaborator in the King's Highway Series. These books were at the time a unique experiment in the inculcation of morals by indirection through stories, poems, pictures, and Bible passages.

In the field of worship Tweedy directed himself both to children and adults. He decried the prevalent laments over a decline in worship due, said he, to a comparison of the ordinary churchman of today with the extraordinary of yesterday. Nevertheless, there are difficulties in the present and the deepest are theological.

"Our little world has lost its unique glory as the center of the universe. . . . Man is no more viewed as the child of yesterday, created suddenly out of the dust by a divine fiat in the year 4004 B.C. He is the last, loveliest and most divine child of a life emerging out of creation's unthinkable beginning, and journeying hopefully along the highways of illimitable time." Hope is dashed, however, by the havoc of unbridled competition, by the relativity of ethics, and faith is benumbed by bewilderment as to the very character of God. "What manner of Deity is this who may have a million earths like our own, starry children who in turn come in and then go out of existence? Can our prayers reach Him? Does He hear us singing,

> O God, our help in ages past,
> Our hope for years to come?"

Doubts have been intensified by the "murky problems and horrible experiences of the Great War." But worship we must. "Worship nothing, and you will come to nothing. The snail has crawled to the tip of the cabbage leaf and fancies that it has reached the pinnacle of earth. Worship low ideals and mean gods, and your pathway slopes downward."[13]

"Worship is entirely natural, growing out of man's awe and wonder and his sense of dependence upon the Power which created him. It is inevitable. . . . When a church ceases to worship, it will become a dead church, no matter how beautiful the liturgy or how eloquent the preaching."[14]

Training in worship is necessary alike for the preacher and for the congregation. He must give diligent attention to his public prayers striving to combine the best from the liturgical and the free traditions. Children should early be guided in prayer. As an aid to parents Tweedy and Weigle brought out a little book entitled *Training the Devotional Life*.[15] Music is one of the great aids. "Even *pure music apart from speech* has its gracious ministry. It is full of religious suggestion and inspiration, and one should learn to worship through listening, as Milton did, until it brought all heaven before his sightless eyes. The prelude to public worship, often badly chosen and rarely heeded, is an example. This should help to set the tone and beget the mood of the hour, and so to prepare for the preacher's message. It rids the mind of cluttering particulars, creates receptivity, and by subjecting the congregation to a common experience aids in organizing a discordant crowd into a worshiping unit."[16]

Tweedy's own hymn book entitled *Christian Worship and Praise*,[17] though incorporating much of the ancient and universal, bespoke also the man and his times. The hymns chosen strike often the notes of radiance, cheer, valor, compassion, and loveliness. The first verse of the hymn "God the Omnipotent" with its line, "Thunder Thy clarion, the lightning Thy sword," is omitted. "Fairest Lord Jesus, ruler of all nature" becomes "lover of all nature." In the General Confession, the affirmation that "there is no health in us" is left out, as well as the phrase "miserable offenders." This was the era of sweetness and light. Today the stress is on contrition and pardon, with perhaps too little of lyrical joy and high resolve.

One hymn of Tweedy's finds a continuing place in hymnody:

> O gracious Father of mankind,
> Our spirits' unseen Friend,
> High heaven's Lord, our hearts' dear Guest,
> To thee our prayers ascend.
> Thou dost not wait till human speech
> Thy gifts divine implore;
> Our dreams, our aims, our work, our lives
> Are prayers Thou lovest more.
>
> Thou hearest these, the good and ill,
> Deep buried in each breast;
> The secret thought, the hidden plan,
> Wrought out or unexpressed.
> O cleanse our prayers from human dross,
> Attune our lives to Thee,
> Until we labor for those gifts
> We ask on bended knee.
>
> Thou seekest us in love and truth
> More than our minds seek Thee;
> Through open gates Thy power flows in
> Like flood tides from the sea.
> No more we seek Thee from afar,
> Nor ask Thee for a sign,
> Content to pray in life and love
> And toil, till all are Thine.   Amen.

RELIGIOUS EDUCATION: E. HERSHEY SNEATH AND YOUNGER COLLEAGUES

Religious education as a separate discipline was a new venture in seminaries, which is not to say that religious education had hitherto been neglected. In the earlier days often the minister had also been the schoolmaster. Witness the elder Dwight. In the colonial period the responsibility for establishing schools rested with the State. If the State failed, the Church stepped in. The schools established by the State were not lacking in religious instruction. But the separation of Church and State, though not motivated by hostility, led to the exclusion of religion from the curriculum of the public schools simply because of the diversity of the religious pattern. There were several ways then in which religious instruction could be imparted. One was in the home, another in the Sunday School, and such schools were well over one hundred years old before the advent of the so-called movement of religious education. Another method was the scheme of released time, whereby pupils were permitted in the public schools to receive instruction in the beliefs of their several faiths at specified hours. This opportunity greatly engaged Benjamin Winchester who gave courses in the Divinity School from 1916 to 1918.[18] There was, however, no objection to moral instruction in the public schools, nor basically to religious education if it were not sectarian, and particularly if it were indirect.

The Divinity School felt the need to explore the possibilities and to provide for the emergency, and to that end invited one of its own graduates, E. Hershey Sneath, who had spent most of his career teaching philosophy at Yale College.[19] He joined the staff of the Divinity School in 1912 and taught there until his retirement in 1923. His approach to religious education was naturally conditioned by his own religious position, a combination of moralism and mysticism. In the booklet entitled *Shall We Have a Creed?*[20] he declared that "according to the teaching of Jesus, the real aim of our religion is the establishment of the Kingdom of God in the world and this Kingdom is a Kingdom of Righteousness." For the Athanasian Creed he would substitute: I believe in Jesus' conception of God as righteous Father. I believe in Jesus' conception of the law of love. I believe in Jesus' conception of the immortality of the righteous soul.

One observes that belief was not in what Jesus was or did, but in the correctness of his conceptions. Jesus was not affirmed to be the Redeemer, nor even the Revealer, and the reason may well have been that for Sneath mysticism provided the basis for faith and assurance. Like Porter, he was affected by the Neoplatonic strain of piety. In a symposium on mysticism he chose to expound Wordsworth,[21] and in an essay on the "Aesthetic Consciousness" went so far as to assert that the sense of the beautiful has cognitive value. "We see [Nature] . . . through the poet's eyes and much of truth that might have escaped us becomes our own."[22] The aesthetic sense, according to Sneath, is a creative energy and the order and beauty which it imposes upon the world of nature is not simply a projection but an intuition of reality which can subsequently be largely verified by observation.[23]

One can readily see how one with these assumptions would stress in religious education on the one hand the moral and on the other hand the approach to God through every channel and not the least through nature. This approach is evident in the two series of graded materials which Sneath edited, the King's Highway Series already mentioned and the Golden Rule Series. Nearly half a million copies of these books were sold.

Sneath did a prodigious amount of editing of works in the field of religion at varying levels. He projected many ventures only some of which were realized. He had an extraordinary capacity for enlisting collaborators and getting from them the best.[24] He was himself a man of independent means and gave his own services to the School. His irresistible enthusiasms enlisted the funds which made possible the Stephen Merrell Clement Professorship in Christian Methods, the Horace Bushnell Professorship of Christian Nurture and the Shattuck and Samuel Thorne Lectureships in Religious Education. His greatest gift to the School was a vindication of his faith in the indirect method. It was he who lured Luther Allan Weigle to shift his interest from philosophy to religious education and thus made possible the invitation to Weigle to join the faculty of the Divinity School of which he was to become the eminent dean.[25]

Weigle's philosophy of religious education stemmed from Horace Bushnell whose *Christian Nurture* he re-edited. Together with his later colleague, Robert Seneca Smith, Weigle deserves largely the credit of saving the Religious Education movement from the instrumentalism of John Dewey then rampant. Weigle conceived the department of Religious Education in a divinity school to assist ministers to think of their entire work in educational terms and specifically to prepare them to train their own Sunday School teachers. In addition some students should be equipped for posts as directors of religious education in the churches, and others for service in higher education or in educational administration.[26]

MISSIONS: HARLAN P. BEACH AND YOUNGER COLLEAGUES

Harlan P. Beach, the first incumbent of the chair of Missions, was a link with the Puritan age. Born in 1854 he was trained for college at Phillips Andover Academy where he saw Harriet Beecher Stowe in the pew and listened to such men in the pulpit as Noah Porter, ex-president Woolsey, Samuel Harris, Wendell Phillips, and Phillips Brooks. At Yale he sat also under Leonard Bacon, George Park Fisher, and heard the preaching of Theodore T. Munger. Beach's diary from 1870 to 1876 is marked by the introspection of the Puritan journal.[27] On January 1, 1873, he reports: "I begin a new year with this clean page, but before the end is through this book will see many blots and so it will be with my life." He notes ruefully having snickered in church when a classmate passed around crackers and then toothpicks, and of suffering himself to be distracted on the day of prayer by the presence of Female Seminarians. A Sabbath had been misspent in that he went in the morning to an Episcopal church and in the evening took a girl walking. "I am sorry I walked with her on Sunday night."

His first impulse to a missionary career was prompted by learning that twenty years before his birth a missionary member of the family had been eaten by South Sea Islanders. In 1883 Beach and his wife were sent to North China by the American Board. There they labored for seven years until her health necessitated a return. During the first year in China Beach mastered two thousand six hundred characters and before he left had a command of five thousand. He was nominated to the committee for the revision of the Mandarin Bible despite his rugged Puritan insistence that no tampering should be allowed with the meaning of the word of God in order to render the Gospel more palatable to the Chinese who took amiss the text, "He that loveth Father and Mother more than me is not worthy of me." On the other hand he was more than ready to avoid needless offense to Oriental suceptibilities, as, for example, in the pictorial representation of Joseph with bare legs. Beach was responsible for founding one of the two first YMCA's in China. The labors of the Beaches bore such fruits that when the Boxer Rebellion broke in 1900 one hundred and fifty of the native martyrs came from their station.

After returning to the United States and teaching for a time, he became a secretary of the Student Volunteer Movement. From 1895 to 1906 he exerted an influence on twleve thousand students. For their instruction he commenced a series of handbooks on the various mission fields and more pretentious works largely of a statistical nature. One which enjoyed an immense vogue was entitled A *Geography and Atlas of Protestant Missions*. When he came to Yale in 1906 he was easily the best-informed man in the world with regard to global Christianity.[28]

On coming to the Divinity School he insisted that he be allowed to devote one-third of his time to the mission fields. In particular he should visit Yale-in-China every third year. This school had grown out of the Student Volunteer Movement. In addition, Beach made a tour of the Levant in 1910, and of Africa in 1912, and in 1916 attended in Panama a conference of Protestant missionaries to South America. The volume reporting the sessions entitled *Renaissant Latin America*[29] was from his pen. Beach's primary concern in missions was evangelization. He believed in the finality of Christianity and shared the urgency of his age to win the world for Christ in that generation. At the same time he was not indifferent to the social impact of missions and in his thinking combined Darwinian evolution, the theory of progress, and Christian evangelization. Fifty years of missionary work in the Hawaiian Islands he averred has "metamorphosed raw heathen into material for a Christian state. Christianity becomes the adjuvant of inexorable law and not only enables the fittest to survive in increasing strength, but also imparts to the unfit that divine capacity which often makes them leaders among the most fit. It takes the outcaste of India whose ancestors since the Laws of pre-Christian Manu have been despised and rejected of men, with little religion and less mentality, and makes him the teacher of Sudra children, or even of Brahmin boys and girls."[30]

Beach had a statesmanlike grasp for missionary problems. In the Far East he was fully alive to incipient nationalism and to the desire of the indigenous churches for independence. He was particularly insistent that missionaries should not present an occidentalized Christianity.[31] He voiced impatience with western denominationalism, for what can those who worship cows and monkeys be expected to grasp of the differences between Anglican and Non-conformists? He reported with enthusiasm those church unions on the mission field which presaged the world-wide ecumenical movement.[32] The role of the missionary as the redresser of wrongs perpetrated by his countrymen touched him especially in Africa where first the whites had stolen Africans from Africa and now were stealing Africa from the Africans. Yet he was never indiscriminate in denunciation and recognized that in a large section of Africa the *Pax Britannica* had occasioned an immense increase in the African population—another problem.

As a teacher Beach was very engaging, a jovial man with an abdominal chuckle. On one of the stunt nights Frank Porter was set over against Beach in a feather-blowing contest. Beach proved to have "superior wind."[33] He had a Chinese leisureliness of speech—said the Chinese

Harlan P. Beach

felt cheated if an address ended in less than three hours. And he knew how to sustain attention by interspersing diverting yarns. He told of an African missionary who was puzzled when a native presented Silias as his name for baptism. The missionary was for changing it to Silas, but the African was right. His master had called him Silly Ass. On the scholarly side one of Beach's greatest works was the building up of the Day Missions Library[34] which did so much to facilitate the distinguished studies of his successor, Kenneth Scott Latourette.

A younger colleague of Beach was John Clark Archer who moved increasingly into the field of comparative religion.

Personal Evangelism: Henry B. Wright

"Christian Methods" was a new field introduced in 1914 to enlist most advantageously the services of Henry B. Wright. It was called the Stephen Merrell Clement chair, the funds, as we have noted, having been secured by Sneath. The teaching career of Henry B. Wright had been spent hitherto in Yale College in the field of classics, both Latin and Greek. Like his father, Dean Wright, Henry had been engaged also in administration, for a time as the secretary of the Yale YMCA and then as secretary of the University until the coming of Anson Phelps Stokes. Wright's excellence as a scholar and an executive passed, however, almost unnoticed because he was so pre-eminently a fisher of men. He was in the succession of the elder Dwight, Nathaniel W. Taylor, and Moses Stuart, and most notably of Chauncey Goodrich, in bringing Yale undergraduates to a Christian decision.

Henry B. Wright

Whether in student conferences, in his office, or in his home he was constantly wrestling with the wayward. George Stewart in his *Life of Henry B. Wright* says: "When men came to him with problems to be solved, he would listen thoughtfully, his dark eyes filled with dignified concern, quickly lighting up with sympathy when the narration of events became difficult or embarrassing for his visitors. He suffered and groped with his friends for solutions to their difficulties, but he was as eager before a vexed moral tangle as the scientist in unraveling one of the mysteries of nature."[35]

There was nothing obtrusive about his winning of souls. Dean Brown said of him: "He was a lovable saint. He was never harsh, censorious, intolerant as saints sometimes have been. Some of the saints may be all right when they get to heaven—I hope so—but they were not comfortable people to have around here on earth. Henry Wright was stern and strict with himself regarding his own conduct, but toward the moral failures of others he was patient, kindly, tolerant. He could always find some extenuating circumstance, some mitigating fact which caused him to look charitably upon the faults of his fellow-men."[36]

Henry Wright's pre-eminence in Christian work on the Yale campus was well known at the Divinity School because when Benjamin Bacon was made pastor of the College Chapel he discovered that actually the unofficial pastor was Henry B. Wright. Bacon all the more gladly welcomed him to the faculty of the Divinity School.

One might wonder whether the subject Henry came to teach could be taught, because he said himself that religion is imparted by contagion, not taught by words. But he did give courses and he had to hammer them out without precedent. The load was the greater because he had only just recovered from an attack of pulmonary tuberculosis. Together with Sneath and Macintosh he gave a course entitled "The Psychology, Message and Methods of Public Evangelism," primarily a study of such men as Edwards, Whitefield, Wesley, Finney, Bushnell, and Moody. Another course was called "The Principles of Personal Evangelism." With William R. Bailey he conducted a course called "Rural Sociology," for which Henry was prepared by his contacts with men in every walk of life in the village of Oakham, Massachusetts. "Leadership of Voluntary Bible Study Groups" was another course. One of the most significant developments was instruction designed to prepare men for trained leadership in the YMCA. This was a layman movement often manned by laymen, distinguished in zeal, deficient in understanding. In the field of religion on the college campus Henry Wright gave two courses, "The Religious Aspects of University Teaching" and "Religious Aspects of Student Problems," and thereby he opened a field to be enormously developed by his successor, Clarence Prouty Shedd.

Religious Literature: Charles A. Dinsmore

In 1920 Charles Allen Dinsmore was given a professorial assignment in the field of Religious Literature, including the Bible as literature, and religion in the poets. Dinsmore had a very sensitive feeling for the literary quality of the Bible and was very insistent that it should be conserved in translation. On the occasion of the Tyndale celebration he remarked, "Tyndale's peculiar contribution to the English Bible is that occult, indefinable something we call charm. If we try to break that illusive word into its elements, charm certainly includes lucidity of expression, the natural rhythm of deep emotion, the inevitable euphony of intense sincerity, the perfect phrase which allows the thought to be revealed, not in utter nakedness, but trailing all its clouds of glory."[37]

The last phrase, of course, is Wordsworthian. One might suppose that when Dinsmore turned to religion in the poets he would, like Porter and Sneath, address himself to Wordsworth among the first. Instead Dinsmore wrote a book entitled *Great Poets and the Meaning of Life*[38] in which he began with Homer, ended with Shakespeare, and centered on Dante. Here lay the passion of his life. To Dante he consecrated several volumes.[39] The kind of religion which one finds in the poets is likely to be different if one starts in the *Inferno* rather than at *Grassmere*.

In 1933 Dinsmore lamented that "for the past two generations there has been a pronounced waning of the consciousness of the exceeding sinfulness of sin. And as for the Atonement, it is not a living issue."[40] To this theme he devoted his work *The Atonement in Literature and Life* in which he affirmed that the atoning death of Christ is something more than that which is repeatable in human experience. "It is God who forgives! and we have an instinctive feeling that there are depths in his pardon which show no recognizable elements in human mercy. It is God who loves! and even the purest and noblest human love fails to image the glory of the divine. It is God who suffers! and the plummet of man's grief drops but a little way in the abyss of that agony. The cross of Christ must perforce be interpreted by human experience, as this affords us our only insight into its meaning, but the power of the cross lies in those depths and heights which transcend experience. All that we see gives us a sense of the unseen, and what brings the penitent to his knees, and then lifts him up and sends him on his way with exceeding joy, is not the clearness of his knowledge, but the compelling consciousness that there are abysses of sorrow which he cannot fathom, and vast ranges of grace which tower where his thought may not climb. The heart is awed in the presence of these unrevealed mysteries, is tempered and exalted by them, and finds their incomprehensible greatness an unfailing source of strength."[41]

In his baccalaureate sermon to the graduating class of the Divinity School in 1933 he declared: "We believe that the light that shone in the face of Jesus Christ was not a transient splendor, but was the grace and truth of a glory that existed before the world began. In him we behold the Eternal. The cross on Calvary is a symbol of a cross that is forever in the heart of God. We believe that the Lamb was slain from the foundation of the world; that the nature of the Infinite which is akin to ours is working in humanity through the ages towards some purpose of unimagined grandeur."[42]

Dinsmore was reaffirming Bushnell with a new emphasis. Bushnell's concern had been to moralize the doctrine of the Atonement against those who held crudely substitutionary views. Dinsmore's concern was to revive the doctrine against those who felt no need for Atonement at all. In his latter days he was a lonely man. He would be better understood today by the rebels against the shallower aspects of Liberalism.

CHAPTER XIX

The Social Life and the
Social Order

The idea of the Holy Commonwealth at Yale never receded into the haze which sometimes obliterates East Rock. But the form continually changed. In the twentieth century Yale was no longer the center of the Connecticut community with a Congregational complexion. The influx of Irish, Poles, and Italians had given the community a Catholic preponderance. The constituency of the Divinity School was less in the immediate environs and more in the country and the world at large. But a sense of community was there, first in the School itself and then distributed throughout the land.

Fellowship within the school was easy to cultivate because the numbers were not great—a student body of around one hundred twenty-five, and a faculty of fourteen. For the most part the students lived in the dormitories, since few were married. Dean Brown strenuously discouraged marriage prior to graduation, declaring that he had seven reasons against it, one for each day of the week.[1] The sacred number since his day has proved quite ineffectual as a deterrent. In the earlier day students all ate at the Commons. Faculty homes were not remote. The Porters were thought to have gone to *Ultima Thule* when they built on Bradley Street. The frontier was further extended when Brown, Bacon, and Walker became established on Edwards Street. Such distances were easy to be encompassed. The "softies," Bacon and Porter, rode bicycles. The "hardies," Walker and Brown, went on foot four times a day. They went home for lunch cutting diagonally across the Pierson Sage Square, then an open field save for the Hillhouse mansion on the crest and the Osborn Laboratory on the corner. Faculty-student relationships were informal and when Professor Porter retired, the men presented him with an armchair, hoisted him into it, and carried chair and professor up to the home on Bradley Street. On Sunday afternoons students sauntered to Edwards Street to call on Mrs. Brown. The Dean was usually off preaching while she graced the table for tea.

Social events may in those days have been no more frequent than now. They stand out the more perhaps by reason of the selectivity of memory. The year opened with a picnic at Double Beach, when the Brownites played ball against the Tweedyites.[2] In 1916 the latter lost through excessive courtesy of the in-field.[3]

During the year stunt night was portentous. The institution was formally inaugurated on the 10th of February, in 1911, with ex-president Dwight delivering words of felicity. The faculty took part. Mockery was directed at the Yale Historical Pageant in which the nineteenth century was represented by Darwin as a monkey in burlap. The creature's tail proved refractory and Darwin was picked up bodily by the outraged faculty and thrown into the hall. Humor today has become more sophisticated. Another "interlude was presented now by the faculty members, under the personal direction of Mrs. Williston Walker. The faculty of the Civil War period were gathered with a handful of students for a formal reception. A discussion of the slavery question speedily began between Professor Leonard Bacon (in the person of Prof. B. W. Bacon, his grandson and successor) and the pastor of the Center Church (Professor Walker under a thicket of gray whiskers). Neither would yield ground and the debate ended in a draw."[4] Thus did the second generation wax merry over the issues which had distracted their fathers.

THE SOCIAL ORDER

By the nineteen twenties the social order in the city of New Haven had come to embrace the submerged groups in new form. There was no longer a Little Algeria near the Quinnipiac. Negroes now occupied the Dixwell Avenue area. The lower Green and Grand Avenue had been taken over by the Italians. The Oak Street area was conglomerate. Churches and settlements endeavored to minister to these groups. The

Church of the Redeemer conducted Welcome Hall on Oak Street. Center Church supported the Davenport Church and settlement in the Italian district on the lower Green. There were several Italian Protestant churches. Mrs. Porter organized Neighborhood House near St. Paul's Church on Chapel Street. Divinity students were engaged in all of these enterprises. Scholarship aid was conditioned upon eight hours a week of such activity. These assignments together with work in the YMCA and supply preaching constituted the field work of that period.

Instruction on social questions was given by William B. Bailey. His attention was directed mainly to amelioration and alleviation. In discussing opportunities for social work he enumerated the efforts to aid the needy and the delinquent through the social agencies, boys clubs, reform schools, and other movements.[5] He was sanguine over the ability of the churches and society to correct social ills and in 1921 expressed the hope that the liquor problem, having been solved, could soon be dropped from the curriculum in favor of the Negro problem.[6] The measure of insight attained by that generation as to the nature of the ills in the social fabric is disclosed in an address by a visiting lecturer in 1924, who enumerated the five great evils menacing our society: prostitution, liquor lawlessness, gambling, sensual movies, political corruption or bossism.[7]

The great social problem of that period was World War I and its aftermath. War is always the enemy of reform because it diverts energies from corrective endeavors and creates so many new maladies to be corrected.

The faculty of the Divinity School all favored American participation in the struggle with Germany. Pacifism has no lineage at Yale and in general throughout American Christianity the mood of that war was crusading. Yale men were indeed more moderate than some of the voices in the pulpits of the land. Basic for all was the belief that war may be an instrument of justice and that in this instance it was. Stories of German atrocities were uncritically accepted. On the part of the United States participation in the war was viewed as "national self-sacrifice for the sake of international redemption." Righteousness, liberty, democracy, abiding peace through a League of Nations, were the sanguine hopes of Allied success.[8]

The faculty served in various roles—Henry Wright as Director of

Religious Work at Camp Devons, Douglas Macintosh went twice as a religious worker with the Canadian troops, Archer was with the YMCA in Mesopotamia, and Dahl at Camp Devons.[9] Macintosh sent to the *Yale Divinity Quarterly* a report of what he had seen in Somme region. "It is difficult to imagine what use can ever be made of this region again. Where towns and villages stood, there is no longer the first sign of a house. Everything has been blown to fragments or buried beneath the chalk which has been churned up over and over again by bursting shells. Over large areas the surface soil has disappeared. . . . Here and there over the battlefield little wooden crosses were to be seen, marking the shell-made graves of unknown soldiers. Some of these shallow graves had been torn open again by exploding shells. Flocks of carrion crows flew hither and thither, competing with rats and the sanitary squads as scavengers. Close up to the edge of the shell hole, where strangely enough a little soil had been left, there bloomed some beautiful blue corn-flowers."[10]

The close of the war brought with it grave social problems and much searching of heart as to the propriety and effectiveness of war as an instrument of international justice and social reform. Macintosh more than any other on the faculty addressed himself to these questions. He was a fine example of the continuing association of the theological, evangelical, and social aspects of Christianity. He wrote several books on theology, one on personal religion, and one on social religion. In this latter work he commenced with an analysis of the social teaching of Jesus, rejecting alike the interpretation of the Sermon on the Mount as an interim ethic by Schweitzer and as a deferred ethic by Dibelius, to be held in abeyance until after the Kingdom was established, though Macintosh recognized that there may be Christian courses of action which are not feasible in a non-Christian society. For this reason the communism of the early Church may have failed. Reinhold Niebuhr was commended by his old teacher for grappling courageously with the ethic of Jesus, and "his idea of the 'relevance of an impossible ethical ideal' despite its paradox and its pessimism" was deemed "considerably closer to being a valid interpretation and application of the Sermon on the Mount than Schweitzer's notion that it is mere interim ethics." Nevertheless, the paradox of the "relevance of an impossible ideal" though apparently profound is actually specious. It is always incumbent upon us to do the best possible and this is possible and it is imperative, and all that the absolute ideal requires of us *now*.[11]

The problem of war engaged Macintosh in the aftermath as it had not during the conflict. He was disillusioned with regard to the atrocity stories and the operations of the "merchants of death," the munition makers. He discerned the vindictiveness of the Treaty of Versailles and became very sympathetic toward a thoroughgoing pacifism. At the same time he felt there might be situations in which the weak could be and should be protected through an exercise of armed force. The war on war would be won only through world government by way of the renunciation of national sovereignty. Within the confines of the nation he would enlarge the role of the state to alleviate the ills of a competitive society. He endorsed heartily the New Deal. Yet he perceived the dangers implicit for the liberties of the citizen and for the decade of the thirties became himself the outstanding symbol of the right of conscience over against totalitarian pretensions on the part of the state. The matter came up in connection with his application for citizenship in the United States. He was asked whether he would promise to take up arms in defense of his country. He had not hitherto been a pacifist. He was not now an absolute pacifist. In this area, as in epistemology, he was a critical pacifist. The record of his statement of the case as presented before the judge in New Haven on June 24, 1929, in response to the question, reads: " 'If necessary, are you willing to take up arms in defense of this country?' I had written, 'Yes, but I should like to be free to judge of the necessity.' . . . I had never taken the position of absolute pacifism, because I could not be sure that never under any possible circumstances would a defensive or police use of military force be justified; on the other hand, I was still surer that it would not be right for me to give a blanket promise beforehand that I would support any and every war in which the future Government of my country might engage. . . . I was ready to give the United States, in return for citizenship, all the allegiance I had ever given or could ever give to any country. Interpreting the will of God, however, as what is right and for the highest well-being of all humanity, I felt that I ought not to put my allegiance to any country, even my own, above my allegiance to the will of God, thus interpreted. I recognized the principle of the submission of the individual citizen to the opinion of the majority in political matters in a democratic country; but I did not believe in having my own moral opinions settled by the majority. . . . I felt that it would be only fair, as well as in accord with the Constitution and the laws of the United States, if I were to be allowed to become a naturalized citizen on the same free ethical basis as that enjoyed by the native-born citizen. In other words, just as the native-born citizen is a citizen without having had to promise beforehand that he will support any and every war which any future Government of the country may engage in during his lifetime, so, it seemed to me, the naturalized citizen should be a citizen who has not been required to make any immoral promise to do what might possibly seem wrong to him when the time came."[12] His petition was denied and the judgment of the Court in New Haven was sustained by the Supreme Court. Subsequently, there has been a reversal and today one who is willing to perform an alternate service may be admitted to citizenship in the United States. Macintosh might have been naturalized, but in the meantime he had suffered a paralytic stroke and was not well enough to avail himself of the new ruling. He died a Britisher.

CHAPTER XX

The Great Quarter of a Century

The last quarter of a century has been the greatest in the history of the Yale Divinity School. Yet despite the distinction of this period it will receive here only a highlighted and impersonal treatment. The reason is that an adequate account would require another volume and in any case a lapse of time is needful for the attainment of perspective.

The period has known two deans. Luther Allan Weigle served for twenty-one years, from 1928 to 1949, when he was succeeded by Liston Pope. The selection of these two men was indicative of a new emphasis. Both were taken, not from the parish ministry, but from the ranks of the teaching profession. Both were already serving on the faculty. At the time of Brown's coming, the decision to call an eminent minister was wise, but in 1928 the need was to raise the educational standards of the school to a par with the other departments of the University.

Dean Weigle and President Angell embarked with hearty accord on this endeavor. The President agreed that the School should share fully in all of the resources of the University and like other departments might operate on a deficit budget. The Divinity School had endowments of its own and Dean Brown had felt obligated to live within their income, but the assumption throughout the University came to be that expansion and the equalization of departments should be financed from general funds. In these the Divinity School was to share, as well as in enlarged benefactions. Five hundred thousand came from the University campaign, a million from John D. Rockefeller, Jr., and two and a half million from the Sterling trustees.

These gifts made possible the new quadrangle on Prospect Street. The old buildings on College and Elm, once heralded as "a permanent habitation," had long since been antiquated, and the site was desired by the University for Calhoun College. The summit of Prospect Street afforded grounds sufficiently spacious for the buildings then to be constructed and for the expansion ultimately contemplated. In Georgian Colonial, a style simple and functional, dormitories were provided for the unmarried men and buildings for administration and teaching in addition to a refectory, gymnasium, library, and a chapel chaste and worshipful. A symbol of the share the alumni accepted in the undertaking is to be found at the intersections of the walks in the millstones shipped from New Hampshire by George Stewart, Jr.

The School, thus handsomely treated by the University, set out to measure up to all of the educational requirements of the institution. Entering students were required to have a B.A. degree and could receive no advanced standing by reason of work done in college. They might, in view of previous courses, be accorded a greater range of electives, but for graduation must complete the full complement. Henceforth students were not to be recruited but attracted by the reputation of the School. The time had come when this step might be ventured because Brown's recruitment had started the flow of a continuing stream and the alumni of the School in churches and colleges already constituted a recruiting agency. Dean Weigle's step was so abundantly justified that in 1930 the decision was reached to limit the enrollment and to practice selective admission. Since then, sometimes one-third and sometimes even one-half of the applicants have had to be denied. The maximum enrollment has advanced, however, from three hundred to four hundred. The war, here as elsewhere, played a large role in the expansion because the students came from military service to complete interrupted professional training and were the better able to do so because of aid under the G. I. bill. The needs of the churches also played a part because throughout the country there was and is a dearth of adequately trained men. Were the School to double its size, all of the graduates could be placed and vacancies in the churches would still remain. But there is a limit to size in educational effectiveness and even the present numbers diminish those intimacies which are of the essence of the learning process. Better to develop other seminaries than that anyone should embark on mass production. The firm resolve of the school is not to exceed four hundred.

In 1931 in the interest of higher educational standards the curriculum was revised and the number of courses taken by a student at a given time was reduced. Prior to Dean Weigle's administration, the student normally took eight courses of two hours each; the year was divided into two semesters. This scheme was replaced by three terms and the normal load came to be four courses with the hours in class variable. Language courses met four times a week, lecture courses three, and seminars two. By this arrangement the student might have as few as eight hours a week in class and seldom more than fourteen. Under Dean Pope the semester plan has been restored in order to conform to the schedule of the University, but the restriction of the courses to four and the flexibility as to hours in class have been retained.

One result of these measures has been to introduce a greater stability into the student body. Whereas previously a high percentage of the students stayed only for one year, the more stringent educational demands persuaded them of the necessity of three continuous years. From 1925 to 1931 the average annual enrollment was two hundred thirty-three of whom only ninety-nine were returning students, whereas from 1931 to 1941, with practically the same enrollment, the number of those returning was one hundred forty-two. The student body under the selective process is of the highest quality, both academically and in every other regard.

In 1932 women were admitted as candidates for the B.D. degree. Since that time they have numbered about 10 per cent. Twenty years later, in 1952, a study of the two hundred fifty-two women who had been enrolled disclosed that only 36 per cent had obtained their degrees. Marriage accounted for 40 per cent of the withdrawals. In academic performance the women are above the average of the school. They are harder to place in field work, earn less and make a greater demand on the scholarship funds of the school. They put their training to good use as ministers' wives, directors of religious education, and teachers of religion in colleges and on the mission field. Recently the degree of M.R.E.,

Master of Religious Education, obtainable in two years, has been introduced primarily to provide a public accreditation to those women who cannot remain for three years, but the degree is open to all students. The degree of S.T.M., Master of Sacred Theology, has been established in recognition of a fourth year of theological study.

The number of married students has advanced since World War II. The percentage just before the war was 29 per cent. In recent years it has become stabilized at around 48 per cent. Academically, the married students do better than the unmarried. Financially they are often in difficulties because they always come on the assumption of optimum conditions.

The student body is derived not primarily from the indigent or the affluent but from the middle brackets with a goodly number from the ranks of the professions. Commonly forty-three states are represented and sometimes as many as sixteen foreign countries. The number of colleges of which the students are graduates numbers as high as two hundred twenty-three. Of late the largest contingent has come from Yale College which is a striking change from earlier years and significant evidence that the School is not without honor in its own University. The number of denominations fluctuates at around thirty-four. The Methodists throughout the quarter of a century and longer have held the lead. For some time the second place was held by the Disciples, then came Baptists, Congregationalists, Presbyterians, Lutherans, and next a sprinkling from varied bodies. Latterly the Congregationalists and Presbyterians have been tied for second place, with the Disciples in the fifth. The Presbyterians have just come into second place. The Episcopalians have come up in six years from one to eighteen regular students in addition to the twenty-five from the Berkeley Divinity School enrolled in courses.

The very complexion of the School makes a great contribution to the ecumenical movement. There is not much shifting of denominational allegiances by reason of this mingling, but there is an advance in mutual understanding and respect. Occasionally there is something of a clash which manifests itself not so much in theology and deportment as in liturgics. Some desire not only a divided chancel but two men, one for the pulpit and one for the reading desk. Some would like an altar rail in a chancel where there is not room to deploy and others wish to stand behind a communion table. Some hanker after vestments, others prefer a plain suit and a not too somber tie. But most are ready to enter devoutly into now one and now another form of worship and there is no chapel service in the country—so say the itinerants—which is better attended or conducted with greater reverence. There are advantages and disadvantages in an interdenominational seminary. The graduate may perhaps feel less intimately bound to his own fellowship, but this tends to be prevented by the provision of courses in the history, doctrines, and polity of the various denominations, taught by officers of these bodies, and by the cultivation of denominational clubs within the seminaries. On the other hand, the graduate is almost certain to find himself afterward in a local ministerial association in which there will be Yale alumni in other pulpits of the same city. Likewise the white and colored pastors in the same area will have had their training in the same school.

The faculty during this quarter century has increased in numbers without diminishing in quality. The achievement in the classroom and the literary output cannot be assayed without extensive personal reference which has been deliberately excluded here. In the affairs of the churches, members of this faculty have been active as sponsors, chairmen, instigators, and architects of such bodies as the American Northern Baptist Convention, the Federal Council of Churches, the National Council of Churches, the World Council of Churches, the American Association of Theological Schools, the International Council of Religious Education, the World Sunday School Association, and the Committee of the Revised Standard Version of the Bible. They cannot be accused of taking their ease in the tranquil retirement of a blissful hilltop.

Abandonment of the old apprenticeship system in 1822 created a deficiency in theological training which was not seriously remedied for over a century. In 1928 a full-time director of field work was appointed with the task of combining educational training and student self-support. Undeniably for a large proportion of the students, field work is an economic necessity. In addition to the rise in living costs the integration of the Divinity School with the University has come to entail a tuition charge of four hundred dollars. The students and their wives are industrious and resourceful. During the year 1954-55 86 per cent were engaged in remunerative field work. The average earnings per student during the school year were just under eight hundred dollars and the earning of students and wives for the entire year totaled $552,775. The director of field work endeavors to secure employment which will provide valuable training. The churches and the YMCA are highly co-operative. An even more important task of the director is to furnish supervision for apprenticeships. Here the director supplements his own endeavors by enlisting the aid of pastors, YMCA directors, visiting fellows and other competent friends. The adjustment of the field work load to the academic schedule of the student is carefully scrutinized. Those heavily involved have long been required to reduce the academic load and remain for a fourth year. None is permitted to take the B.D. degree without a period of field work regardless of remuneration.

The war brought special problems and opportunities. The Divinity School remained in session during the summer throughout the war years to prepare men more rapidly for service in the chaplaincy and in the churches. Special training was given to candidates for the naval chaplaincy under a program devised by the navy. The war and its attendant convulsions together with the spread of communism have occasioned drastic changes in the status of missions, the requisite qualifications of missionaries, and the openings available in various lands. In consequence the rethinking of missions has become an annual assignment. Here Yale has been to the fore.

An increasing contribution of the Divinity School has been the preparation of men at the graduate level for teaching in colleges and seminaries. The alumni of the Divinity School have always been able to take a doctor's degree but until 1920 could do so only through the departments of Philosophy and Semitics. In that year in Dean Brown's administration two new departments were added, Religion and Religious Education. Douglas Macintosh was the prime mover in the first and Luther Weigle in the second. Recently these two have been merged. A survey made in 1954 of the Ph.D.'s in Religion, Religious Education, and cognate fields, such as Semitics, disclosed a total of three hundred seventy-two. Of this number thirty-five were college presidents and deans, one hundred and twenty-eight were college teachers, four were preparatory schoolteachers, fifteen were presidents or deans of theological seminaries, seventy were teaching in theological seminaries, thirteen were college chaplains, thirty-four were executives of denominational or inter-denominational organizations, thirty-one were pastors—observe that by no means all went into the teaching profession—fourteen were missionary teachers, four military chaplains, and the remaining twenty-four fall into miscellaneous categories.

Closely related to the preparation of teachers for colleges and seminaries is the development of religion in higher education. Yale has been pioneering in the creation of a department concerned to fit men to serve as college chaplains, campus YMCA workers, and teachers. During the thirty years prior to 1952-54, more than six hundred students had taken courses in this area. Many of them have since been located in teaching posts in colleges and have contributed no little to the revival of interest in religion on the part of undergraduates. The professors of the Divinity School in this field keep constant touch with the colleges and themselves conduct a veritable placement bureau.

Of the developments in Dean Pope's administration, the first is the stabilization of the faculty-student ratio. When Weigle became dean, the ratio was one faculty member to something over seventeen students. He brought it down to eleven, but the enormous increase of the students widened the gap in the year of his retirement to eighteen to one. Under Pope it was then reduced again to thirteen. This rectification of the balance was achieved by extensive appointments to the faculty of younger men. Between 1948 and 1954 the faculty increased 50 per cent and the average age was reduced from fifty-three to forty-four. The ages are now so well spaced that there is no reason to fear a devastating decimation of the faculty by anything short of a Black Death.

The other conspicuous achievement of the present deanship is the realization of the long-cherished plan for the extension of the plant. The increase of the student body from three to four hundred since the building of the quadrangle was most acutely felt in the library. The Corporation appropriated funds for linking the library with the gymnasium and converting the handball and squash courts into stacks. A gift from the Sealantic Fund has made possible the erection of a dormitory for unmarried women, three apartment houses for married students, and a residence for a faculty member.

With regard to the subjects peculiarly enlisting contemporary interest, the Bible and Biblical theology have experienced a renaissance. Although Hebrew and Greek are no longer required, they are voluntarily taken by at least 10 per cent. There are forty studying Greek. A seminar on Romans by a Continental exegete can command an attendance of over one hundred. In Biblical studies source analysis and form criticism have about reached their limit. Attention is now focused partly on archeology —witness the enormous interest aroused by the discovery of the Dead Sea Scrolls—but even before that, Gerash, Jericho, and Dura had excited the specialist. The other great interest is in the improvement of the Biblical text by the exploration of patristic data.

Theology has focused on the depravity of man and the revelation of God in Christ. Church history has turned to the discovery of meaning in the whole process, a philosophy of history. American church history has taken its place alongside European. At Yale the history of the expansion of Christianity has been accorded monumental treatment. In social ethics much attention of necessity is devoted to the contemporary questions of race relations and communism. The ethic of war was much canvassed when war was closer.

The study of human personality, handled with distinction by Hugh Hartshorne during the deanships of Brown and Weigle, has since developed in the direction of psychiatry and with specific reference to pastoral counseling.

The faculty of the School exhibits no uniformity and no cliques. There is a healthy interchange and none is of Paul, Cephas, or Apollos. The annual gathering at the commencement of the year at Seabury House provides two days of interchange continued throughout the year in evening discussions.

The achievement of a school is to be found in its alumni. Quite another volume would be required to describe their services to the churches. Dean Pope in his report for 1952-54 observed that no statistics can convey the quality of leadership which they exercise. "They are to be found," said he, "among the outstanding ministers in nearly every important city of the nation, as well as in other pastorates of small renown but high service. They are conspicuous in any missionary or ecumenical gathering. Four of the last seven Moderators of the Congregational Christian Churches have been alumni of the school (and eleven of the twenty-four clergymen to hold that post, the highest in Congregationalism, since 1865). The alumni rolls also include the names of the last Moderator of the Presbyterian Church, U. S.; the principal executive officers of the American Baptist Convention and the International Convention of the Disciples of Christ; the General Secretary of the National Council of Churches, and the chief educational officer of that organization; and the principal American in the secretariat of the World Council of Churches. The names of several bishops are included, and those of more than thirty college presidents and deans."

When over a quarter of a century ago Henry B. Wright completed his biographical catalog of the alumni he indulged in reflections which are even more abundantly true today. These are his words: "The writer's high privilege . . . [has been] to live over again with the 3,600 former students of the School their careers in pulpit and in parish, in class room, in executive's office, and in editor's chair. He has followed pioneer trails of undaunted souls, across and ever in advance of the receding national frontier. He has journeyed with lonely but brave hearts on sea and land, to the frozen North and over scorching desert sands. He has observed great-hearted, patient men putting their guiding hands, not upon eyes and ears and lips, but upon the groping fingers of blind and deaf and dumb, bidding them again see and hear and speak. . . . He has stood long by the scholar's desk and beheld the painstaking labor of years issue at last in revelations of living truth to perplexed human hearts through the ministry both of interpretation and translation. He has heard the ring of the excavator's pick and spade on the walls of buried cities and seen them yield their hidden treasures for our clearer understanding of the past. By the watchfires of circling camps in one generation, and in the darkness of mud-filled, shell-swept trenches in the next, in prisoner's cell, on ships that do business in great waters, to soldier, and sailor, and immigrant, to black man and red man and brown man and yellow man, in crowded city slum and in lonely farmhouse, he has heard the ministers of a living God proclaim the message of hope and opportunity for all. And he has never once forgotten that the men who were willing to do these things were trained for the Christian ministry."

Notes

Chapter I. This Grand Errand

1. Increase Mather, *Ichabod* (Boston, 1702), pp. 71, 86. Samuel Willard, *The Peril of the Times Displayed* (Boston, 1700).
2. Cotton Mather, *Magnalia Christi Americana* (reprint Hartford, 1820), I, 59.
3. Solomon Stoddard, *The Efficacy of the Fear of Hell* (Boston, 1713), p. 9.
4. Mather, *Magnalia*, I, 26.
5. *Calvini Opera*, XLV, 49-50.
6. Thomas Lechford, *Plain Dealing* (London, 1642); reprint Boston, 1867, ed. J. H. Trumbull, p. 19.
7. Cf. Isabel M. Calder, "The Authorship of a Discourse . . . ," *American Historical Review* XXXVII (1931-32), 267-69.
8. Edward Winslow, *Good Newes from New-England* (London, 1624), end of the dedication.
9. William Bradford, *Of Plymouth Plantation*, Samuel Eliot Morison, ed. (New York, 1952), pp. 75-76.
10. Stoddard, *A Treatise Concerning Conversion* (Boston, 1719), pp. A2-A3.
11. Stoddard, *The Efficacy of the Fear of Hell*.
12. Art. "Solomon Stoddard," *Dictionary of National Biography*.
13. Stoddard, *The Doctrine of Instituted Churches* (London, 1700), p. 27.
14. Charles Chauncy, *God's Mercy Shewed to His People* (Cambridge, New England, 1655).
15. Mather, *Magnalia*, II, 281-82.
16. Charles McLean Andrews, *The Colonial Period of American History* (New Haven, 1936), II, 104-5.
17. Williston Walker, *The Creeds and Platforms of Congregationalism* (New York, 1893), pp. 502-3.
18. Franklin Bowditch Dexter, *Documentary History of Yale University* (New Haven, 1916), pp. 164, 170.
19. Edwin Oviatt, *The Beginnings of Yale* (New Haven, 1916), p. 57.
20. Dexter, *op. cit.*, p. 17.
21. *Ibid.*, p. 27. Italics mine.
22. The first attempt to identify the books donated in 1701 was made by Ezra Stiles in 1784 (College Records, Yale Library MS Vault Sect. VII. Drawer 1.).
23. Dexter, *op. cit.*, p. 32.
24. Ames, *Medulla Theologica* (Amsterdam, 1648), p. 182.
25. Dexter, *op. cit.*, p. 193.

26. Anne Pratt, "The Books Sent by Jeremiah Dummer to Yale College," in *Papers in Honor of Andrew Keogh* (New Haven, 1938), p. 435.
27. *Ibid.*, p. 424.
28. *Ibid.*, p. 464.
29. See Dummer's protestation that the list was not weighted, in Dexter, *op. cit.*, p. 241.
30. Pratt, *op. cit.*, p. 439.
31. *Ibid.*, p. 455.
32. *Ibid.*, p. 444.
33. Mather, *Magnalia*, I, 229, and preface by John Higginson, p. 11.
34. Herbert and Carol Schneider, ed., *Samuel Johnson, His Career and Writings* (New York, 1929), I, 13.
35. *Ibid.*, p. 14.
36. Dexter, *op. cit.*, p. 226.
37. Thomas Clap, *The Annals or History of Yale College* (New Haven, 1766), p. 32.
38. Joshua L. Chamberlain, *Yale University* (Boston, 1900), p. 57.
39. Franklin, Bowditch Dexter, ed., *The Literary Diary of Ezra Stiles* (New York, 1901), I, 205-6. All quotes from this work appearing here have been modernized.
40. Andrew Keogh, *Bishop Berkeley's Gift of Books to Yale in 1733* (Oslo, 1933), p. 129.
41. Schneider, *op. cit.*, I, 27.
42. George Hunston Williams, ed., *The Harvard Divinity School* (Boston, 1954), pp. 295-351.
43. Clifford K. Shipton, ed. *Sibley's Harvard Graduates* (Boston, 1945), VII, 33.
44. *Ibid.*, VII, 45.
45. New London, 1754.
46. *Some Considerations tending to put an end to the Differences that have been about Singing by Rule*, Yale University Manuscript Collection (Z 36/218).

CHAPTER II. THE GREAT AWAKENING

Bibliography
Alexander V. G. Allen, *Jonathan Edwards* (Boston, 1890).

Leonard Bacon, *Thirteen Historical Discourses* (New Haven, 1839).

Ernst Benz, "The Pietist and Puritan Sources of Early Protestant World Missions (Cotton Mather and A. H. Francke)." *Church History* XX (1951), 23-55.

Charles Chauncy, *Seasonable Thoughts on the State of Religion in New England* (Boston, 1743).

Clarence H. Faust and Thomas H. Johnson, *Jonathan Edwards, Representative Selections* (New York, 1935).

John C. Feaver, *Edward's Concept of God as Redeemer* (Yale dissertation, 1949, unpublished).

Clyde Amos Holbrook, *The Ethics of Jonathan Edwards* (Yale dissertation, 1944, unpublished).   .

Samuel Johnson, *Samuel Johnson, His Career and Writings*, ed. Herbert and Carol Schneider, 3 vols. (New York, 1929).

Peter Y. de Jong, *The Covenant Idea in New England Theology* (Grand Rapids, 1945).

William Wakefield McKee, *The Idea of the Covenant in Early English Puritanism 1580-1643* (Yale Dissertation, 1948, unpublished).

Perry Miller, "The Half Way Covenant," *New England Quarterly* VI (1933), pp. 676-715.

Jonathan Edwards (New York, 1949).

Jonathan Edwards, Images or Shadows of Divine Things, ed. (New Haven, 1948).

"Jonathan Edwards on the Sense of the Heart," *Harvard Theological Review* XLI (1948), pp. 123-45.

"Jonathan Edwards and Emerson," *New England Quarterly Review* XIII (1940), pp. 589-617.

"The Marrow of Puritan Divinity," *Colonial Society of Massachusetts Publication* XXXII (1935), pp. 247-   .

The New England Mind, The Seventeenth Century (New York, 1939).

The New England Mind from Colony to Province (Cambridge, Mass., 1953).

Orthodoxy in Massachusetts (Cambridge, Mass., 1933).

"Preparation for Salvation in Seventeenth Century New England," *Journal of the History of Ideas* IV (1943).

"Solomon Stoddard, 1643-1729," *Harvard Theological Review* XXXIV (1941), pp. 277-320.

The Transcendentalists (Cambridge, Mass., 1950).

Donald Hosea Rhoades, *Jonathan Edwards: Experimental Theologian* (Yale, dissertation, 1945, unpublished).

Gottlob Schrenk, "Gottesreich und Bund im älteren Protestantismus," *Beiträge zur Förderung christlicher Theologie* 2 Reihe V (Gütersloh, 1923).

Harriet Beecher Stowe, *Old Town Folks* (Cambridge, Mass., 1896).

Leonard J. Trinterud, "The Origins of Puritanism," *Church History* XX (March, 1951), pp. 37-57.

Ola Elizabeth Winslow, *Jonathan Edwards* (New York, 1940).

1. Ola Winslow, *op. cit.*, p. 71.

2. *Ibid.*, p. 93.

3. Edwards, "Justification by Faith Alone," *Works* (Worcester, 1808-9), VII, 56, 128. Edwards was not at this point repudiating the Covenant theology which at its best was not contractual. Calvin did indeed suggest (*Opera* XLI, 131-35) that God fulfills the covenant to those who keep His commandments but John Ball asserted that God acts out of sheer grace (*A Treatise on the Covenant of Grace* [London, 1645]). John Preston said the covenant is not a compact forfeited by man's disobedience (*The New Covenant* [London, 1629], pp. 215, 19, 223, 99). Thomas Blake indeed insisted that faith, repentance, and sincerity are conditions (*Vindiciae Foederis; or a Treatise of the Covenant of God Entered with Man-Kinde* [London, 1653], pp. 26, 74-75, 93, 105, 112), but Tobias Crisp considered these to be no more than accompaniments (*Christ Alone Exalted* [London, 1755], I, 134, 151, 140-41) and such was the view of Edwards.

4. Edwards, "The Importance and Advantage of a Thorough Knowledge of Divine Truth," *op. cit.*, VIII, 9.

5. *Ibid.*, "A Divine and Supernatural Light," VIII, 298.

6. Cf. Samuel Willard, *A Compleat Body of Divinity* (Boston, 1726).

7. Edwards, "Memoirs of Mr. Edwards Life," *op. cit.*, I, 34-36.

8. Alexander V. G. Allen, *Jonathan Edwards* (Boston, 1890), p. 189.

9. Perry Miller, *HTR* XLI (1948), pp. 142-43.

10. G. P. Fisher, ed., *An Unpublished Essay of Edwards on the Trinity* (New York, 1903).

11. Edwards, "Dissertation Concerning the End for which God Created the World," *op. cit.*, VI, 31-124.

12. *Calvini Opera*, VIII, 606-7.
13. Edwards, "Sinners in the Hands of an Angry God," *op. cit.*, VII, 496.
14. *Ibid.*, "Men Naturally God's Enemies," p. 165.
15. *Ibid.*, p. 198.
16. Miller, *Jonathan Edwards*, pp. 84-93, and Allen, pp. 309-10, quoting Edwards, (Worcester, 1808, VI, 448-51).
17. Edwards, "Religious Affections," *ibid.*, IV, 183.
18. *Ibid.*, "True Grace Distinguished from the Experience of Devils," VII, 261.
19. *Ibid.*, "Religious Affections," IV, 201.
20. *Ibid.*, p. 203.
21. *Ibid.*, "The Excellency of Christ," VII, 280-81.
22. Edwards, *Remarks* (Edinburgh, 1796), p. 377-81.
23. Edwards, "Men Naturally God's Enemies," *Works* (Worcester, 1808), VII, 206.
24. *Ibid.*, "Justification by Faith Alone," pp. 19-21.
25. *Ibid.*, "Religious Affections," IV, 44.
26. Stowe, "Old Town Folks," *Writings* (Cambridge, 1896), IX, 29.
27. Edwards, "Sinners in the Hands of an Angry God," *Works*, VII, 495.
28. *Ibid.*, p. 496.
29. *Ibid.*, pp. 501-2.
30. Ola Winslow, *op. cit.*, p. 192.
31. Joseph Tracy, *The Great Awakening* (Boston, 1842), p. 13.

CHAPTER III.   NEW LIGHTS AND OLD

1. Edwards, *An Account of the Life of Mr. David Brainerd* (Edinburgh, 1798), pp. 24-25.
2. Cotton Mather, *Magnalia Christi Americana*, I, 503.
3. Stoddard, *QUESTION, Whether God is NOT Angry with the Country for Doing So Little Towards the Conversion of the Indians?* (Boston, 1723), p. 8.
4. Edwards, *Brainerd*, pp. 118-19.
5. *Ibid.*, pp. 499-500.
6. Joseph Tracy, *History of the American Board of Commissioners for Foreign Missions* (New York, 1842), pp. 7-10.
7. Edwards, *Brainerd*, p. 409.
8. *Ibid.*, p. 376.
9. *Ibid.*, p. 452.
10. *Ibid.*, p. 254.
11. *Ibid.*, pp. 36-37.
12. Ola Winslow, *op. cit.*, p. 188.
13. Allen, *op. cit.*, p. 134.
14. Edwards, *A History of the Work of Redemption* (Edinburgh, 1788), p. 341, and Ernst Benz, "The Pietist and Puritan Sources of Early Protestant World Missions (Cotton Mather and A. H. Francke)," *Church History*, XX (1951), 23-55.
15. Charles Chauncy, *Seasonable Thoughts on the State of Religion in New England* (Boston, 1743), pp. 98, 220-21, 249-50.
Cf. Leonard Bacon, *Thirteen Historical Discourses* (New Haven, 1839), p. 213.
16. Schneider, *op. cit.*, 1, 28.
17. Edwards, "Narrative of Surprising Conversions," *Works* III, 77-78.
18. *Ibid.*, "Religious Affections," IV, 79, 155.
19. *Ibid.*, "True Grace Distinguished from the Experience of Devils," VII, 248-49.
20. *Ibid.*, "Religious Affections," p. 167.

21. *Ibid.*, p. 170, slightly rearranged.
22. *Ibid.*, "True Grace Distinguished from the Experience of Devils," p. 247.
23. *Ibid.*, "Religious Affections," pp. 369-70.
24. *Ibid.*, p. 109.
25. *Ibid.*, p. 112.
26. George Leon Walker, "Jonathan Edwards and the Half-way Covenant," *New Englander* XLIII (1884), pp. 601-14.
27. Ola Winslow, *op. cit.*, pp. 221, 246.
28. Bacon, *op. cit.*, "Discourse XII."
29. Edwards, *Brainerd*, pp. 98-100.
30. Franklin Bowditch Dexter, *Documentary History of Yale University* (New Haven, 1916), p. 368-69.
31. *Ibid.*, pp. 369-70, November 19, 1744.
32. George Stewart, Jr., *A History of Religious Education in Connecticut . . .* (New Haven, 1924), p. 149.
33. *Ibid.*, Chap. V.
34. *Supra* p.
35. *Sibley's Harvard Graduates*, Clifford K. Shipton, ed. (Boston, 1945), VII, 39-40.

Chapter IV. A Learned Ministry

1. Clap, *The Annals or History of Yale-College in New Haven . . .* (New Haven, 1766), p. 84.
2. Stowe, "Old Town Folks," *The Writings of Harriet Beecher Stowe* (Cambridge, 1896), IX, 304-5.
3. *The Literary Diary of Ezra Stiles*, III, 102-3.
4. On Wollebius in the curriculum see William L. Kingsley, *Yale College* (New York, 1879), II, 496-98.
5. Stowe, *op. cit.*, p. 257.
6. Edwards A. Park, *Memoir of Nathanael Emmons* (Boston, 1861), p. 100, slightly recast.
7. *Works of Nathanael Emmons* (Boston, 1842), I, clviii-ix.
8. *The Original Library of Yale College*, Yale Library, Rare Book Room, MS Vault Sect. VII, Drawer 1, p. 19.
Through bindings and other marks Miss Anne Pratt was able to augment somewhat the list of Stiles. Her notes are in manuscript in the Memorabilia Room. She refers to but does not reproduce the original list in *The Library Gazette* XV, 2 (Oct., 1940), pp. 29-40.
9. *Papers in Honor of Andrew Keogh* (New Haven, 1938), contains:
Anne S. Pratt, "The Books Sent from England by Jeremiah Dummer to Yale College," pp. 7-44.
Louise May Bryant and Mary Patterson, "The List of Books Sent by Jeremiah Dummer," pp. 423-92.
Donald G. Wing and Margaret L. Johnson, "The Books Given by Elihu Yale in 1718," *Yale Library Gazette*, XII (1939), pp. 46-67.
Anne S. Pratt and Andrew Keogh, "The Yale Library of 1742," *Yale Library Gazette* XV (1941), pp. 29-40.
The List of Gifts by Sir John Davies, Yale Library, Rare Book Room, MS Vault Sect. 17:1.
"Bishop Berkeley's Gift of Books in 1733," *Yale Library Gazette* VIII, I (July, 1933), pp. 1-41.
Andrew Keogh, *Bishop Berkeley's Gift of Books to Yale in 1733* (Oslo, 1933).

10. Clap, A *Catalogue of the Library of Yale College in New Haven* (New London, 1743), preface.
11. Perkins, *The Whole Treatise of the Cases of Conscience* (London, preface 1606), p. 51.
12. Clarke, *Golden Apples* (London, 1659), p. 71.
13. Wollaston, *The Religion of Nature Delineated* (London, 1731), p. 79, slightly rearranged.
14. Davenport, *God's Call to His People to Turn Unto Him* (Cambridge, 1669), pp. 18-20.
15. *The Protestant Almanack for the Year from the Incarnation of Jesus Christ,* 1668 . . . (London 1668). Calendar for February.
16. John Ollyffe.
17. Thomas Paybody.
18. Sir John Hayward, *David's Teares* (London, 1623), p. 283.
19. Thomas Wilson, *Lord Bishop of Sodor and Man, The Knowledge and Practice of Christianity Made Easy . . . for the Indians* (London, 1741), p. 3.
20. John Clarke.
21. William Gouge, *Of Domesticall Duties* (London, 1622), pp. 235-36.
22. MS, Rare Book Room, Yale Library.
23. William L. Kingsley, *Yale College* (New York, 1879), I, 107.
24. Charles Hart Handschin, *The Teaching of Modern Languages in the United States of America* (Washington, 1913), pp. 17-24.

CHAPTER V. THE SCHOOLS OF THE PROPHETS

1. Mary Latimer Gambrell, *Ministerial Training in 18th Century New England* (New York, 1937), p. 138. William Orpheus Shewmaker, "The Training of the Protestant Ministry in the United States of America, Before the Establishment of Theological Seminaries," *Papers of the America Society of Church History* 2nd Ser. VI (1921).
2. Samuel Hopkins, *The Life and Character of the Late Reverend, Learned and Pious Mr. Jonathan Edwards* (Edinburgh, 1799), pp. 49-51.
3. Emmons, *Sermons* (Wrentham, Mass., 1800), pp. 234, 237-38, 245, 304.
4. Bellamy, *Works* (New York, 1811), I, 89-92. Hopkins, *Works* (Boston, 1852), II, 466-99.
5. Bellamy, *op. cit.*, I, 264-65.
6. Hopkins, *Works*, I, 249.
7. *Ibid.*, I, 512.
8. Emmons, *op. cit.*, p. 201.
9. *Ibid.*, p. 321.
10. Hopkins, *Works*, II, 295.
11. For Edwards' correspondence with his students see Stanley Williams, "Six Letters of Jonathan Edwards to Joseph Bellamy," *New England Quarterly* I (1928), pp. 226-42.
12. MS 1794, p. 14, Yale Sterling Library, Rare Book Room.
13. This passage from the manuscript has been supplied by the courtesy of Thomas A. Schafer who is preparing the definitive edition of the *Miscellanies* for the Yale Press. The passage with somewhat different readings is available in Harvey Gates Townsend, ed., *The Philosophy of Jonathan Edwards from his Private Notebooks* (University of Oregon, 1955), pp. 235-36.
14. Sereno E. Dwight, *The Life of President Edwards* (New York, 1830), pp. 173-85.
15. *Ibid.*, p. 159.

16. Stephen West, ed., *Sketches of the Life of the Late Rev. Samuel Hopkins* (Hartford, 1805), p. 65.
17. Hopkins, *Works*, I, 59.
18. Bellamy, *op. cit.*, I, 24.
19. Benjamin Trumbull, *History of Connecticut* (New Haven, 1818), II, 159-60.
20. Gambrell, *op. cit.*, pp. 108-15.
21. Bellamy, *Works* (Boston, 1853), I, lviii-lix. Gambrell, *op. cit.*, p. 135.
22. Helen Evertson Smith, *Colonial Days and Ways* (New York, 1901), pp. 226-29.
23. Emmons, *Works* (Boston, 1842), I, lviii-lix.
24. Edwards A. Park, *Memoir of Nathanael Emmons* (Boston, 1861), p. 112.
25. Emmons, *Works*, I, cxxii, cxxiv.
26. *Ibid.*, I, cxl.
27. *Ibid.*, I, lxiv.
28. *Ibid.*, I, clviii-xix.
29. Emmons, *Sermons*, pp. 291-92.
30. Emmons, *Works*, I, cxxxvi-cxlv. Some slight rephrasing.
31. *Ibid.*, I, cxxx.

Chapter VI. Revolution, Enlightenment, and New Light Restored

1. Henry Phelps Johnston, *Yale and Her Honor-roll in the American Revolution* (New York, 1888), pp. 8-11.
2. *Ibid.*, p. 95. William L. Kingsley, *Yale College* (New York, 1879), I, p. 100.
3. Johnston, *op. cit.*, pp. 107-8.
4. Ebenezer Baldwin, *History of Yale College* (New Haven, 1841), p. 103.
5. *Records of the Colony of New Plymouth in New England* (Boston, 1859), X, 26; Arthur H. Buffinton, "The Puritan View of War," *Publications of the Colonial Society of Massachusetts*, XXVIII (1930-33), pp. 67-86.
6. Cotton Mather, *Souldiers Counselled and Comforted* (Boston, 1689), p. 37.
7. James Cogswell, *God, the Pious Soldier's Strength and Instructor* (Boston, 1757), p. 7.
8. Amos Adams, *The Expediency and Utility of War* (Boston, 1759), p. 14.
9. Thomas Bridge, *The Knowledge of God, Securing from Flattery* (Boston, 1705), p. 50.
10. Thomas Prince, *Extraordinary Events the Doings of God, and Marvelous in Pious Eyes* (Boston, 1745), pp. 118, 23.
11. Samuel Woodward, *A Sermon Preached October 9, 1760, Being a Day of Public Thanksgiving on Occasion of the Reduction of Montreal and the Entire Conquest of Canada.* (Boston, 1760). Nathaniel Appleton, *A Sermon Preached October 9, Being a day of Public Thanksgiving Occasioned by the Surrender of Montreal, and all Canada* (Boston, 1760).
12. Roland H. Bainton, "Congregationalism—from the Just War to the Crusade in the Puritan Revolution," *Andover Newton Theological School Bulletin* (April, 1943).
13. Alice Mary Baldwin, *The Clergy of Connecticut in Revolutionary Days* (New Haven, 1936), p. 7.
14. *Ibid.*, pp. 8-9.
15. *Ibid.*, pp. 10-11, 16-17.
16. *Ibid.*, p. 28.
17. "Letters of a Westchester Farmer (1774-75), by the Reverend Samuel Seabury (1729-1796)," Clarence H. Vance, ed., *Publications of the Westchester County Historical Society* VIII (1930), pp. 45-46, 48 slightly rephrased, 61, 87.

18. E. Edwards Beardsley, *Life and Correspondence of the Right Reverend Samuel Seabury, D.D.* (Boston, 1881).
19. Samuel Griswald Goodrich, *Recollections of a Lifetime* (New York, 1856), I, 191 footnote.
20. Franklin Bowditch Dexter, ed., *The Literary Diary of Ezra Stiles* (New York, 1901), II, 209.
21. Abiel Holmes, *The Life of Ezra Stiles* (Boston, 1798), p. 79.
22. *Literary Diary*, III, 24-25.
23. *Ibid.*, II, 103.
24. *Ibid.*, I, 62.
25. *Ibid.*, II, 314.
26. *Ibid.*, I, 378 and III, 399-400.
27. *Ibid.*, II, 230.
28. *Ibid.*, I, 192.
29. *Ibid.*, I, 433.
30. Abiel Holmes, *op. cit.*, p. 78.
31. *Literary Diary*, II, 113-15.
32. *Ibid.*, III, 7-8.
33. The above topics are mentioned in the *Literary Diary* as follows: predestination II, 521; lie II, 389; war II, 323, 387 III, 148; polygamy III, 50, 309, 334; flood III, 333; unregenerate II, 509; sin II, 518; women in government III, 15, II, 490; toleration II, 287, III, 205, 255; censorship III, 291; slavery II, 395, III, 305; navigation III, 315; Shay's rebellion III, 256; Yale Corporation, III, 231.
34. *Ibid.*, III, 273-75.
35. Lyman Beecher, *Autobiography* (New York, 1864), I, 43.
    On Deism: Herbert M. Morais, *Deism in Eighteenth Century America* (New York, 1934); Gustav Adolph Koch, *Republican Religion* (New York, 1933); Woodbridge Riley, "The Rise of Deism in Yale College," *The American Journal of Theology*, IX (1905), pp. 474-83, is not very useful because he equates "natural religion" with Deism.
36. Timothy Dwight, *Travels; in New England and New York* (New Haven, 1821), IV, 365-68.
37. *Ibid.*, IV, 390-91.
38. S. G. Goodrich, *Recollections*, I, 348-49. On Dwight consult the sketch in the *DAB* and more particularly Charles E. Cuningham, *Timothy Dwight* (New York, 1942).
39. Timothy Dwight, *Theology Explained and Defended* (New York, 1830), I, 283-85.
40. *The Writings of Harriet Beecher Stowe*, "Old Town Folks" (Cambridge, 1896), IX, 126.
41. Timothy Dwight, *A Discourse on Some Events of the Last Century* (New Haven, 1801), p. 45.
42. George Park Fisher, *Life of Benjamin Silliman* (Philadelphia, 1866), I, 83.
43. Charles Roy Keller, *The Second Great Aweakening in Connecticut* (New Haven, 1942), p. 42.
44. *President Dwight's Decisions of Questions Discussed by the Senior Class in Yale College in 1813 and 1814* (New York, 1833), condensed.
45. Timothy Dwight, *Greenfield Hill* (New York, 1794), p. 41.

CHAPTER VII. THE DIVINITY SCHOOL

1. The history of the Divinity School for this period is covered by John Terrill Wayland, *The Theological Department in Yale College, 1822-1858* (unpublished Yale Ph.D. dissertation, 1933). Sketches of the faculty for this period are given by Timothy Dwight, *Memories of Yale Life and Men 1845-1899* (New York, 1903). *The Semi-Centennial Anniversary of the Divinity School of Yale College, May 15th and 16th, 1872* (New Haven, 1872) contains a historical address by George Park Fisher and sketches of the faculty.
2. William Warren Sweet, "The Rise of Theological Schools in America," *Church History* VI (1937), pp. 260-73.
3. Franklin Bowditch Dexter, ed., *The Literary Diary of Ezra Stiles* (New York, 1901), II, 415-16.
4. Consult the biography by Sidney Earl Mead, *Nathaniel William Taylor 1786-1858* (Chicago, 1942), and *Memorial of Nathaniel W. Taylor* (New Haven, 1858) with tributes by Leonard Bacon, S. W. S. Dutton and G. P. Fisher.
5. William B. Sprague, *Annals of the American Pulpit* (New York, 1859), II, 163.
6. Leonard Bacon in *Memorial of Nathaniel W. Taylor*, pp. 6-10.
7. Theodore Thornton Munger, "Dr. Nathaniel W. Taylor—Master Theologian," *Yale Divinity Quarterly* V, 3 (February, 1909), pp. 233-40.
8. Dwight, *Memories of Yale Life and Men 1845-1899*, pp. 274 and 76-83.
9. Wayland, *The Theological Department in Yale College, 1822-1859*, p. 92.
10. *Semi-Centennial*, pp. 74-75.
11. James Hadley, *Diary, 1843-1852* (New Haven, 1951), *passim*.
12. *Semi-Centennial*, pp. 76, 78.
13. Eleazar T. Fitch, *Sermons, Practical and Descriptive, Preached in the Pulpit of Yale College* (New Haven, 1871), pp. 8-9, 3.
14. Dwight, *Memories*.
15. Chauncey Goodrich, "Narrative of Revivals of Religion in Yale College," *American Quarterly Register* X (February, 1838), pp. 306-7.
16. Hadley, *Diary*, pp. 156-57.
17. *Semi-Centennial*, p. 83.
18. Dwight, *Memories*, pp. 265-66, 270-72.
19. Wayland, *The Theological Department*, p. 195.
20. Josiah Willard Gibbs, "Catholic Complaints against the Early Protestant Versions of the Scriptures," *The New Englander* X, N. S. IV (1852), pp. 300-308. Identified in Dexter, *Biographies 1805-15*, p. 255.
21. Dwight, *Memories*, pp. 20, 41-52.
22. *Ibid.*, pp. 181-184, 192.
23. *Ibid.*, p. 174.
24. Consult George Park Fisher, *Life of Benjamin Silliman*, 2 vols. (New York, 1866), II, 23-24.
25. Sarah Stuart Robbins, *Old Andover Days* (Boston, 1908), pp. 163-66.
26. John C. Schwab, "The Yale College Curriculum 1701-1901," *Educational Review* (June, 1901), pp. 12-13.
27. Robbins, *op. cit.*, p. 179.
28. Claude M. Fuess, *An Old New England School* (Boston, 1917), p. 317.
29. Robbins, *op. cit.*, pp. 39-40, slightly condensed.
30. "Moses Stuart," *The New Englander* X, N. S. IV (1852), pp. 42-55 (anonymous), and Mrs. M. H. Cornelius, "A Chapter of Reminiscences: Moses Stuart," *The New Englander* XXXII (July, 1873), pp. 550-60. (Cf. John

Giltner, *Moses Stuart: 1780-1852* (unpublished Yale dissertation, 1956), now the best treatment.
31. Edwards A. Park, A *Discourse Delivered at the Funeral of Professor Moses Stuart* (Andover, 1852).
32. William Adams, A *Discourse on the Life and Services of Professor Moses Stuart* (New York, 1852), pp. 59-60.
33. Consult Theodore Davenport Bacon, *Leonard Bacon, A Statesman in the Church* (New Haven, 1931). For the statements in the following sketch see pp. 288, 122, 136, 138, 157, 163, 53. The hymn is at the front.

CHAPTER VIII. THE NEW HAVEN THEOLOGY

1. Sydney E. Ahlstrom, "The Scottish Philosophy and American Theology," *Church History* XXIV, 3 (September, 1955), pp. 257-72.
2. Taylor's views on this subject are recorded in student notes on his lectures transcribed in manuscript from earlier and anonymous notes by R. C. Learned and others in 1838-40, entitled *"Notes" on Mental Philosophy, Ethics. . . .* These notes are deposited in the library of the Yale University Divinity School and will hereafter be referred to as *Manuscript Notes.*
3. *Ibid.*, II, 117-18.
4. Samuel Rogers Andrew, "What Is the Real Difference between the New Haven Divines and Those Who Oppose Them?" *Quarterly Christian Spectator*, 3rd Series V, no. 5 (New Haven 1833), p. 666.
5. Summary in George Park Fisher, *Discussions in History and Theology* (New York, 1880), pp. 321-22.
6. Bennet Tyler, "An Address to the Alumni of the Theological Institute of Connecticut, July 15, 1857," in *Tyler, Harvey . . . Letters* (Hartford, 1857), p. 11, slightly recast.
7. H. Shelton Smith, *Changing Conceptions of Original Sin* (New York, 1955).
8. Taylor, *Manuscript Notes*, II, 145-46.
9. *Ibid.*, I, 154-55.
10. Dutton, in *Memorial of Nathaniel W. Taylor*, pp. 16-17.
11. Taylor, "On the Means of Regeneration," *Quarterly Christian Spectator* III, 1 (New Haven, 1829), pp. 704, 711, condensed.
12. Taylor, *Concio ad Clerum* (New Haven, 1828), p. 38.
13. Lyman Beecher, *Autobiography, Correspondence, . . .* (New York, 1864-65), I, 49.
14. *Ibid.*, II, 237.
15. Rebecca Taylor Hatch, *Personal Reminiscences and Memorials* (New York, 1905), pp. 27-28.
16. L. Beecher, *op. cit.*, I, 524.
17. Hatch, *op. cit.*, pp. 28-29.
18. Ibid., pp. 32-33.
19. L. Beecher, *op. cit.*, II, 516.
20. *Ibid.*, I, 70.
21. Reference lost.
22. L. Beecher, *op. cit.*, I, 75.
23. *Ibid.*, II, 505.
24. *Ibid.*, I, 161-63.
25. *Ibid.*, II, Introduction.
26. *Ibid.*, I, 344.
27. *Ibid.*, I, 560.

28. L. Beecher, *Works* (Boston, 1852-53), III, 196.
29. William Adams, *A Discourse on the Life and Services of Professor Moses Stuart* (New York, 1852), p. 34.
30. Josiah Willard Gibbs, "Critical Miscellanies" (November, 1857), in *Published Writings* II, p. 668. For detailed evidence see the unpublished dissertation of John Giltner, *Moses Stuart: 1780-1852* (Yale dissertation, 1956).
31. Theodore Davenport Bacon, *Leonard Bacon, A Statesman in the Church* (New Haven, 1931), p. 39.
32. S. G. Goodrich, *Recollections of a Lifetime*, 2 vols. (New York, 1856), I, 356-59.
33. Benjamin Silliman, *Consistency of the Discoveries of Modern Geology, with the Sacred History of the Creation and the Deluge* (New Haven, 1833).
34. Theodore Thornton Munger, "Dr. Nathaniel W. Taylor—Master Theologian," *Yale Divinity Quarterly* V, 3 (February, 1909), p. 234.
35. Moses Stuart, "Critical Examination of Some Passages in Genesis I," *Biblical Repository* VII (1836), pp. 46-106. Condensed and slightly paraphrased.
36. Harriet Beecher Stowe, "Old Town Folks," in *The Writings of Harriet Beecher Stowe*, X, 64.
37. Jarvis Means Morse, *A Neglected Period of Connecticut's History* 1818-1850 (New Haven, 1933).
38. H. B. Stowe, *op. cit.*, IX, 69.
39. L. Beecher, *op. cit.*, I, 88.
40. *Ibid.*, I, 105.
41. *Ibid.*, I, 86.
42. Lyman Beecher Stowe, *Saints, Sinners and Beechers* (Indianapolis, 1934), p. 31.
43. *Ibid.*, p. 46.
44. *Ibid.*, pp. 86, 92, 96.
45. *Ibid.*, p. 97.
46. Hatch, *op. cit.*, p. 34.
47. H. B. Stowe, *op. cit.*, IX, 84.
48. H. B. Stowe, "The Minister's Wooing," in *Writings*, V, pp. 247-48.
49. *Ibid.*, V, 253-54.

Chapter IX. Coming to Terms

Bibliography
> Mary Bushnell Cheney, Ed., *Life and Letters of Horace Bushnell* (New York, 1880).
> Theodore Thornton Munger, *Horace Bushnell, Preacher and Theologian* (New York, 1899).
> Warren Seymour Archibald, *Horace Bushnell* (Hartford, 1930).

Four unpublished Yale Dissertations
> Vincent Henry Daniels, *The Thought of Horace Bushnell up to the Publication of "Nature and the Supernatural"* (1939).
> Edward C. Gardner, *Man as Sinner in Nineteenth Century New England Theology* (1952).
> Ralph O. Harpole, *The Development of the Doctrine of Atonement in American Thought from Jonathan Edwards to Horace Bushnell* (1924).
> Rachel Henderlite, *The Theological Basis of Horace Bushnell's "Christian Nurture"* (1947).

Works of Bushnell cited
> *The Age of Homespun* (Litchfield ?, 1851 ?).
> *An Argument for "Discourses on Christian Nurture"* (Hartford, 1847).

Barbarism the First Danger (New York, 1847, reprinted in *Work and Play*
  [New York, 1881]).
Christ and His Salvation (New York, 1864).
Christ in Theology (Hartford, 1851).
Discourses on Christian Nurture (Boston, 1847).
God in Christ (Hartford, 1849).
Nature and the Supernatural (New York, 1858).
Sermons for the New Life (New York, 1858).
Sermons on Living Subjects (New York, 1873).
The Spirit in Man (New York, 1903 and 1907).
The Vicarious Sacrifice (New York, 1866).
Work and Play (London & New York, 1864, reprint New York, 1881).

1. Horace Bushnell, "The Age of Homespun," in *Work and Play* (New York, 1881)
   p. 391.
2. *Ibid.*, pp. 396-97.
3. Bushnell, *The Spirit in Man* (New York, 1907), p. 125.
4. Bushnell, *Christ in Theology*, p. 170-71.
5. Mary Bushnell Cheney, ed., *Life and Letters of Horace Bushnell* (New York,
   1880), p. 90.
6. William Ellery Channing, "The Moral Argument against Calvinism," *Complete
   Works* (London, 1885), p. 377.
7. Bushnell, *Sermons for the New Life*, p. 324.
8. Bushnell, *The Vicarious Sacrifice*, pp. 42, 44.
9. *Ibid.*, p. 42.
10. *Ibid.*, p. 73.
11. Moses Stuart, *Letters on the Eternal Generation of the Son of God* (Andover,
    1822).
12. Consult John Giltner, *Moses Stuart* (MS), p. 343.
13. Bushnell, *Christ in Theology*, pp. 169-70.
14. Bushnell, *God in Christ*, pp. 138-39.
15. Bushnell, *Sermons for the New Life*, pp. 150-51.
16. Bushnell, *God in Christ*, p. 139.
17. Bushnell, *Christ in Theology*, pp. 167-68.
18. Bushnell, *God in Christ*, p. 175.
19. Bushnell, *Christ in Theology*, pp. 173-75.
20. Charles Coulston Gillispie, "Genesis and Geology," *Harvard Historical Studies*
    LVIII (Cambridge, 1951).
21. Edward Hitchcock, *The Religion of Geology and Its Connected Sciences*
    (Boston, 1852), p. 105.
22. Conrad Wright, "The Religion of Geology," *New England Quarterly* XIV
    (1941), pp. 335-58.
23. Bushnell, *The Vicarious Sacrifice*, p. 249.
24. Bushnell, *Nature and the Supernatural*, pp. 76-78.
25. *Ibid.*, p. 206.
26. Samuel Taylor Coleridge, *Confessions of an Inquiring Spirit* (London, 1849),
    p. 11.
27. Bushnell, *God in Christ*, pp. 158-59.
28. Bushnell, *The Spirit in Man*, pp. 77-78.
29. Bushnell, *God in Christ*, p. 73.
30. Josiah Willard Gibbs, *Philological Studies* (New Haven, 1857), pp. 14-15.
31. Bushnell, *Christ in Theology*, p. 24.
32. Bushnell, *God in Christ*, p. 55.

33. *Ibid.*, p. 74.
34. *Ibid.*, pp. 75-76.
35. *Ibid.*, pp. 82-83.
36. In *Polemics* (bound volume of tracts in the Yale Sterling Library), reprinted from the *New York Evangelist*, 1849.
37. Ralph Waldo Emerson, *Nature* (London, 1845), pp. 10, 17. Cf. Perry Miller, "The Romantic Dilemma in American Materialism and the Concept of Nature," *Harvard Theological Review* XLVIII, 4 (October, 1955), pp. 239-53.
38. Cheney, *op. cit.*, pp. 115-16.
39. *Ibid.*, p. 264.
40. Bushnell, *Nature and the Supernatural*, p. 336.
41. *Ibid.*, p. 491, and Chap. XV.
42. Bushnell, *Christian Nurture*.
43. Bushnell, *Nature and the Supernatural*, pp. 163-64.
44. Bushnell, *Barbarism the First Danger* (New York, 1847), reprinted in *Work and Play* (New York, 1881), pp. 229-51.
45. Bushnell, *Nature and the Supernatural*, p. 183.
46. H. Shelton Smith, *Changing Conceptions of Original Sin* (New York, 1955), pp. 156-57.
47. Bushnell, *Nature and the Supernatural*, p. 128.
48. *Ibid.*, p. 104.
49. *Ibid.*, p. 138. Italics mine.
50. *Ibid.*, p. 237.
51. Bushnell, *Christ and His Salvation*, pp. 130-31.
52. Bushnell, *Nature and the Supernatural*, p. 236.
53. Bushnell, *Sermons for the New Life*, p. 108.
54. *Ibid.*, p. 118.
55. Bushnell, *An Argument for "Discourses on Christian Nurture,"* p. 16.
56. Bushnell, *Sermons for the New Life*, pp. 236-37. Italics mine.
57. Bushnell, *The Spirit in Man*, pp. 350-51.

CHAPTER X.   NEW OCCASIONS TEACH NEW DUTIES

1. Edition of Boston, 1788. Pequot Collection, No. 422, Rare Book Room, Sterling Library, Yale University. This extensive collection of *New England Primers* was assembled by the Rev. William Holman of Southport, Conn.
2. Cf. Paul Leicester Ford, *The New England Primer* (New York, 1897), p. 29.
3. Harry R. Warfel, *Noah Webster* (New York, 1936), pp. 91, 397.
4. New Haven, 1830.
5. *Annual Report of the Connecticut Sunday School Union, Second Annual Meeting* (New Haven, 1826), Vols. 2 and 3; *Report of the Doings of the First State Convention of Sabbath School Teachers Held at Hartford* (1857); Edwin Wilbur Rice, *The Sunday-School Movement . . . 1780-1927* (Philadelphia, 1927); George Stewart, Jr., *A History of Religious Education in Connecticut* (New Haven, 1924).
6. Oliver Wendell Elsbree, *The Rise of the Missionary Spirit in America 1790-1815* (Williamsport, Penna., 1928), pp. 148-50; George Leon Walker, *Some Aspects of the Religious Life of New England* (New York, 1897), pp. 152 f.
7. Elsbree, *op. cit.*, p. 56.
8. *A Plea for the West* (Cincinnati, 1835), especially pp. 10-12.
9. Colin Brummitt Goodykoontz, *Home Missions on the American Frontier* (Caldwell, Idaho, 1939), p. 181, quoting Calvin Stowe.

10. Julian M. Sturtevant, *Autobiography* (New York, 1896), pp. 138-39.
11. Goodykoontz, *op. cit.*, p. 250.
12. David George Gelzer, *Mission to America Being a History of the Work of the Basel Foreign Missions Society in America* (Unpublished dissertation, Yale, 1952).
13. E. W. Dwight, *Memoir of Obookiah* (New York, n.d.), and Hiram Bingham, *A Residence of Twenty One Years in the Sandwich Islands* (Hartford, 1847).
14. These letters are all in the Yale manuscript vault under the name of Josiah Willard Gibbs.
15. Timothy Dwight, *A Sermon on Duelling* (New York, 1805).
16. L. Beecher, *The Remedy for Duelling* (Sag-Harbor, N.Y, 1807), pp. 37-38.
17. L. Beecher, *Autobiography* I, 150-54.
18. Consult Roland H. Bainton, "The Churches and Alcohol," *Quarterly Journal of Studies on Alcohol* VI (June, 1945), pp. 45-58; Daniel Dorchester, *The Liquor Problem in All Ages* (New York, 1884); John Allen Krout, *The Origins of Prohibition* (New York, 1925); August F. Fehlandt, *A Century of Drink Reform in the United States* (Cincinnati, 1904).
19. *Tischreden* (Weimar ed.), III, 338, no. 3468.
20. Krout, *op. cit.*, p. 19.
21. L. Beecher, *Autobiography*, I, 245-53.
22. "On Drunkenness," *Religious Tract Society*, No. 300.
23. Dorchester, *op. cit.*, p. 197.
24. *First Annual Report of the Executive Committee of the Connecticut Temperance Society May 19, 1830* (Middletown, 1830), p. 20.
25. New Haven, 1829.
26. Krout, *op. cit.*, p. 151.
27. Fehlandt, *op. cit.*, pp. 80-81.
28. Cf. the tract of 1830, *Essay on the Prize-Question, Whether the Use of Distilled Liquors or Traffic in Them Is Compatible, at the Present Time with Making a Profession of Christianity* (New York, 1830) with the tract of 1848, *Scriptural View of the Wine-Question* (New York, 1848).
29. Krout, *op. cit.*, pp. 194-95.
30. James Hadley, *Diary*, p. 155.
31. *A Discourse on the Traffic in Spiritous Liquors* (New Haven, 1838), specific references to pp. 49 and 22.
32. *Letters on the Maine Liquor Law*, American Temperance Union (New York, 1851).

CHAPTER XI.   MINE EYES HAVE SEEN THE COMING

1. Park, "Memoir" in Samuel Hopkins, *Works* (Boston, 1852), I, 115-18.
2. *Ibid.*, I, 110.
3. Hopkins, *op. cit.*, II, 553-81, condensed.
4. Park, "Memoir," in *ibid.*, I, 118. Cf. *The Works of Joseph Bellamy* (Boston, 1853), I, liii.
5. Leonard Bacon's review of "The Minister's Wooing," *The New Englander*, XVIII (New Haven, 1860), pp. 155-56.
6. Rebecca Taylor Hatch, *Personal Reminiscences* (New York, 1905), p. 25, and Lyman Beecher, *Autobiography and Correspondence* (New York, 1865), I, 136-37.
7. Jonathan Edwards, Jr., *The Injustice and Impolicy of the Slave Trade, and of the Slavery of the Africans, September 15, 1791* (New Haven, 1833).
8. Ralph Foster Weld, *Slavery in Connecticut*, Connecticut Tercentenary Commission, XXXVII (New Haven, 1935).

9. Two Broadsides 1790 and 1792. Yale Sterling Library Rare Book Room, Broadside 40.
10. Bernard C. Steiner, "History of Slavery in Connecticut," in *Labor, Slavery, and Self-Government,* Johns Hopkins University Studies, XI (Baltimore, 1893), p. 84.
11. John Terrill Wayland, *The Theological Department in Yale College 1822-1858* (unpublished Yale dissertation, 1933), pp. 298-99.
12. Claude M. Fuess, *An Old New England School* (Boston, 1917), p. 226.
13. Early Lee Fox, *The American Colonization Society, 1817-1840* (Baltimore, 1919), p. 138.
14. Robert Austin Warner, *New Haven Negroes* (New Haven, 1940), p. 11.
15. George Park Fisher, *A Sermon Preached . . . January 4, 1861* (New Haven, 1861), p. 16.
16. *The African Repository* VIII (Washington, August, 1832), pp. 169-70.
17. *Slavery Discussed in Occasional Essays* (New York, 1846), pp. 200 and 243 (condensed and slightly paraphrased).
18. Arthur Young Lloyd, *The Slavery Controversy 1831-1860* (Chapel Hill, 1939), pp. 18-20.
19. Warner, *op. cit.,* p. 63.
20. Declaration of the "American Society of Free Persons of Colour, 1830," in *ibid.,* pp. 49-51.
21. Fox, *op. cit.,* p. 140.
22. Review of pamphlets on "Slavery and Colonization," *Quarterly Christian Spectator,* III, No. 5 (New Haven, 1833), presumably by Leonard Bacon.
23. "A Letter to the Secretaries of the American Tract Society" (New Haven, 1858), in *Slavery Pamphlets* 55, No. 14, p. 3, Rare Book Room, Yale Sterling Library.
24. Robert C. Senior, *New England Congregationalism and the Anti-Slavery Movement 1830-1860* (unpublished Yale dissertation, 1954).
25. *American Anti-Slavery Almanac,* Vol. I, No. 3 (Boston, 1838).
26. *The Liberator,* XIV, No. 3 (Boston, January 19, 1844).
27. *Iibid.,* XIX, No. 45 (Boston, November 9, 1849), p. 180.
28. *Ibid.,* XIV, No. 16 (Boston, April 19, 1844), p. 63.
29. "Present State of the Slavery Question," in *Slavery Discussed,* p. 98.
30. Alice Felt Tyler, *Freedom's Ferment* (Minneapolis, 1944), p. 475.
31. *Slavery Discussed,* p. 74.
32. Theodore Davenport Bacon, *Leonard Bacon* (New Haven, 1931), pp. 269-71.
33. Warner, *op. cit.,* p. 46.
34. *Annual Report of the Connecticut Sunday School Union* (New Haven, 1826), p.16.
35. *The Connecticut Journal,* LXIV (Sept. 13, 1831), condensed.
36. Warner, *op. cit.,* pp. 53-58.
37. Gilbert Hobbs Barnes, *The Antislavery Impulse 1830-1844* (New York, 1933), pp. 72-73.
38. The first account of the *Amistad* captives was by John W. Barber, *A History of the Amistad Captives* (New Haven, 1840). The Yale Library has a box of clippings from contemporary newspapers as well as pencil sketches of many of the prisoners.

    William A. Owens, in his *Slave Mutiny: The Revolt on the Schooner Amistad* (New York, 1953), has produced a very vivid undocumented account, slightly fictionalized in that narrative is often turned into conversation. Transcripts of his sources have been deposited with the New Haven Historical Society. Samuel Flag Bemis gives a detailed and documented recital with especial attention to legal and political aspects in *John Quincy Adams and the Union* (New York, 1956).

39. *The African Repository,* VIII, No. 6 (Washington, August, 1832), p. 174.
40. *The New Englander* XII (New Haven, 1854), p. 222.
41. Joseph C. Lovejoy, *Memoir of Rev. Charles T. Torrey* (Boston, 1847), p. 364.
42. Wayland, *op. cit.,* pp. 299-300.
43. James Hadley, *Diary,* p. 123. "Mac" is Alexander McWhorter who finished the Yale Divinity School in 1844, "Bush" is George Bushnell who finished in 1846.
44. *Conscience and the Constitution* (Boston, 1850).
45. *A Sabbath Scene,* a broadside, June, 1850. In the edition of 1854 these lines were expunged.
46. Frank Haywood Hodder, *The Genesis of the Kansas-Nebraska Act* (Madison, 1913).
47. *Supra* note 24.
48. *Speeches and Other Proceedings at the Anti-Nebraska Meetings Held in New Haven, Connecticut, March 8 and 10, 1854* (New Haven, 1854), pp. 10-13, 15-18, partially condensed.
49. Mary Hewitt Mitchell, *History of the United Church of New Haven* (New Haven, 1942), pp. 97-98.
50. *The Independent* (New York, March 27, 1856), pp. 98-99.
51. Theodore Davenport Bacon, *op. cit.,* p. 463.

CHAPTER XII.   A PERMANENT HABITATION

1. The material for the first portion of this chapter when not otherwise indicated is drawn from the unpublished Yale dissertation of Gerald Everett Knoff, *The Yale Divinity School 1858-1899* (1936). Cf. also George Wilson Pierson, *Yale College 1871-1921* (New Haven, 1952).
2. George E. Day, in *Addresses at the Laying of the Corner Stone of the Divinity Hall . . .* (New Haven, 1869), pp. 7, 12.
3. *The Semi-Centennial Anniversary of the Divinity School of Yale College . . . 1872* (New Haven, 1872), p. 23.
4. *Addresses at the Laying of the Corner Stone, op. cit.,* p. 6.
5. *Yale Courant* (New Haven, Sept. 21, 1870), p. 12. *College Courant* (New Haven, Dec. 25, 1869), pp. 381-82.
6. Cited in Knoff, *op. cit.,* pp. 284-85.
7. *Yale Divinity Quarterly,* V, 2 (November, 1908), p. 213.
8. Knoff, *op. cit.,* p. 44, and *passim.*
9. *Noah Porter; A Memorial by Friends,* ed. George S. Merriam (New York, 1893).
10. *Ibid.,* review by Duncan, pp. 197-252.
11. *Agnosticism, A Doctrine of Despair, A Baccalaureate Sermon, June 27, 1880,* American Tract Society (New York, 1880).
12. *Ibid.,* pp. 25-27.
13. *Noah Porter; A Memorial,* pp. 110, 127-28.
14. Knoff, *op. cit.,* p. 92, and George Park Fisher in *Leonard Bacon, Pastor of the First Church in New Haven* (New Haven, 1882).
15. Samuel Harris, *The Self-Revelation of God* (New York, 1887), p. 172.
16. Newell M. Calhoun, *Yale Divinity Quarterly,* II, 2 (October, 1905), p. 63.
17. Harris, *The Self-Revelation of God,* pp. 145-47.
18. Knoff, *op. cit.,* p. 339. Cf. F. W. Whittaker's MS on Harris, Yale Ph.d. 1950.

19. Samuel Harris, *Enoch Pond, D.D., A Memorial Discourse* (Bangor, 1882), p. 18.
20. *The Philosophical Basis of Theism* (New York, 1883), pp. 1, 14-15, 5.
21. "The Demands of Infidelity Satisfied by Christianity," *Bibliotheca Sacra* (1856), pp. 281-83.
22. *The Kingdom of Christ on Earth* (Andover, 1874), p. 255.
23. "Demands of Infidelity," p. 314.

CHAPTER XIII. THE ESTABLISHED DISCIPLINES: BIBLE AND HOMILETICS

1. Vergilius Ferm, ed., *Contemporary American Theology*, 2 vols. (New York, 1932-33), I, 4, 12-13.
2. Consult my article "Yale and German Theology in the Middle of the Nineteenth Century," *Zeitschift für Kirchengeschichte*, LXV, III (1954) which publishes much of George Park Fisher's journal for 1852-53.
3. Ferm, *op. cit.*, pp. 15-16.
4. *Timothy Dwight . . . Memorial Addresses* (New Haven, 1917).
5. *Ibid.*
6. Robert Dudley French, *The Memorial Quadrangle* (New Haven, 1929), pp. 191-92.
7. Edward L. Curtis, "An Address in Memory of Prof. George Edward Day . . ." in *Memorial Addresses, Yale Divinity School, December 17, 1905*. Also found in *Yale Divinity Quarterly*, II, 3 (January, 1906), pp. 85-95.
8. *The Literary Diary of Ezra Stiles*, Franklin Bowditch Dexter, ed. (New York, 1901), I, 73.
9. *Holy Bible* (New Haven, 1833), iii-xvi.
10. "Common Version and Biblical Revision," *American Quarterly Register*, XVII (May, 1859), pp. 489-528.
11. Ferm, *Contemporary American Theology*, I, 11, 32.
12. Edward L. Curtis, *The Interior* (Sept. 16, 1886).
13. Edward L. Curtis, *Address to the Students of the Yale Divinity School, May 15, 1895*. This manuscript is the property of Mrs. George Dahl.
14. Edward L. Curtis, *A Critical and Exegetical Commentary on the Books of Chronicles* in the International Critical Commentary (New York, 1910).
15. Edward L. Curtis, "The Old Testament in Religious Education," *The Biblical World*, n.s. XXII, 6 (December, 1903), pp. 424-35.
16. Charles C. Torrey, *The Composition and Historical Value of Ezra-Nehemiah* (Giessen, 1896).
17. Charles C. Torrey, *The Second Isaiah* (New York, 1928).
18. But Newman Smyth learned this from Beyschlag (*Recollections and Reflections*, 1926, p. 92), and said so in 1879 (*Old Faiths in New Lights*, p. 36).
19. George Barker Stevens, *The Christian Doctrine of Salvation* (New York, 1905), p. 131.
20. George Barker Stevens, *The Theology of the New Testament* (New York, 1899), p. 172.
21. *Ibid.*, pp. 154-62.
22. George Barker Stevens, *The Christian Doctrine of Salvation*, pp. 131, 535.
23. Frank Chamberlin Porter, "The Yeçer Hara; A Study in the Jewish Doctrine of Sin," in *Biblical and Semitic Studies, Yale Bicentennial Publications* (New York, 1901).
24. Gerald Everett Knoff, *The Yale Divinity School 1858-1899* (unpublished Yale dissertation, 1936), p. 344.

25. James M. Hoppin, *The Office and Work of the Christian Ministry* (2nd ed., New York, 1870), pp. 53-54.
26. Lewis O. Brastow, *The Modern Pulpit* (New York, 1906), pp. 325, 329-31.
27. Jay T. Stocking, *Yale Divinity Quarterly*, IV, 1 (May, 1907), pp. 20-21.
28. Samuel Silas Curry, *Lessons in Vocal Expression* (Boston, 1895), p. 50.
29. Edgar DeWitt Jones, *The Royalty of the Pulpit* (New York, 1951), pp. xxiv-xxvii and xiv.
30. *Ibid.*, p. 5.
31. Henry Ward Beecher, *Yale Lectures on Preaching* (New York, 1872), pp. 43, 46.

Chapter XIV. The New Disciplines

1. Egbert Smyth, *The Value of the Study of Church History in Ministerial Education* (Andover, 1874).
2. Frederick H. Lynch, *The One Great Society; A Book of Recollections* (New York, 1918), chapter on Fisher, pp. 74-81.
3. See note 2, p. 285.
4. *Yale Divinity Quarterly*, VI, 3 (January, 1910), p. 78.
5. Benjamin W. Bacon, *Dictionary of American Biography*, article on "George Park Fisher."
6. George Park Fisher, *Manual of Natural Theology* (New York, 1893), pp. 35-36.
7. Leonard Bacon, *Thirteen Historical Discourses* (New Haven, 1839), preface, and p. 17.
8. Gerald Everett Knoff, *The Yale Divinity School 1858-1899* (1936, unpublished Yale dissertation), pp. 275, 304, 348, 366. Cf. *The Independent* (March 4, 1897), p. 281.
9. Cf. *The Register* (Sept. 27, 1894).
10. Newman Smyth, *Recollections*, pp. 135-43.
11. Knoff, *op. cit.*, p. 367.
12. *The Semicentennial Anniversary of the Divinity School of Yale College* . . . (New Haven, 1872), pp. 38-63, 104.
13. *Yale Alumni Weekly*, Bicentennial Issue, XI, 14 (January, 1902), pp. 145-50.
14. *Yale Divinity News*, XVII, 3 (March, 1921).
15. Edward S. Ninde, *The Story of the American Hymn* (New York, 1921), p. 212.
16. George B. Bacon, *Exercises at the Opening of the Lowell Mason Library of Music in the Yale Divinity School, May 11, 1875*, p. 12. In the Yale Sterling Library bound in College Pamphlets, No. 1980.
17. Ninde, *op. cit.*, p. 120.
18. Arthur Loundes Rich, *Lowell Mason* (Chapel Hill, 1946), p. 12.
19. George B. Bacon, *op. cit.*
20. Knoff, *op. cit.*, pp. 312, 371, 375-76, 374.
21. John Addison Porter, *Sketches of Yale Life* (Washington, D.C., 1886), pp. 15-16.

Chapter XV. The Age of the Deans

1. James Glover Johnson, *The Yale Divinity School 1899-1928* (unpublished Yale dissertation, 1926), p. 123.
2. *Yale Alumni Weekly*, XVI, 9 (Nov. 21, 1906), p. 175.
3. Johnson, *op. cit.*, pp. 33-44.
4. *Ibid.*, pp. 78-79, 145-47.
5. The preceding two paragraphs rely on Johnson in this order: pp. 149, 151, 162-65, 50-51, 141-42.
6. *Ibid.*, pp. 69, 87-88.

7. William DeWitt Hyde, "Reform in Theological Education," *The Atlantic Monthly*, LXXXV (January, 1900), pp. 16-26.
8. *The Congregationalist*, LXXXIV (Boston, Sept. 28, 1899), p. 454.
9. "The Actual Service of Our Theological Seminaries," *The Congregationalist*, LXXXV (Boston, Jan. 11, 1900), pp. 51-52.
10. "Our Schools of Theology," *The Congregationalist*, LXXXV (Jan. 11, 1900), p. 42.
11. *The Congregationalist*, LXXXIV (Sept. 28, 1899), p. 448, and Johnson, *op. cit., p.* 86.
12. *Ibid.*, pp. 122-38.
13. *Ibid.*, p. 127.
14. *Ibid.*, p. 150.
15. *Yale Divinity Quarterly*, VIII, 1 (May, 1911), p. 25.
16. "The Year and Its Ending at Yale Divinity," *The Congregationalist* (June 17, 1911), p. 839, signed H. A. B.
17. Johnson, *op. cit.*, p. 139.
18. Charles Reynolds Brown, *The Social Message of the Modern Pulpit* (New York, 1906), pp. 5-8.
19. *Ibid.*, pp. 78-79.
20. Charles Reynolds Brown, *My Own Yesterdays* (New York, 1931), pp. 141-42, slightly condensed.
21. Johnson, *op. cit.*, pp. 445, 591.
22. *Ibid.*, pp. 78, 242.
23. *Yale Divinity News*, XVII, 1 (November, 1920), pp. 1-2.
24. Johnson, *op. cit.*, pp. 260-61.
25. *Ibid.*, p. 255.
26. Benjamin W. Bacon, *The Yale University School of Religion* (1914).
27. Johnson, *op. cit.*, pp. 374-75, 197-98.
28. Newman Smyth, *The Place of Death in Evolution* (New York, 1897), and *The Meaning of Personal Life* (New York, 1916).
29. *Yale Alumni Weekly*, XVII, 17 (Jan. 15, 1908), p. 395.
30. *Yale Divinity Quarterly*, IV, 3 (December, 1907), pp. 114-15.

Chapter XVI. The Biblical Phalanx

1. Charles C. Torrey, *Our Translated Gospels* (New York, 1936), pp. 99, 105.
2. Torrey, *Documents of the Primitive Church* (New York, 1941).
3. Benjamin W. Bacon, *Jesus and Paul* (New York, 1921), pp. 20-22.
4. Bacon, *The Beginnings of Gospel Story* . . . (New Haven, 1909), pp. 79-83.
5. Bacon, *Jesus and Paul*, pp. 7-10.
6. Bacon, "The Gospel Paul 'Received,'" *American Journal of Theology* XXI, 1 (January, 1917), pp. 15-42. This passage on p. 28.
7. Bacon, "The Treatment of Mark 6:14-8:26 in Luke," *Journal of Biblical Literature*, XXVI, II (1907), 132-50.
8. Bacon, *Jesus and Paul*, p. 29.
9. Bacon, "Ultimate Problems of Biblical Science," *Journal of Biblical Literature*, XXII, 1 (1903), 1-14.
10. Bacon, *Jesus and Paul*, pp. 31-32.
11. *Ibid.*, p. 123, and "The Gospel Paul 'Received,'" pp. 15-42.
12. Bacon, *Is Mark a Roman Gospel?* (Cambridge, 1919).
13. Bacon, *The Development of the Synoptic Tradition.* . . , typewritten manuscript p. 548.

14. *Ibid.,* p. 64.
15. Bacon, *Jesus and Paul,* p. 247, and Bacon, *The Gospel of the Hellenists,* Carl Kraeling, ed. (New York, 1933).
16. Bacon, *The Development of the Synoptic Tradition,* pp. 567-68.
17. Bacon, "The Return to Theology," in *Christianity and Modern Thought* (New Haven, 1924), p. 115.
18. *Contemporary American Theology,* Virgilius Ferm, ed. (New York, 1932-33), I, 40. The entire article is a valuable autobiography.
19. *Yale Divinity News,* XXVIII, 3 (March, 1932), p. 2.
20. *Yale Divinity News,* XXIX, 1 (November, 1932), pp. 1-3.
21. *Yale Divinity News,* XIX, 1 (November, 1922), pp. 1-2.
22. Frank Chamberlin Porter, *The Messages of the Apocalyptical Writers* (New York, 1905).
23. Porter, *The Mind of Christ in Paul . . .* (New York, 1930).
24. Porter, "The Liberal and the Ritschlian Theology of Germany," *The Andover Review,* XIX (July, 1893), pp. 440-61.
25. *Yale Divinity Quarterly,* V, 4 (March, 1909), p. 264.
26. Samuel Taylor Coleridge, *Confessions of an Inquiring Spirit* (London, 1849), p. 38.
27. William Wordsworth, *Prefaces and Essays on Poetry* (Boston, 1892), p. 16.
28. Porter, "The Place of the Sacred Book in the Christian Religion," *Yale Divinity Quarterly,* V, 4 (March, 1909), p. 266. Cf. Porter, "The Bearing of Historical Studies on the Religious Use of the Bible," *Harvard Theological Review,* II, 3 (July, 1909), pp. 275-76.
29. "The Bearing of Historical Studies," p. 258.
30. Porter, "The Religious and the Historical Uses of the Bible," *The New World,* III, 10 (June, 1894), pp. 258-59.
31. These excerpts are taken from an unpublished manuscript by Frank Chamberlin Porter in the Library of the Yale Divinity School entitled *The Place of the New Testament in the Christian Religion.*
32. Ferm, *op. cit.,* II, 227.
33. *Yale Divinity News,* XVII, 4 (May, 1921), p. 3.
34. Porter, "The Religious and the Historical Uses of the Bible," p. 254.
35. Porter, "Inquiries Concerning the Divinity of Christ," *American Journal of Theology,* VIII (1904), p. 24.
36. Porter, "The Sufficiency of the Religion of Jesus," *American Journal of Theology,* XI, (1907), p. 89.
37. Porter, "Inquiries Concerning the Divinity of Christ," p. 18.
38. Porter, *The Place of the New Testament.*

Chapter XVII.　Theology and Church History

1. Eugene G. Bewkes, Julius Seelye Bixler, Robert Lowry Calhoun, *et al, The Nature of Religious Experience; Essays in Honor of Douglas Clyde Macintosh* (New York, 1937).
2. Douglas C. Macintosh, *Personal Religion* (New York, 1942). The first section is drawn from family history.
3. Macintosh, *The Reasonableness of Christianity* (New York, 1928), pp. 135-37.
4. Cf. the review by R. L. Calhoun, *Yale Divinity News,* XXII, 2 (January, 1926), p. 3.
5. Macintosh, *The Reasonableness of Christianity,* pp. 163-65, condensed.
6. See the discussion by Eugene Bewkes in *The Nature of Religious Experience.*

7. Macintosh's epistemology in philosophy and theology is set forth in two works: *The Problem of Knowledge* (New York, 1915), and *The Problem of Religious Knowledge* (New York, 1940).
8. Macintosh, *Theology as an Empirical Science* (New York, 1919).
9. Macintosh, *The Pilgrimage of Faith in the World of Modern Thought* (Calcutta, 1931), pp. 223-24.
10. *The Nature of Religious Experience*, pp. 50, 72, 76, 125, and 198.
11. George Leon Walker, *Some Aspects of the Religious Life of New England* . . . (New York, 1897).
12. Williston Walker, "The Services of the Mathers in New England Religious Development," *Papers of the American Society of Church History*, V (New York, 1893), pp. 61-85.
13. *Yale Divinity Quarterly*, VIII, 1 (May, 1911), p. 12.
14. *Yale Divinity News*, XVIII, 3 (March, 1922).
15. W. Walker, *The Creeds and Platforms of Congregationalism* (New York, 1893).
16. W. Walker, "The Sandemanians of New England," *American Historical Association, Annual Report I* (1902), pp. 131-62.
17. W. Walker, "Why Did Not Massachusetts Have a Saybrook Platform?" *The Yale Review* (May, 1892), pp. 68-86.
18. W. Walker, *John Calvin* . . . (New York, 1906).
19. W. Walker, *The Reformation* (New York, 1901).
20. W. Walker, *A History of the Christian Church* (New York, 1918).

Chapter XVIII. The Making of a Minister

1. Charles Reynolds Brown, *The Making of a Minister* (New York, 1927), p. 41.
2. Brown, *The Art of Preaching* (New York, 1922), pp. 11, 15, and 5.
3. Brown, *My Own Yesterdays* (New York, 1931), pp. 62 and 65.
4. Brown, *The Art of Preaching*, pp. 106-7.
5. *Ibid.*, p. 179.
6. Brown, *Yale Talks* (New Haven, 1920), p. 19.
7. Brown, *The Art of Preaching*, p. 164.
8. Brown, *The Making of a Minister*, p. 214.
9. Brown, *The Art of Preaching*, p. 22.
10. *Ibid.*, pp. 23-24.
11. Henry Hallam Tweedy, "Unrighteous Forgetfulness," in *Sermons I Have Preached*. . . , Sidney A. Weston, ed. (Boston, 1931), pp. 148-49, 155-56.
12. Tweedy, "The Ministry," in H. H. Tweedy, *et al, Christian Work as a Vocation* (New York, 1922), p. 19.
13. Tweedy, "Training in Worship," in *Education for Christian Service*, by Members of the Faculty of the Divinity School of Yale University (New Haven, 1922), pp. 165-206.
14. Tweedy, in the foreword to *Christian Worship and Praise* (New York, 1939), pp. v-vi.
15. Luther Allen Weigle and Henry Hallam Tweedy, *Training the Devotional Life* (New York, 1919).
16. *Ibid.*, p. 34.
17. Tweedy, *Christian Worship and Praise* (New York, 1939).
18. Benjamin S. Winchester, *Religious Education and Democracy* (New York, 1917).
19. *Yale Divinity News*, XIX, 4 (May, 1923).
20. E. Hershey Sneath, *Shall We Have A Creed?* (New York, 1925), pp. 34-35.
21. *At One with the Invisible*. . . , E. Hershey Sneath, ed. (New York, 1921), pp. 260-293.

22. Sneath, "The Importance of the Aesthetic Consciousness and Its Bearing on Religious Education," in *Education for Christian Service*, p. 212.
23. Sneath, *The Mind of Tennyson*. . . , (New York, 1900), p. 8.
24. Cf. The Tribute by Luther Allan Weigle, *Yale Divinity News* XVIII, 2 (January, 1922), pp. 1-2.
25. Weigle, "Retirement of Professor Sneath," *Yale Divinity News*, XIX, 4 (May, 1923), pp. 1-2.
26. See his article "Departments of Religious Education in Theological Seminaries," *Organized Sunday School Work in North America* 1918-22, Official Report of the Sixteenth International Sunday School Convention, Kansas City, Mo., 1922 (Chicago, 1922), pp. 427-32.
27. In the Divinity School Library.
28. John C. Archer in *Yale Divinity News*, XVII, 3 (March, 1921), pp. 1-2.
29. Harlan Beach, *Renaissant Latin America* (New York, 1916).
30. Beach, "The Foreign Missionary's Calling," in *Christian Work as a Vocation*, pp. 45 and 15-16.
31. *Yale Divinity Quarterly*, III, 2 (October, 1906), 56-59.
32. Beach, in *Christian Work as a Vocation*, pp. 21-22.
33. *Yale Divinity Quarterly*, V, 3 (February, 1909), p. 253.
34. See the article on Beach by Kenneth Scott Latourette in *Dictionary of American Biography*, supplement one.
35. George Stewart, Jr., *The Life of Henry B. Wright* (New York, 1925), p. 4.
36. *Yale Divinity News*, XX, 2 (January, 1924), pp. 1-2.
37. *Yale Divinity News*, XXII, 2 (January, 1926), p. 1. Cf. Charles A. Dinsmore, *The English Bible as Literature* (Boston, 1931), p. 83.
38. Dinsmore, *The Great Poets and the Meaning of Life* (Boston, 1937).
39. Dinsmore, *Life of Dante Alighieri* (Boston, 1919); *The Teachings of Dante* (Boston, 1901); *Aids to the Study of Dante* (Boston, 1903).
40. *Yale Divinity News*, XXIX, 4 (May, 1933), p. 1.
41. Dinsmore, *Atonement in Literature and Life* (Boston, 1906), pp. 14-15.
42. *Yale Divinity News*, XXIX, 4 (May, 1933), p. 1.

CHAPTER XIX. THE SOCIAL LIFE AND THE SOCIAL ORDER

1. *Yale Divinity Quarterly*, IX, 1 (May, 1912), pp. 17-19.
2. *Ibid.*, IX, 1 (May, 1912), p. 62.
3. *Ibid.*, XIII, (November, 1916), p. 178.
4. *Ibid.*, XIII, 3 (January, 1917), p. 210.
5. William B. Bailey, "Opportunities for Social Work," in *Modern Christian Callings*, E. Hershey Sneath, ed. (New York, 1922).
6. *Yale Divinity News*, XVII, 2 (January, 1921), p. 5.
7. *Ibid.*, XX, 2 (January, 1924), address by C. G. Twomley.
8. George Stewart, Jr., and Henry B. Wright, *The Practice of Friendship* (New York, 1918), p. 14, and E. Hershey Sneath, ed., *Religion and the War by Members of the Faculty of the School of Religion, Yale University* (New Haven, 1918).
9. Cf. Henry B. Wright on "The Record of the Yale School of Religion in the War," *Yale Divinity Quarterly* XVI, 3 (March, 1920), pp. 115-17.
10. *Yale Divinity Quarterly*, XIII, 1 (May, 1916), pp. 198-203.
11. Douglas C. Macintosh, *Social Religion* (New York, 1939), pp. 65 and 73.
12. *Ibid.*, pp. 285-87.

Index

Adam, 20, 22, 51, 61, 98, 119, 125, 129
Adams, John Quincy, 154-55
Allen, Ethan, 163
Alumni, ix, 49, 265-68
Ames, William, 9, 39
Amherst College, 119
Amistad, 152-55
Andover Seminary, 79, 90, 92, 105, 134, 146, 186, 195
Angell, James Rowland, 260
Aquinas, Thomas, 45, 71
Aramaic originals, 212, 213, 218, 219
Archer, John Clark, xi, 208, 249
Arminian, 11, 71
Arnold, Gottfried, 187
Atonement, 22, 44, 51, 52, 78, 101, 112, 115, 116, 168, 180, 185, 215-17, 252
Auburn Seminary, 79
Augustine, -tinian, 98
Awakening, First great, x, 24, ch. II-III, 28, 29, 34, 42, 57, 132
  Second, x, 77, 80, 90, 97, 132

Bacon, Benjamin W., 164, 173-78, 181, 182, 189, 190, 198, 200, 204, 213-19, 225, 251, 254, 255
Bacon, David, 93
Bacon, George, 196
Bacon, Leonard, 81, 90, 93-96, 106, 124, 131, 138, 140, 146, 150, 151, 155, 158-60, 161-63, 165, 168, 169, 190, 194, 196, 207, 213, 247, 255

Bailey, William, 200, 208, 251, 256
Bainton, Roland H., xi, 209
Baldwin, Roger, 154
Bangor Seminary, 79
Baptism, 5, 15, 32, 215
Baptists, 35, 70, 71, 73, 128, 131, 140, 147, 203, 207, 227, 263, 268
Barlow, Joel, 85
Basel Mission, 134
Battell Chapel, 188, 199
Baur, Ferdinand C., 171, 187, 214, 215
Beach, Harlan P., 195, 200, 246 49
Beecher, Catherine, 110, 111, 151
Beecher, Harriet, see Stowe
Beecher, Harriet Porter, 110
Beecher, Henry Ward, 151, 158, 159, 183-85
Beecher, Lyman, 72, 101-4, 108, 109, 127, 132, 135, 138, 146, 151, 172, 183, 196
Beecher, Roxana, 109
Beecher Lectureship, 183-85, 191, 205
Bellamy, Joseph, 50-53, 57-59, 97, 115, 127, 143, 144
Berkeley, George, 11, 14, 40
Berkeley Divinity School, 263
Bewkes, Eugene, 227
Beza, Theodore, 9
Bible
  Criticism, 88, 106, 129, 130, 171, 178, 228
  in Curriculum, 41, 173-82, ch. XVI
  in education, 36
  in preaching, 238

291